Animals in Our Lives

Animals in Our Lives

Human–Animal Interaction in Family, Community, and Therapeutic Settings

edited by

Peggy McCardle, Ph.D., M.P.H.
Eunice Kennedy Shriver National Institute
of Child Health and Human Development
Rockville, MD

Sandra McCune, Ph.D.
WALTHAM Centre for Pet Nutrition
Leicestershire, United Kingdom

James A. Griffin, Ph.D.
Eunice Kennedy Shriver National Institute
of Child Health and Human Development
Rockville, MD

Layla Esposito, Ph.D.
Eunice Kennedy Shriver National Institute
of Child Health and Human Development
Rockville, MD

and

Lisa S. Freund, Ph.D.
Eunice Kennedy Shriver National Institute
of Child Health and Human Development
Rockville, MD

·P A U L·H·
BROOKES
PUBLISHING CO®

Baltimore • London • Sydney

Paul H. Brookes Publishing Co.
Post Office Box 10624
Baltimore, Maryland 21285-0624
USA

www.brookespublishing.com

Typeset by Aptara, Inc., Falls Church, Virginia.
Manufactured in the United States of America by
Versa Press, Inc., East Peoria, Illinois.

This work may be reproduced in whole or in part for the official use of the U.S. government or any authorized agency thereof. The following materials were written by U.S. government employees within the scope of their official duties and, as such, shall remain in the public domain: Preface, Introduction, Chapter 1, Chapter 4, Chapter 6, Chapter 9, and Chapter 13.

The views expressed in this book are those of the authors and do not necessarily represent those of the National Institutes of Health, the *Eunice Kennedy Shriver* National Institute of Child Health and Human Development, the U.S. Department of Health and Human Services, or Mars, Inc.

The individuals described in this book are composites or real people whose situations are masked and are based on the authors' experiences. In all instances, names and identifying details have been changed to protect confidentiality or are used with permission.

Library of Congress Cataloging-in-Publication Data

Animals in our lives: human–animal interaction in family, community, and therapeutic settings/edited by Peggy McCardle . . . [et al.]
   p. ; cm.
Includes bibliographical references and index.
ISBN-13: 978-1-59857-157-8
ISBN-10: 1-59857-157-5
1. Animals—Therapeutic use.   2. Human-animal relationships.   I. McCardle, Peggy D. II. Title.
[DNLM: 1. Animal Assisted Therapy.   2. Bonding, Human-Pet. WM 450.5.A6 A598 2010]
RM931.A65A62 2010
615.8'5158—dc22   2010025322

British Library Cataloguing in Publication data are available from the British Library.

2014   2013   2012   2011   2010
10   9   8   7   6   5   4   3   2   1

Contents

About the Editors

Peggy McCardle, Ph.D., M.P.H., Chief, Child Development and Behavior Branch, *Eunice Kennedy Shriver* National Institute of Child Health and Human Development, National Institutes of Health, 6100 Executive Boulevard, Suite 4B05, Rockville, MD 20852-7510. Dr. McCardle has been a classroom teacher and has served as faculty at various universities and as a speech-language pathologist in hospitals and medical centers. In addition to her duties as Branch Chief, she directs the Language, Bilingualism and Biliteracy Program and developed various branch programs in literacy. She is a co-editor of several volumes and has served as guest editor of thematic journal issues on reading, bilingualism, and English language learner research. She is committed to the importance of ongoing research on child health, development, and learning and to ensuring that important research results are shared with the practice community so that they can improve the lives of children.

Sandra McCune, Ph.D., WALTHAM Program Manager, Human–Animal Interaction Research, WALTHAM Centre for Pet Nutrition, Freeby Lane, Waltham-on-the-Wolds, Melton Mowbray, Leicestershire, LE14 4RT, United Kingdom. Dr. McCune heads up the WALTHAM research program on Human–Animal Interaction at the WALTHAM Centre for Pet Nutrition in Leicestershire, United Kingdom. She manages a large global portfolio of research projects across many aspects of human–animal interaction.

James A. Griffin, Ph.D., Deputy Chief, Child Development and Behavior Branch, *Eunice Kennedy Shriver* National Institute of Child Health and Human Development, National Institutes of Health, Director, Early Learning and School Readiness Program, 6100 Executive Boulevard, Suite 4B05, Rockville, MD 20852-7510. Dr. Griffin holds a bachelor of arts degree *summa cum laude* in psychology from the University of Cincinnati and a doctoral degree with honors in child clinical psychology from the University of Rochester. He completed a postdoctoral fellowship in psychiatric epidemiology at The Johns

Hopkins University School of Public Health. Dr. Griffin's career has focused on research and evaluation efforts related to service systems and early intervention programs designed to enhance the development and school readiness of children from at-risk and disadvantaged backgrounds.

Layla Esposito, Ph.D., Health Scientist Administrator, *Eunice Kennedy Shriver* National Institute of Child Health and Human Development, National Institutes of Health, 6100 Executive Boulevard, Suite 4B05, Rockville, MD 20852-7510. Dr. Esposito holds a doctoral degree from Virginia Commonwealth University. She is a child psychologist and is currently a project officer at the *Eunice Kennedy Shriver* National Institute of Child Health and Human Development. In this role, she oversees a portfolio of grants in human–animal interaction (HAI). Her other research interests include socioemotional development and childhood obesity.

Lisa S. Freund, Ph.D., Associate Branch Chief for Neurobiological Research, *Eunice Kennedy Shriver* National Institute of Child Health and Human Development, National Institutes of Health, 6100 Executive Boulevard, Suite 4B05, Rockville, MD 20852-7510. Dr. Freund is a developmental neuropsychologist who is known for her neuroimaging studies with children from different clinical populations and was a *Eunice Kennedy Shriver* National Institute of Child Health and Human Development (NICHD)–supported scientist for several years. She came to the NICHD from The Johns Hopkins University School of Medicine and the Kennedy Krieger Institute, where she was Associate Professor of Psychiatry. Within the Child Development and Behavior Branch at the NICHD, Dr. Freund is responsible for a multifaceted research and training program to promote investigations, both basic and applied, to gain a deeper understanding of the linkages among genes, the developing brain, and behavior. Dr. Freund is an avid equestrian and has been involved with equine-assisted therapy in her private practice.

About the Contributors

Alan M. Beck, Sc.D., Dorothy N. McAllister Professor of Animal Ecology, Purdue University School of Veterinary Medicine, 725 Harrison Street, West Lafayette, IN 47907-2027. Dr. Beck directed the animal programs for the New York City Department of Health for five years and then was Director of the Center for the Interaction of Animals and Society at the University of Pennsylvania School of Veterinary Medicine for 10 years. In 1990, Dr. Beck became Director of the Center for the Human–Animal Bond at the Purdue University School of Veterinary Medicine.

Ann Berger, M.D., M.S.N., Chief, Pain and Palliative Care, National Institutes of Health, Clinical Center, 10 Center Drive, Room 21733, Building 10, Bethesda, MD 20292. Dr. Berger completed her undergraduate degree with a bachelor of science degree in nursing from New York University, a master of science degree in oncology nursing from University of Pennsylvania, followed by a doctor of medicine degree from Medical College of Ohio. As Assistant Professor in medicine and anesthesiology at Cooper Hospital/University of Medicine and Dentistry in New Jersey, Dr. Berger founded the palliative care service that provided consultative patient care and supported education and research. Dr. Berger's national and international work includes service as chair of the National Institutes of Health Clinical Center Pain and Palliative Care Collaborative Working Group and steering committee member for the National Palliative Care Consensus Project. Since 2004, Dr. Berger has published several books for professionals on pain and other symptom care.

Octavia J. Brown, Ed.M., D.H.L., Associate Professor of Equine Studies, Centenary College, 59 Mendham Road, Gladstone, NJ 07934. Dr. Brown has been in the field of equine-assisted activities/therapies since 1970. She is Associate Professor of Equine Studies at Centenary College, Hackettstown, New Jersey, where she directs a North American Riding for the Handicapped Association (NARHA)-approved therapeutic riding instructor training course. Dr. Brown is a NARHA Master Instructor and is Past President of the Federation of Riding for the Disabled International.

Preston R. Buff, Ph.D., Senior Scientist, The Nutro Company, 1550 West McEwen Drive, Franklin, TN 37067-1769. Dr. Buff received his bachelor of science degree in biology from Southwest Missouri State University in 1995, his master of science degree in animal science from the University of Missouri in 1999, and his doctor of philosophy degree in animal science from the University of Missouri in 2001. He became board certified with the American College of Animal Nutrition in 2006. Prior to joining Mars, Inc., in 2008, he was Assistant Professor at Mississippi State University in the Department of Animal and Dairy Sciences. Dr. Buff lives on a horse farm in Tennessee with his wife and their five dogs and three cats.

Aubrey H. Fine, Ed.D., Professor of Education, California Polytechnic State University, 3801 West Temple Avenue, Pomona, CA 91768. Psychologist Dr. Aubrey Fine has been in the field of animal-assisted therapy (AAT) for more than 25 years. He has been on the faculty of the California Poly State University since 1981 and is presently Professor of Education.

Nancy R. Gee, Ph.D., Associate Professor, Department of Psychology, State University of New York at Fredonia, Fredonia, NY 14063. Dr. Gee is a cognitive psychologist who began her career doing research on basic memory processes. Her lifelong hobby has been training dogs, and she has successfully competed at the highest levels of dog agility, earning 19 championship titles, placements at national competitions, and appearances on Animal Planet and Fox television. Her current research weds her love of dogs with the scientific investigation of the impact of the presence of a dog on the development of cognitive and motor skills in preschool children.

Temple Grandin, Ph.D., Professor, Department of Animal Sciences, Colorado State University, Fort Collins, CO 80523-1171. Temple Grandin is Professor of Animal Science at Colorado State University. She is also a person with autism. She is the author of *Thinking in Pictures, Animals in Translation,* and *Animals Make Us Human.*

Lynne Haverkos, M.D., M.P.H., Program Director, *Eunice Kennedy Shriver* National Institute of Child Health and Human Development, 6100 Executive Boulevard, Suite 4B05, Rockville, MD 20852-7510. Dr. Haverkos, a pediatrician and fellow of the American Academy of Pediatrics, directs the Pediatric Behavior and Health Promotion

Research Program in the Child Development and Behavior Branch at the *Eunice Kennedy Shriver* National Institute of Child Health and Human Development. She oversees research and training grants in the areas of health promotion, disease prevention, and risk behaviors.

Karyl J. Hurley, D.V.M., DACVIM, DECVIM-CA, Director of Global Scientific Affairs, Mars Petcare, 6885 Elm Street, McLean, VA 22101. Dr. Hurley is a specialist in small animal internal medicine, with a strong interest in the impact of pets on society and in the lives of individuals. She manages the WALTHAM Foundation, which provides research funds to promote the health and welfare of pets worldwide, and directs the global Scientific Affairs for Petcare on behalf of Mars, Inc.

Valerie Maholmes, Ph.D., Program Director, *Eunice Kennedy Shriver* National Institute of Child Health and Human Development, 6100 Executive Boulevard, Suite 4B05, Rockville, MD 20852-7510. Dr. Maholmes is currently Program Director for the Social and Affective Development/Child Maltreatment and Violence Research Program in the Child Development and Behavior Branch at the *Eunice Kennedy Shriver* National Institute of Child Health and Human Development. In this capacity, she provides scientific leadership on research and research training relevant to normative social, affective, and personality development in children from the newborn period through adolescence and on the impact of specific aspects of physical and social environments on the health and psychological development of infants, children, and adolescents.

Patricia B. McConnell, Ph.D., C.A.A.B., Adjunct Associate Professor, University of Wisconsin–Madison, Department of Zoology, 1117 West Johnson Street, Madison, WI 53706. Dr. McConnell is a certified applied behaviorist and internationally known expert on canine behavior and human–animal relationships. She teaches biology and philosophy of human–animal relationships at the University of Wisconsin–Madison; has written 12 books on training and behavior; has advised clients for more than 20 years about serious behavioral problems, specializing in canine aggression; and presents speeches and training seminars around the world.

F. Ellen Netting, Ph.D., M.S.S.W., Professor and Samuel S. Wurtzel Chair in Social Work, School of Social Work, 1000 West Franklin Street, Richmond, VA 23284-2027. Dr. Netting received her bachelor of arts degree in sociology from Duke University, her master of science degree in social work from the University of Tennessee in Knoxville, and her doctor of philosophy degree from the University of Chicago. Her scholarship has focused on health and human service delivery issues, as well as nonprofit management concerns. She is the co-author or co-editor of 16 books and has published more than 160 book chapters and refereed journal articles.

Anke Prothmann, M.D., Pediatric Resident, Technische Universitaet Muenchen, University Hospital recths der Isar, Department of Pediatrics, Koelner Platz 1, D-80804 München, Germany. After finishing medical school residency in child and adolescent psychiatry, Dr. Prothmann served for 10 years as leader of Germany's first university research group in animal-assisted therapy and human medicine. Her doctoral thesis concerned behavioral traits of children with psychological disorders during animal-assisted therapy, and her current research topics are pets and child development, pets in child health and child care, and pets as adjuvant therapy in human medicine. She has extensive experience in scientific research as well as in lectures and training programs for pedagogues, physicians, teachers, nurses, biologists, and soldiers. Dr. Prothmann is the author of the first German textbook concerning animal-assisted child psychotherapy, *Animal–Child Psychotherapy: Theory and Practice of Animal-Assisted Therapy in Children and Adolescents.*

James A. Serpell, Ph.D., Professor of Humane Ethics and Animal Welfare, School of Veterinary Medicine, Director, Center for the Interaction of Animals and Society, University of Pennsylvania, 3900 Delancy Street, Philadelphia, PA 19104-6010. Dr. Serpell is the Marie A. Moore Professor of Humane Ethics and Animal Welfare at the School of Veterinary Medicine, University of Pennsylvania, where he also directs the Center for the Interaction of Animals and Society. His research focuses on the behavior and welfare of companion animals, the development of human attitudes to animals, and the history of human–animal relationships. In addition to publishing more than 80 articles and book chapters on these and related topics, he is the author, editor, or co-editor of several books, including *Animals and Human Society: Changing Perspectives* (1994), *The Domestic Dog: Its Evolution, Behaviour and Interactions with People* (1995), *In the Company of Animals* (1986, 1996), and *Companion Animals and Us* (2000).

Stephen J. Suomi, Ph.D., Chief, Laboratory of Comparative Ethology, the *Eunice Kennedy Shriver* National Institute of Child Health and Human Development, National Institutes of Health, 6100 Executive Boulevard, Suite 4B05, Rockville, MD 20852-7510. Dr. Suomi is Chief of the Laboratory of Comparative Ethology at the *Eunice Kennedy Shriver* National Institute of Child Health and Human Development, National Institutes of Health, in Bethesda, Maryland. Dr. Suomi's initial post-doctoral research successfully reversed the adverse effects of early social isolation, previously thought to be permanent, in rhesus monkeys. His subsequent research at the University of Wisconsin led to his election as Fellow in the American Association for the Advancement of Science "for major contributions to the understanding of social factors that influence the psychological development of nonhuman primates." Throughout his professional career, Dr. Suomi has been the recipient of numerous awards and honors, the most recent of which include the Donald O. Hebb Award from the American Psychological Association, the Distinguished Primatologist Award from the American Society of Primatologists, and the Arnold Pfeffer Prize from the International Society of Neuropsychoanalysis.

Philip Tedeschi, M.S.S.W., Clinical Associate Professor, Clinical Director, Institute for Human–Animal Connection, Graduate School of Social Work, University of Denver, 2148 South High Street, Denver, Colorado 80208. Dr. Tedeschi is Clinical Director and Co-founder of the Institute for Human–Animal Connection at the University of Denver's Graduate School of Social Work, where he serves as Clinical Associate Professor specializing in the human–animal bond and conservation social work.

Roland J. Thorpe, Jr., Ph.D., Assistant Scientist, Johns Hopkins Bloomberg School of Public Health, 624 North Broadway, Suite 441, Baltimore, MD 21205. Dr. Thorpe is Assistant Scientist in the Department of Health Policy and Management at The Johns Hopkins Bloomberg School of Public Health and Core Faculty of the Hopkins Center for Health Disparities Solutions. Dr. Thorpe is a gerontologist and epidemiologist whose research focuses on how social and behavioral factors influence the health and functional status of middle-age and older adults.

Kate Trujillo, M.S.W., ABD, Doctoral Candidate and Leadership Education in Neurodevelopmental and Related Disabilities (LEND) Fellow, 2148 South High Street, Denver, Colorado 80208. Kate Trujillo is a doctoral candidate at the University of Denver and is currently studying how the role of companion animals influences the development of emotional security for children. She is also a professor for the Institute of Human–Animal Connection at Denver University and a LEND fellow at the University of Colorado.

James Herbert Williams, Ph.D., M.S.W., M.P.A., Dean and Professor, Graduate School of Social Work, University of Denver, 2148 South High Street, Denver, CO 80208. Dr. Williams is Dean and Professor at the Graduate School of Social Work at the University of Denver. His research and scholarship focus on K–12 academic performance, youth violence, delinquency prevention, race and gender disparities, and mental health service needs and utilization patterns of urban children.

Lisa Jane Wood, Ph.D., B.Com, The University of Western Australia, 35 Stirling Highway, Crawley, Western Australia 6009. Dr. Wood is a research fellow at the Centre for the Built Environment and Health (School of Population Health) at The University of Western Australia. In addition to researching the social and health benefits of pets, her research interests include social capital, neighborhoods and health, and mental health promotion. She has a strong interest and commitment to research that is useful and relevant to the "real world."

Preface

This book grew out of the activities of a Public–Private Partnership, initiated by Mars, Inc., with the *Eunice Kennedy Shriver* National Institute of Child Health and Human Development (NICHD). This partnership between NICHD and the WALTHAM Centre for Pet Nutrition, a division of Mars, Inc., is based on a mutual appreciation of and concern for the health, development, and welfare of both children and animals. The partnership takes a strong interest in the science that could be brought to bear on how the interactions between people (especially children and youth) and animals influence the people's health and development. This area, generally referred to as human–animal interaction (HAI), is of great mutual interest to the WALTHAM Centre and the NICHD.

Mars, Inc., is privately held and has within its corporate culture a long-standing and deep respect for peer-reviewed, fundamental research. This strong respect for the value of science has enabled the company to patiently fund long-term research on its core business and essential raw ingredients. As the world's largest pet-care company, Mars has sought to develop knowledge on all aspects of pets and pet ownership through its research and training facility in the United Kingdom, the WALTHAM Centre for Pet Nutrition. Since the 1980s, through its sponsorship and collaborative studies, WALTHAM has pioneered the study of the HAI phenomenon. As this and other work progressed, professionals in the field began to call for more research, larger studies, and greater methodological rigor. At that point, the WALTHAM team sought a partner whose "business" was funding research and who took an interest in child health and well-being: the NICHD.

The NICHD, established by Congress in 1962, is one of the 27 institutes and centers that compose the National Institutes of Health, the world's largest funder of biomedical and behavioral research. The NICHD conducts and supports research on topics that are related to the health and well-being of children, adults, families, and populations. Some of the topics of this research include reducing infant deaths; improving the health of children, parents, and families; learning about growth and development; examining, preventing, and treating problems such as intellectual, learning, and developmental disabilities; understanding typical development and promoting healthy development; and enhancing people's well-being throughout their life spans with optimal rehabilitation research.

At the invitation of Mars staff, a research partnership exploration team was formed in early 2008. It was agreed that an initial exercise to "take stock" of current HAI research was essential. A public–private partnership was formed between the WALTHAM Centre and the NICHD that was based on the commitment to this activity. After a preliminary literature review of the HAI field and a look back at the 1987 National Institutes of Health consensus conference report on the health benefits of pets, the group proposed a workshop to develop a research agenda in HAI. That workshop, which took place in Rockville, Maryland, in October 2008, brought together researchers who were already working in HAI, as well as many who were not, from a variety of disciplines, including veterinary and pediatric medicine, nursing, gerontology, animal behavior, developmental psychology, and others. A second workshop was held in August 2009 at the WALTHAM Centre for Pet Nutrition in Waltham-on-the-Wolds, United Kingdom. The two workshops resulted not only in a rigorous and ambitious research agenda, but also in a strong desire to inform others about the potential of this field of research. One major outcome of the workshops is this volume, which all contributors hope will help to inform those who are unaware of HAI and to promote a movement toward gathering evidence that can inform the therapeutic use of animals, potentially providing an evidence base for that area of clinical treatment. Ultimately, of course, the contributors to the volume hope that it will in some way enhance the lives of children, youth, and families and their pets or therapy animals, as humans and animals continue to interact.

Acknowledgments

This volume is based largely on two foundational workshops. Directions in Human–Animal Interaction Research: Child Development, Health and Therapeutic Interventions, was held in Rockville, Maryland, on September 30, 2008–October 2, 2008. Directions in Human–Animal Interaction Research II: The Role of Pets in the Socioemotional and Biobehavioral Development of Children, was held August 3–5, 2009, in Waltham-on-the-Wolds, United Kingdom. Both meetings were sponsored through the Public–Private Partnership between the WALTHAM Centre for Pet Nutrition, a division of Mars, Inc., and the *Eunice Kennedy Shriver* National Institute of Child Health and Human Development (NICHD), a partnership that was established to promote and support research on human–animal interaction (HAI). The editors acknowledge both partners for supporting the workshops and making this book possible.

The WALTHAM Centre for Pet Nutrition in the United Kingdom is the hub of Mars, Inc.'s global research activities on animal nutrition and health, which support their various brands of pet foods but also support science more generally. The Centre's scientists have pioneered important breakthroughs in pet nutrition and have shared their findings in more than 1,500 research publications. Their facility in the United Kingdom uniquely integrates office and research space for pets and people. Affiliated with the Centre is the WALTHAM Foundation, formed in 2001, which is dedicated to scientific research on the nutrition and healthy longevity of companion animals. The foundation has funded research in more than 20 countries, providing research grants to improve the health and welfare of companion animals. WALTHAM–Mars have supported various conferences and meetings, as well as research studies examining a range of aspects of HAI. In 2008, the organization initiated the current PPP with the NICHD.

The NICHD was established to investigate the broad aspects of human development as a means of understanding developmental disabilities, including intellectual disability, and developmental problems that occur during pregnancy. Today, the NICHD conducts and supports research on all stages of human development, from preconception to adulthood, to better understand the health of children, adults, families, and communities. The NICHD's mission is to ensure that every person is born healthy and wanted; that women suffer no harmful effects from reproductive processes; that all children have the chance to achieve their full potential for healthy and productive lives, free from disease or disability; and that all people achieve health, productivity, independence, and well-being through optimal rehabilitation.

We also acknowledge several individuals who have contributed substantial effort to making this volume a reality. First, for their efforts in establishing the partnership and suggesting the workshops on which this volume is partially based, we thank John Lunde and Megan Sibole of Mars, Inc. For making the workshops take place as efficiently as they did, we thank Tiffany Ray, Wanda Hawkes, and Fuambai Ahmadu at the NICHD and Sarah Wright of the WALTHAM Centre. Finally, for patiently assisting us in finalizing a book prospectus and for guiding us through the production process, a special cheer for Sarah Shepke, our acquisitions editor, whose enthusiasm for the subject of the book was instrumental in its publication!

This book is dedicated to Laraine Freund
(July 27, 1990–January 1, 2010).

We dedicate this book to Laraine Freund. This alert, fun-loving, hard-working 19-year-old volunteered for the Child Development and Behavior Branch at the *Eunice Kennedy Shriver* National Institute of Child Health and Human Development during the summer of 2009, when the branch was particularly hard hit with additional workload but, due to fiscal constraints, could not hire summer interns. Laraine came in and went to work, and everyone in the branch not only deeply appreciated her hard work and dedication but became very fond of her. Laraine knew that the team was working on books about the science of human–animal interaction (HAI) and even did some reference checking on chapters. Her mother is a member of the branch, and we learned that both mother and daughter were horse enthusiasts who had developed a special relationship with their horses and with each other as they shared this activity. We wanted to have a party for Laraine when she was through working for us, but never got the chance. Laraine, who received a heart transplant at a very young age, began to have health problems. She was hospitalized and suffered a prolonged illness. During this time, her strength and good cheer were amazing, and her mother set up a web site that the branch, our Mars HAI partners, and others watched to track her progress. After a brave battle, Laraine died on New Year's Day 2010. Horses and family pets were an important part of Laraine's life, and we think she would be honored to have this book, which seeks to scientifically understand the beneficial role that animals can play in our lives, dedicated to her.

Introduction

LAYLA ESPOSITO, PEGGY McCARDLE,
VALERIE MAHOLMES, SANDRA McCUNE, AND JAMES A. GRIFFIN

For many people, the most vivid memories of childhood involve a family pet, including the arrival of a new puppy or kitten, shared adventures (and misadventures), the giving and receiving of affection, and often the first experience of loss and mourning. Pets have been part of human culture for millennia (Knight & Herzog, 2009; Serpell, 2008), and many pet owners tend to attribute many of their human thoughts and emotions to both domestic and wild animals as they interact with them and observe their behaviors. Pets have moved from the yard into the household in many communities, and pet ownership is on the rise (American Pet Products Association, 2008).

The American Pet Products Association reported in the 2009–2010 National Pet Owners Survey that of the 72 million households that include a pet, 64% have dogs, 53.5% have cats, and 5.5% own horses. Several other types of animals are also commonly kept as pets, such as fish, reptiles, and rodents. Current statistics suggest that there may be more pets than children in the United States and that a child is more likely to grow up in a household with a pet present than with a father (Melson, 2004; see also Chapters 4 and 11).

Animals are not only often considered part of the family in the homes in which they reside, but they also continue to provide personal service in traditional roles (e.g., Seeing Eye dogs) and more novel situations (e.g., alerting dogs that can tell when a sleeping child with diabetes is in danger of chemical imbalance and can wake the child and/or parents). Animals are found in schools and in therapeutic settings. Teachers frequently include pets in classroom lessons and activities, and psychotherapists may use animals to facilitate patient interaction and conversation.

Given the various ways in which animals are involved in the daily lives of children and families, it is imperative that the field of human–animal interaction (HAI) be well studied and that the therapeutic involvement of animals be based on scientific evidence. Although there has been interest in HAI for decades, there has not been a commensurate amount of systematic research. Anecdotes and small studies indicate that there is the potential for HAI to provide benefits to human health and development; however, more evidence is needed to confirm such benefits.

In 1987, the National Institutes of Health (NIH) held a Consensus Conference to examine the available research on the health benefits of pets. Experts from a variety of disciplines reviewed the research in five topic areas to identify concepts that needed a stronger scientific base. The areas were the role of pets in child development, the role of pets in cardiovascular health, health correlates of pet ownership in older people, the role of pets in social and therapeutic situations, and safety and risks in people–pet relationships.

The experts agreed that definitive conclusions on possible benefits of companion animals would require much larger sample sizes and more rigorous experimental designs than existed in the studies that had been conducted at that time. Studies reviewed by the expert panel suggested that pets could benefit some children by facilitating stable relationships with the children's peers and with adults, yet these studies were limited by small sample sizes and disproportionate samples from upper and middle classes. The panel recommended that prospective longitudinal studies be conducted across racial and socioeconomic boundaries to determine long-term consequences of pet ownership and to identify specific populations, with or without pets, of children who were at risk for developing problems in social, emotional, and cognitive development, as well as conditions and experiences that might put children at risk for these problems.

The body of HAI research has matured since the early 1970s from anecdotal studies and individual case histories to peer-reviewed science. Although many studies use the scientific method, it often remains difficult to draw definitive conclusions from them. Because studies have often used small sample sizes, lacked statistical power, or lacked adequate controls, the potential of the HAI field to deliver health benefits has yet to be fully realized. The field has great promise and relevance to people's lives, and a focus on quality is vital to ensure that the theoretical work can be applied to greatest effect.

In 2008, the National Institute of Child Health and Human De- velopment (NICHD) and the WALTHAM Centre for Pet Nutrition, a division of Mars, Inc., cosponsored a series of meetings that brought together researchers and practitioners who were working on animal behavior or child health and development with those who were studying or clinically applying principles of HAI. Drawing from those meetings, this book describes the human and animal sides of HAI, presents the available science, and calls for evidence-based practice in a field that is growing rapidly.

In this volume, HAI refers to the mutual and dynamic relation- ships between people and animals and the ways in which these inter- actions may affect physical and psychological health and well-being. The concept has also been termed the human–animal bond or the human–companion animal bond. Within the domain of HAI, various groups and subfields use different terminology.

Animal-assisted therapy (AAT) describes the intentional inclusion of an animal in a treatment plan to facilitate healing and recovery of patients who have acute or chronic conditions. AAT is goal directed, is based on the individual's personalized treatment plan, should be car- ried out by a trained professional, and should be evaluated periodically to monitor progress. AAT is often used to enhance a variety of other types of more traditional treatments, such as occupational therapy, speech therapy, physical rehabilitation, or even psychotherapy. The anticipated outcomes of AAT can include improvements in cognition, emotion regulation or affect, social competence, or physical abilities. Animal-assisted activities (AAAs), however, involve animals in a recre- ational or educational situation, do not have specific treatment goals, and can be carried out without the direction of a professional. AAAs are less formal and structured than AAT, and typically no data are collected on the impact of the interaction (Delta Society, 2009). Together, AAT and AAA make up animal-assisted intervention (AAI). AAI may be very important in guiding and intervening in the lives of children and youth, but many people are unfamiliar with it, and even those who know of it may fail to see the need for research or an evidence base for such practices. This book seeks to address those gaps in understanding.

This volume takes a multidisciplinary perspective and includes an international group of authors, including psychologists, psychiatrists, nurses, and educators who provide and/or study child development and/or AAI; psychologists, ethologists, and veterinarians who study animal behavior; and social scientists and public health researchers who study population-level impacts of animals on human health and behavior. We as researchers hope that the presentation of the material in a single volume of data drawn from multiple disciplines, research methodologies (e.g., survey research, experimental studies), and countries will accomplish two goals: 1) provide information to clinicians, teachers, and the public about the science behind HAI and the value that it can have for children when it is properly understood and guided; and 2) provide a basis for features that researchers might consider including in their studies. For example, they might include questions about pet ownership and observations of child–animal interaction as well as strictly human–human interaction. They might also focus on experimental methodologies to evaluate AAI that have been shown to have some benefit for children with disabilities, acute or chronic health conditions, or social or emotional difficulties.

The authors who contributed to this volume present research findings that could form the evidence base for practice in the therapeutic involvement of animals to promote better health and development in children. They also provide future directions for research that is needed to continue to build this evidence base, including foundational work to move the field toward a deeper understanding of the nature of HAI and clinical trials of the use of HAI with children. Section I sets the context for the volume, addressing the role that animals play in human lives and in child development. Section II addresses the involvement of animals in human therapies. Therapists have noted that animals seem to have facilitative effects, and as noted earlier, animals are already frequently included in various therapeutic settings. The chapters in Section II examine some of these situations and interactions and the research that has been done to examine them. The third and final section of the book discusses why it is important for research on HAI to provide an evidence base showing its effectiveness, both for clinical practices and to advise parents and teachers about promoting healthy interactions between children and animals. The chapters present approaches, illustrated with data, on how existing programs can and should be evaluated and can serve as a resource for researchers as well as being informative for practitioners.

Overall, it is hoped that this volume stimulates an increased level of interest in the field of HAI and results in an increased number of high-quality studies that can examine the essence of the interactions between animals and children and youth. If they are done correctly, it is expected that such studies will demonstrate the capacity of HAI to improve human health and sustain and promote healthy development. They will provide an evidence base for therapeutic involvement of animals in human treatment and rehabilitation.

REFERENCES

American Pet Products Association. (2009). *2009–2010 national pet owners survey.* Byrum, CT: Author.

Delta Society. (2009). *Animal assisted activities & animal assisted therapy.* Retrieved November 3, 2009, from http://www.deltasociety.org/Page.aspx?pid=317

Knight, S., & Herzog, H. (2009). All creatures great and small: New perspectives on psychology and human–animal interaction. *Journal of Social Issues, 65*(3), 451–461.

Knight, S., & Herzog, H. (Eds.). (2009). New perspectives on human–animal interactions: Theory, policy, and research. *Journal of Social Issues, 65*(3), 451–633.

Melson, G. (2004). *Why the wild things are: Animals in the lives of children.* Cambridge, MA: Harvard University Press.

National Institutes of Health. (1987). *The health benefits of pets.* Retrieved December 7, 2009, from http://consensus.nih.gov/1987/1987HealthBenefits Petsta003html.htm

Serpell, J. (2008). *In the company of animals: A study of human–animal relationships.* Cambridge, United Kingdom: Cambridge University Press.

Animals in Our Lives

A photograph of a child playing melts most people's hearts. Puppies and kittens evoke similar emotional responses, as evidenced by their inclusion in modern advertising. Humans attribute many emotions to animals, even considering them members of the family. Money spent on veterinary care, special pet food, and toys denote the love felt for pets. How did this love affair with pets begin and is the relationship mutually beneficial?

The chapters in this section address these topics. In Chapter 1, James A. Serpell, an ethologist in a school of veterinary medicine, traces the history of pet ownership in Western culture, from the ancient Greeks and Romans to the modern day and across various socioeconomic levels. He explains how pets can serve as sources of social support, describes the value of social support for health in general, and examines how pets in their social support role can improve their owners' health, citing available evidence.

In Chapter 2, Australian sociologist Lisa Jane Wood examines pets' impact on communities. She discusses her research on the role of pets in building *social capital* (a social science concept that refers to connections within and between social networks, such as residents of a neighborhood) and sense of community.

In Chapter 3, Alan M. Beck, a professor of animal ecology, provides an overview of the ways in which animals can affect children's health. He covers the intentional interactions of children with pets, human attitudes toward animals in general, the inclusion of animals in therapeutic settings, and biomedical ethical issues related to the use of therapy animals in public health research.

Chapter 4 gets more specific about the public health implications of pets for children. It is authored by Lynne Haverkos, trained in pediatrics and public health and now a research administrator in health promotion and risk prevention; Karyl J. Hurley, trained in veterinary medicine; Sandra McCune, trained in animal behavior; and Peggy McCardle, trained in public health. These authors delineate both the potentially positive and negative impacts of animals on children's health, provide health statistics on injuries caused by animals (e.g., the incidence of dog bites, which are most frequent among preschool children), and discuss *zoonoses*, infections that can be transmitted between animals and humans. Zoonoses are a source of fear that can affect how humans and animals interact; pet owners and parents in general (and really all people) should know what they are, how they are usually transmitted, and what can be done to reduce the possibility of transmission. The chapter also includes advice about pet selection and information about resources on safety and health issues that can guide parents, practitioners advising parents, and therapists who use animals in their practices.

In Chapter 5, Patricia B. McConnell, an ethologist and Certified Applied Animal Behaviorist, discusses the relationship between humans and dogs and gives insights about animal behavior, including how to "read" dog moods and temperament, how to tell when dogs are feeling threatened, and how to guide safe and successful interactions between children and dogs.

Twelve-year-old Keisha was a very shy little girl. She struggled to make friends in her class and often ate alone in the school cafeteria. Keisha performed well academically and had good relationships with her teachers and other adults in the school, but she had trouble in social situations with peers.

When Keisha's family moved to a new city because her father's job was transferred, her parents worried that she might have even more difficulty making friends in her new school. To help her adjust, they decided to buy her a puppy. She named him Buddy. Keisha walked around her new neighborhood with Buddy to explore the surroundings and learn her way around. She found a playground and saw groups of kids playing basketball and other kids just hanging out. Keisha threw her Frisbee and Buddy ran to catch it. He scooped it up in his mouth and brought it back to Keisha. She threw the Frisbee again. Some of the kids noticed Keisha and Buddy and came over to talk to her. Suddenly Keisha was barraged with questions: "What's his name? He's so cute—how old is he? Does he do any other tricks? Can I throw the Frisbee and see if he'll bring it back to me?"

The next day was Keisha's first day at her new school. She entered her homeroom classroom and saw two of the kids she had met at the playground. As they shouted greetings to her from across the room, she waved shyly. After class, the kids approached Keisha to ask about Buddy. Keisha and her new friends walked to the next class together.

CHAPTER 1

Historical and Cultural Perspectives on Human–Pet Interactions

JAMES A. SERPELL

Most domesticated animals are valued for the practical services and economic resources that they provide for their owners. The rewards of pet ownership, in contrast, derive principally from the relationship itself. People value their pets, not because they are useful, but primarily because their company fulfills social and emotional needs that are comparable, though not necessarily identical, to the needs fulfilled by human companions. Although the term *pet* expresses mainly the affective (or occasionally aesthetic) aspects of humans' relationships with certain animals, clearly there are cases (e.g., working sheepdogs, guide dogs) in which an animal may be valued simultaneously for practical and emotional reasons (Serpell, 2004).

Perhaps because it frequently appears to serve no obvious practical function, the phenomenon of pet keeping is often trivialized or dismissed as a largely modern, bourgeois activity associated with Western affluence and materialism (Serpell, 1996). In reality, the practice of keeping animals as pets is neither a modern phenomenon nor a predominantly Western one. Pet keeping, in the sense used herein, has ancient roots and may have been a prelude to the domestication of some animals (Serpell, 1989b).

HISTORICAL AND CULTURAL PERSPECTIVES

Some of the oldest known archaeological remains of domestic wolf-dogs, dating from the Upper Paleolithic period around 11,000–14,000 years ago, were found buried together with humans in a manner that is indicative of strong mutual bonds of attachment (Benecke, 1987; Davis & Valla, 1978; Morey, 2006). Similar dog–human burials from early Amerindian sites suggest that affectionate relationships between humans and dogs may also have existed more than 8,000 years ago in the North American Midwest (Morey, 1992). Likewise, the discovery of nonindigenous cat remains buried in association with humans on the Mediterranean island of Cyprus about 9,500 years ago provides evidence that people were taking tame wildcats on ocean voyages several thousand years before those animals became household pets or the objects of religious veneration in ancient Egypt (Malek, 1993; Serpell, 2000; Vigne, Guilaine, Debue, Haye, & Gérard, 2004). The notion that late Paleolithic and early Neolithic humans were in the habit of capturing and taming wild animals and keeping them as pets is entirely consistent with the observed behavior of more modern hunting and gathering peoples. According to numerous reports by explorers and anthropologists, pet keeping among hunting and gathering peoples is the norm rather than the exception, and it is typically characterized by intense emotional attachments for the animals involved, as well as by strong moral taboos against killing or eating them. This is even the case when the animals belong to species that are hunted routinely for food (Erikson, 1987, 2000; Serpell, 1989b).

Pictorial and documentary evidence further suggests that pet keeping has been practiced continuously throughout human history, although its popularity has waxed and waned somewhat unpredictably over time and from place to place. It is clear that many prominent ancient Egyptians, Greeks, and Romans were ardent pet lovers and that pet dogs and cats were frequent and long-standing denizens of the imperial households of both China and Japan (although not necessarily at the same time) (Serpell, 1996). In Europe and colonial North America, pet keeping did not become widely respectable until the mid- to late 18th century. Medieval and renaissance moralists and theologians regarded any kind of physical intimacy between people and animals as morally suspect and generally condemned the practice of keeping animals exclusively for companionship. Consequently, pet keeping remained chiefly the province of the upper classes and ruling elite until the end of the early modern period, when the emergence of both enlightenment attitudes and an urban middle class saw the gradual spread of pets into all sectors of Western society (Grier, 2006; Harwood, 1928/2002; Kete, 1994;

Ritvo, 1987; Salisbury, 1994; Serpell, 1996; Thomas, 1983). This change in animal-related attitudes and behavior can be partly attributed to the steady migration of Europeans and Americans out of rural areas and into towns and cities at that time. The rural exodus helped distance growing sectors of the population from direct involvement in the consumptive exploitation of animals, thereby eliminating the need for value systems that were designed to segregate humans and nonhumans into separate moral domains (Serpell, 1996; Serpell & Paul, 1994; Thomas, 1983).

THE HISTORY OF ANIMAL-ASSISTED INTERVENTIONS

The notion that relationships with pet animals could serve a therapeutic or socializing function also surfaced during the early modern period (Serpell, 2006). Writing in 1699, for example, John Locke advocated giving children "dogs, squirrels, birds or any such things" to look after as a means of encouraging them to develop tender feelings and a sense of responsibility for others (Locke, 1699/1964, p. 154). Compassion and concern for animal welfare also became one of the favorite didactic themes of early children's literature during the 18th and early 19th centuries, where its clear purpose was to inculcate an ethic of kindness and gentility, particularly among boys (Grier, 1999; Ritvo, 1987; Turner, 1980). In the late 18th century, theories concerning the socializing influence of animal companionship also began to be applied to the treatment of mental illness.

The earliest well-documented experiment in animal-assisted therapy took place in England at the York Retreat and was the brainchild of a progressive Quaker named William Tuke. The Retreat employed treatment methods that were exceptionally enlightened compared with the standards of the period. Patients were permitted to wear their own clothing and were encouraged to engage in handicrafts, to write, and to read books. They were also allowed to wander freely around the Retreat's courtyards and gardens, which were stocked with a variety of small tame or domestic animals. In his *Description of the Retreat*, Samuel Tuke, the founder's grandson, described how the internal courtyards of the Retreat were supplied

> with a number of animals; such as rabbits, sea-gulls, hawks, and poultry. These creatures are generally very familiar with the patients: and it is believed they are not only the means of innocent pleasure; but that the intercourse with them, sometimes tends to awaken the social and benevolent feelings. (1813/1964, p. 96)

During the 19th century, pet animals became increasingly common features of mental institutions in England and elsewhere. According to an article published in the *Illustrated London News* of 1860, the women's

ward at the Bethlem Royal Hospital in London was at that time "cheer-
fully lighted, and enlivened with prints and busts, with aviaries and
pet animals," whereas in the men's ward the same fondness was man-
ifested "for pet birds and animals, cats, canaries, squirrels, greyhounds
&c. . . . . [some patients] pace the long gallery incessantly, pouring out
their woes to those who listen to them, or, if there be none to listen, to
the dogs and cats" (as cited in Allderidge, 1991, p. 760).

The therapeutic effects of animal companionship in the treatment
of physical ailments also appear to have been recognized at this time.
In her 1860 *Notes on Nursing*, for instance, Florence Nightingale
observed that a small pet "is often an excellent companion for the sick,
for long chronic cases especially" (Nightingale, 1860, p. 103). However,
despite the apparent success of 19th-century experiments in animal-
assisted interventions, the advent of scientific medicine largely elimi-
nated animals from hospital settings by the early decades of the 20th
century (Allderidge, 1991). For the next 50 years, virtually the only
medical contexts in which animals were mentioned were discussions
concerned with zoonotic disease and public health or psychoanalytic
theories concerning the origins of mental illness, in which animals
were symbolic referents (Freud, 1959).

The recent revival of interest in the health and therapeutic benefits
of pet keeping can be attributed largely to the writings of the child psychologist Boris Levinson. Although Levinson (1972) speculated at considerable length on the potential beneficial influence of pets on human
development, his chief contribution was the entirely novel idea of
using pets as co-therapists during psychotherapeutic counseling.
Levinson observed that many of his more withdrawn patients readily
related to, and interacted with, his pet dog Jingles, although they were
unwilling or unable to interact with Levinson himself. He found that,
by carefully involving himself in this animal–child relationship, he was
able to break down the child's initial hostility and reserve and to establish therapeutic rapport far more rapidly than was otherwise possible.
Pets not only served as icebreakers in this context, but also seemed to
provide the child with a relatively neutral medium through which to
express unconscious emotional conflicts, worries, and fears (Levinson,
1962, 1969).

Perhaps surprisingly, Levinson did not endorse the popular idea
that children instinctively identify more easily with animals than with
adult humans. Instead, he favored the view that children with an emotional health disability who have experienced difficulties in their relationships with adults relate more easily or quickly to animals
(Levinson, 1969). The reason for this, he argued, was primarily an animal's ability to offer the child nonthreatening, nonjudgmental, and

essentially unconditional attention and affection. This ability enabled the pet to serve as an adequate substitute companion and provider of comfort when other relationships failed. Although Levinson regarded that temporary role of the pet as important to the child's psychological well-being, he was not convinced that such attachments were necessarily always beneficial in the long-term. Indeed, he detected among adult pet owners some individuals who seemed to have become permanently fixated on animals in preference to humans. To Levinson, therefore, the relationship between the child with an emotional disturbance and the pet represented a kind of bridge that, if carefully exploited, could be used to reawaken the child's enthusiasm for interpersonal relationships (Levinson, 1967, 1969, 1972). Although Levinson's early publications on pet-facilitated psychotherapy received a distinctly lukewarm response from his peers (Levinson, 1983), many of his original ideas have been substantially vindicated by the results of subsequent research.

WHY PEOPLE KEEP PETS

Although it appears that people of all cultures have enjoyed keeping pets and that the practice has existed for thousands of years, it is unlikely that pet keeping ever previously attained the level of popularity that it currently enjoys in North America. According to recent surveys, there are now about 77.5 million pet dogs in America living in roughly 45.6 million homes; 93.6 million cats in 38.2 million homes; 171.7 million freshwater fish in 13.3 million homes; millions of pet ferrets, rabbits, guinea pigs, hamsters, rats, mice, gerbils, birds of various kinds; and a wide assortment of reptiles and amphibians (American Pet Products Association, 2008). Pet keeping is now a majority activity in the United States, with 62% of U.S. households owning at least one pet and 45% owning more than one.

So what explains the enduring popularity of pets and the apparent willingness of people to incur the various costs of keeping them? Certainly, from an evolutionary perspective, this phenomenon can be hard to explain (Archer, 1997). According to evolutionary theory, the process of natural selection favors individuals who behave in ways that are likely to maximize their own survival and reproductive success and/or that of their own close relatives (Hamilton, 1964). Because pets do not belong to the same species, much less the same kin group as their owners, it is difficult to see why pet keeping evolved in the first place or why it persists, given the costs or potential costs to individual pet owners and the communities in which they live.

One of the more common responses to this evolutionary puzzle is the argument that pets are essentially social parasites, animals that have evolved specialized techniques for persuading humans to care for them by releasing and exploiting the innate parenting instincts (Archer, 1997; Budiansky, 2000; Gould, 1979). The superficially infantile appearance of some pets—and the so-called cute responses they appear to evoke in people—appear to lend support to this idea, but clearly there is more to it than that. Although pet owners may find their dogs and cats irresistibly cute, even the most besotted owners would probably acknowledge that they are not in fact nurturing their own biological offspring (Serpell, 1996). Even if humans are in some way innately predisposed to find pets appealing, it does not follow from this that these relationships are necessarily detrimental. On the contrary, *mutualistic* relationships—relationships in which two different species of organism derive mutual benefit by associating with each other—are probably the norm rather than the exception in nature (Herre, Knowlton, Mueller, & Rehner, 1999), and human–pet relationships may represent another, albeit rather unique, example of this type of association. If this is the case, however, it is important to specify the kinds of benefits that might accrue to both participants. The benefits to the animals are obvious. By providing them with food, water, shelter, care, and protection from danger, humans have enabled these animals to expand into a new ecological niche in which they have become hugely successful in evolutionary terms. However, what kinds of nonmaterial benefits might people derive from the company of pets that could potentially outweigh the costs of caring for them?

An important key to answering this question may lie in the phenomenon of social support. Social support is a theoretical construct that expresses the degree to which individuals are socially embedded and have a sense of belonging, obligation, and intimacy with others (Cobb, 1976; Schwarzer & Knoll, 2007). Some authors distinguish between *perceived social support* and *social network* characteristics. The former term represents a largely qualitative description of a person's level of satisfaction with the support that he or she receives from particular social relationships, whereas the latter term is a more quantitative measure incorporating the number, frequency, and type of a person's overall social interactions (Eriksen, 1994). In practice, both kinds of social support tend to break down into different components, including 1) *emotional support,* the sense of being able to turn to others for comfort in times of stress or the feeling of being cared for by others; 2) *social integration,* the feeling of being an accepted part of an established group or social network; 3) *esteem support,* the sense of receiving positive, self-affirming feedback from others regarding one's value, competence, abilities, or worth; 4) *practical, instrumental, or informational support,* the knowledge that others will provide financial, practical, or informational assistance when it is needed; and 5) *opportunities for nurturance and protection,* the sense of being needed or depended on by others (Collis & McNicholas, 1998).

No matter how it is defined, it is now clear that social support (or a lack of it) has a profound impact on human mental and physical health (House, Landis, & Umberson, 1988; Kiecolt-Glaser & Newton, 2001; Lim & Young, 2006; Monroe, Bromet, Connell, & Steiner, 1986). The importance of social relationships to human well-being has been acknowledged implicitly throughout history; witness the long-standing use of exile and solitary confinement as forms of punishment. Since the 1980s, however, a growing body of scientific evidence has emerged that confirms a strong, positive link between social support and enhanced health and survival. In particular, social support factors have been shown to protect people against cardiovascular disease and strokes, rheumatic fever, diabetes, nephritis, pneumonia, and most forms of cancer, as well as depression, schizophrenia, and suicide (see, e.g., Eriksen, 1994; Esterling, Kiecolt-Glaser, Bodnar, & Glaser, 1994; House et al., 1988; Kikusui, Winslow, & Mori, 2006; Sherbourne, Meredith, Rogers, & Ware, 1992; Uchino, 2006; Vilhjalmson, 1993). The precise mechanisms underlying these lifesaving effects of social support are the subject of ongoing research, but most experts agree that at least some of the benefits arise from the phenomenon of social buffering, which is the capacity of supportive social relationships to buffer or ameliorate the deleterious health consequences of psychosocial stress. It is well established that prolonged psychosocial stress results in chronically elevated levels of glucocorticoid (stress) hormones in the blood and that these in turn can have a damaging impact on the body's immune system (Ader, Cohen, & Felten, 1995; Kikusui et al., 2006; Uchino, 2006). Additional evidence suggests that these effects of social support may be mediated by the neuropeptide hormones oxytocin and vasopressin, which appear to play critical roles in the modulation of attachment behavior and social bonding in mammals (Donaldson & Young, 2008; Lim & Young, 2006). Furthermore, the elevation in oxytocin levels that is associated with pleasurable social interactions appears to have a down-regulating effect on the hypothalamo–pituitary–adrenal axis that regulates the stress response (Heinrichs, Baumgartner, Kirshbaum, & Ehlert, 2003; Kikusui et al., 2006).

In general, the findings of research on the possible role of pets in people's lives seem to fit this social support/social buffering paradigm. For instance, pet owners have been shown to possess fewer physiological risk factors (e.g., high blood pressure, high levels of serum triglycerides and cholesterol) for cardiovascular disease than nonowners, and they exhibit improved survival and longevity following heart attacks (Anderson, Reid, & Jennings, 1992; Friedmann, Thomas, & Eddy, 2000; Garrity & Stallones, 1998). They also appear to be more resilient in the face of stressful life events, so they experience fewer health problems and fewer visits to doctors for treatment (Headey, 1998; Siegel, 1990). The acquisition of a new pet has been found to be associated with improvements in owners' mental and physical health and with sustained reductions in their tendency to overreact to stressful situations and stimuli (Allen, Blascovich, Tomaka, & Kelsey, 1991; Serpell, 1991). Significantly, pet owners who report being very attached to their pets tend to benefit more from pet ownership than those who are less attached, and dog owners tend to do better than cat owners, perhaps because the attachment for dogs, on average, is stronger (Freidmann & Thomas, 1995; Ory & Goldberg, 1983; Serpell, 1991). Although interpreting such findings is difficult, and further research is needed to clarify these apparent links between pets and human health, most authorities now agree that these are the kinds of results that would be expected if pets are serving their owners primarily as sources of nonhuman social support (Collis & McNicholas, 1998; Garrity & Stallones, 1998; Serpell, 1996; Virués-Ortega & Buela-Casal, 2006).

Some recent findings also suggest that the mechanisms underlying these salutary effects of pet ownership may be similar to the mechanisms that are thought to be responsible for the social buffering effect in human relationships. Two studies demonstrated significant increases in plasma oxytocin levels in human subjects following interactions with their own dogs, but not with unfamiliar dogs (Miller et al., 2009; Odendaal & Meintjes, 2003). In another recent study, significantly elevated levels of urinary oxytocin were detected among dog owners who received greater amounts of visual attention (gaze) from their dogs in an experimental situation. Interestingly, the same owners professed to feeling stronger attachments for their dogs than did other owners involved in the study (Nagasáwa, Kikusui, Onaka, & Ohta, 2009).

Such studies illustrate the importance of acknowledging that not all human–pet relationships are likely to be equal in terms of their psychological and physiological impact on owners. Just as interpersonal relationships vary greatly in quality, depending on the particular dyadic interactions that take place between two people (Hinde, 1979), the same is true of people's relationships and interactions with animals (Budge, Spicer, Jones, & St. George, 1998; Serpell, 1989a, 2003). Unfortunately, the majority of studies that have looked at the effects of pets on people have tended to ignore this important source of variation. Further progress in this field will likely require studies that address more complex and interesting questions: Why, for example, are some human–pet relationships more or less rewarding than others? Why do some quickly end in "divorce," whereas others are remembered with intense feelings of loss many years after the animal's death? Also, can the quality of these individual relationships be related to their supposed benefits? Finding answers to questions such as these will help to move the field beyond the idea of pets as some sort of universal panacea and toward a more nuanced understanding of both the benefits and disadvantages of these unique interspecies relationships.

Finally, the social buffering hypothesis may help to provide some explanation for the explosion in the popularity of pets since the early 1970s and 1980s. The results of a variety of social and public health surveys have documented the gradual collapse or fragmentation of traditional social support systems in the United States, particularly since the 1960s. Such trends have been marked by a dramatic rise in the number of Americans living alone, especially in urban areas; escalating divorce rates and an increase in the number of couples who choose not to have children or to have fewer children; people spending less time socializing with their friends or getting involved in their local communities; and families dispersing so that fewer close relatives now live within easy reach of one another (Putnam, 2000). In light of these trends, it seems plausible to argue that the recent growth of the pet population at least partly reflects people's attempts to augment their traditional support systems by using companion animals as alternative sources of social support.

REFERENCES

Ader, R.L., Cohen, N., & Felten, D. (1995). Psychoneuroimmunology: Interactions between the nervous system and the immune system. *The Lancet, 345*, 99–103.

Allderidge, P.H. (1991). A cat, surpassing in beauty, and other therapeutic animals. *Psychiatric Bulletin, 15,* 759–762.

Allen, K.M., Blascovich, J., Tomaka, J., & Kelsey, R.M. (1991). Presence of human friends and pet dogs as moderators of autonomic responses to stress in women. *Journal of Personality and Social Psychology, 61,* 582–589.

American Pet Products Association. (2008). *APPA National Pet Owners Survey: 2007–2008*. Greenwich, CT: Author.

Anderson, W.P., Reid, C.M., & Jennings, G.L. (1992). Pet ownership and risk factors for cardiovascular disease. *Medical Journal of Australia, 157,* 298–301.

Archer, J. (1997). Why do people love their pets? *Evolution and Human Behavior, 18,* 237–259.

Benecke, N. (1987). Studies on early dog remains from northern Europe. *Journal of Archaeological Science, 14,* 31–39.

Budge, R.C., Spicer, J., Jones, B., & St. George, R. (1998). Health correlates of compatibility and attachment in human–companion animal relationships. *Society & Animals, 6,* 219–234.

Budiansky, S. (2000). *The truth about dogs: An inquiry into the ancestry, social conventions, mental habits, and moral fiber of* Canis familiaris. New York: Viking.

Cobb, S. (1976). Social support as a moderator of life stress. *Psychosomatic Medicine, 38,* 300–314.

Collis, G.M., & McNicholas, J. (1998). A theoretical basis for health benefits of pet ownership. In C.C. Wilson & D.C. Turner (Eds.), *Companion animals in human health* (pp. 105–122). Thousand Oaks, CA: Sage.

Davis, S.J.M., & Valla, F. (1978). Evidence for domestication of the dog 12,000 years ago in the Natufian of Israel. *Nature, 276,* 608–610.

Donaldson, Z.R., & Young, L.J. (2008). Oxytocin, vasopressin, and the neurogenetics of sociality. *Science, 322,* 900–904.

Eriksen, W. (1994). The role of social support in the pathogenesis of coronary heart disease: A literature review. *Family Practice, 11,* 201–209.

Erikson, P. (1987). De l'apprivoisement à l'approvisionnement: Chasse, alliance et familiarisation en Amazonie Amérindienne. *Techniques et Cultures, 9,* 105–140.

Erikson, P. (2000). The social significance of pet-keeping among Amazonian Indians. In A.L. Podberscek, E.S. Paul, & J.A. Serpell (Eds.), *Companion animals and us: Exploring the relationships between people and pets* (pp. 7–26). Cambridge, MA: Cambridge University Press.

Esterling, B.A., Kiecolt-Glaser, J., Bodnar, J.C., & Glaser, R. (1994). Chronic stress, social support, and persistent alterations in the natural killer cell response to cytokines in older adults. *Health Psychology, 13,* 291–328.

Freidmann, E., & Thomas, S.A. (1995). Pet ownership, social support, and one-year survival after acute myocardial infarction in the Cardiac Arrhythmia Suppression Trial (CAST). *American Journal of Cardiology, 76,* 1213–1217.

Friedmann, E., Thomas, S.A., & Eddy, T.J. (2000). Companion animals and human health: Physical and cardiovascular influences. In A.L. Podberscek, E. Paul, & J.A. Serpell (Eds.), *Companion animals and us: Exploring the relationships between people and pets* (pp. 125–142). Cambridge, MA: Cambridge University Press.

Freud, S. (1959). *The interpretation of dreams* (J. Strachey, Trans.). New York: Basic Books.

Garrity, T.F., & Stallones, L. (1998). Effects of pet contact on human well-being: Review of recent research. In C.C. Wilson & D.C. Turner (Eds.), *Companion animals in human health* (pp. 3–22). Thousand Oaks, CA: Sage.

Gould, S.J. (1979). Mickey Mouse meets Konrad Lorenz. *Natural History, 88,* 30–36.

Grier, K.C. (1999). Childhood socialization and companion animals: United States, 1820–1870. *Society & Animals, 7,* 95–120.

Grier, K.C. (2006). *Pets in America: A history.* Chapel Hill: University of North Carolina Press.

Hamilton, W.D. (1964). The genetical evolution of social behavior. *Journal of Theoretical Biology, 7,* 1–32.

Harwood, D. (2002). *Love for animals and how it developed in Great Britain.* Lampeter: Edwin Mellen Press. (Original work published 1928)

Headey, B. (1998). Health benefits and health cost savings due to pets: Preliminary estimates from an Australian national survey. *Social Indicators Research, 47,* 233–243.

Heinrichs, M., Baumgartner, T., Kirshbaum, C., & Ehlert, U. (2003). Social support and oxytocin interact to suppress cortisol and subjective responses to stress. *Biological Psychiatry, 54,* 1389–1398.

Herre, E.A., Knowlton, N., Mueller, U.G., & Rehner, S.A. (1999). The evolution of mutualisms: Exploring the paths between conflict and cooperation. *Trends in Ecology and Evolution, 14,* 49–53.

Hinde, R.A. (1979). *Towards understanding relationships.* New York: Academic Press.

House, J.S., Landis, K.R., & Umberson, D. (1988). Social relationships and health. *Science, 241*, 540–545.

Kete, K. (1994). *The beast in the boudoir: Pet keeping in nineteenth-century Paris.* Berkeley: University of California Press.

Kiecolt-Glaser, J.K., & Newton, T.L. (2001). Marriage and health: His and hers. *Psychological Bulletin 127*(4), 472–503.

Kikusui, T., Winslow, J.T., & Mori, Y. (2006). Social buffering: Relief from stress and anxiety. *Philosophical Transactions of the Royal Society of London, Series B, 361*(1476), 2215–2228.

Levinson, B.M. (1962). The dog as co-therapist. *Mental Hygiene, 46*, 59–65.

Levinson, B.M. (1967). The pet and the child's bereavement. *Mental Hygiene, 51*, 197–200.

Levinson, B.M. (1969). *Pet-oriented child psychotherapy.* Springfield, IL: Charles C Thomas.

Levinson, B.M. (1972). *Pets and human development.* Springfield, IL: Charles C Thomas.

Levinson, B.M. (1983). The future of research in relationships between people and their animal companions. In A.H. Katcher & A.M. Beck (Eds.), *New perspectives on our lives with companion animals* (pp. 536–550). Philadelphia: University of Pennsylvania Press.

Lim, M.M., & Young, L.J. (2006). Neuropeptide regulation of affiliative behavior and social bonding in animals. *Hormones and Behavior, 50*, 506–517.

Locke, J. (1964). *Some thoughts concerning education. Reprinted with an introduction by F.W. Garforth.* London: Heinemann. (Original work published 1699)

Malek, J. (1993). *The cat in ancient Egypt.* London: British Museum Press.

Miller, S.C., Kennedy, C., DeVoe, D., Hickey, M., Nelson, T., & Kogan, L. (2009). An examination of changes in oxytocin levels before and after interactions with a bonded dog. *Anthrozoös, 22*, 31–42.

Monroe, S.M., Bromet, E.J., Connell, M.M., & Steiner, S.C. (1986). Social support, life events, and depressive symptoms: A 1-year prospective study. *Journal of Consultative Clinical Psychology, 54*(4), 424–431.

Morey, D.F. (1992). Size, shape and development in the evolution of the domestic dog. *Journal of Archaeological Science, 19*, 181–204.

Morey, D.F. (2006). Burying key evidence: The social bond between dogs and people. *Journal of Archaeological Science, 33*, 158–175.

Nagasawa, M., Kikusui, T., Onaka, T., & Ohta, M. (2009). Dog's gaze at its owner increases owner's urinary oxytocin during social interaction. *Hormones & Behavior, 55*, 434–441.

Nightingale, F. (1860). *Notes on nursing: What it is, and what it is not.* New York: D. Appleton & Co.

Odendaal, J., & Meintjes, R. (2003). Neurophysiological correlates of affiliative behaviour between humans and dogs. *The Veterinary Journal, 165*, 296–301.

Ory, M.G., & Goldberg, E.L. (1983). Pet possession and life satisfaction in elderly women. In A.H. Katcher & A.M. Beck (Eds.), *New perspectives on our lives with companion animals* (pp. 303–317). Philadelphia: University of Pennsylvania Press.

Putnam, R.D. (2000). *Bowling alone.* New York: Simon & Schuster.

Ritvo, H. (1987). *The animal estate: The English and other creatures in the Victorian Age.* Cambridge, MA: Harvard University Press.

Salisbury, J.E. (1994). *The beast within: Animals in the Middle Ages.* London & New York: Routledge.

Schwarzer, R., & Knoll, N. (2007). Functional roles of social support within the stress and coping process: A theoretical and empirical overview. *International Journal of Psychology, 42*, 243–252.

Serpell, J.A. (1989a). Humans, animals, and the limits of friendship. In R. Porter & S. Tomaselli (Eds.), *The dialectics of friendship* (pp. 111–129). London: Routledge.

Serpell, J.A. (1989b). Pet keeping and animal domestication: A reappraisal. In J. Clutton-Brock (Ed.), *The walking larder: Patterns of animal domestication, pastoralism and predation* (pp. 10–21). London: Unwin Hyman.

Serpell, J.A. (1991). Beneficial effects of pet ownership on some aspects of human health and behaviour. *Journal of the Royal Society of Medicine, 84*, 717–720.

Serpell, J.A. (1996). *In the company of animals: A study of human–animal relationships* (2nd ed.). Cambridge, MA: Cambridge University Press.

Serpell, J.A. (2000). Domestication and history of the cat. In D.C. Turner & P.P.G. Bateson (Eds.), *The domestic cat: The biology of its behavior* (pp. 180–192). Cambridge, MA: Cambridge University Press.

Serpell, J.A. (2003). Anthropomorphism and anthropomorphic selection— beyond the "cute response." *Society & Animals, 11*, 83–100.

Serpell, J.A. (2004). Factors influencing human attitudes to animals and their welfare. *Animal Welfare, 13*, S145–S151.

Serpell, J.A. (2006). Animal-assisted interventions in historical perspective (2nd ed.). In A.H. Fine (Ed.), *Handbook on animal-assisted therapy* (pp. 3–20). New York: Academic Press.

Serpell, J.A., & Paul, E.S. (1994). Pets and the development of positive attitudes to animals. In A. Manning & J.A. Serpell (Eds.), *Animals and human society: Changing perspectives* (pp. 127–144). London: Routledge.

Sherbourne, C.D., Meredith, L.S., Rogers, W., & Ware, J.E. (1992). Social support and stressful life events: Age differences in their effects on health-related quality of life among the chronically ill. *Quality of Life Research, 1*, 235–246.

Siegel, J.M. (1990). Stressful life events and use of physician services among the elderly: The moderating role of pet ownership. *Journal of Personality and Social Psychology, 58*, 1081–1086.

Thomas, K. (1983). *Man and the natural world: Changing attitudes in England, 1500–1800*. London: Allen Lane.

Tuke, S. (1964). *Description of the Retreat*. Reprinted with an introduction by R. Hunter & I. Macalpine. London: Dawsons. (Original work published 1813)

Turner, J. (1980). *Reckoning with the beast: Animals, pain, and humanity in the Victorian mind*. Baltimore: Johns Hopkins University Press.

Uchino, B.N. (2006). Social support and health: A review of physiological processes potentially underlying links to disease outcome. *Journal of Behavioral Medicine, 29*, 377–387.

Vigne, J.-D., Guilaine, J., Debue, K., Haye, L., & Gérard, P. (2004). Early taming of the cat in Cyprus. *Science, 304*, 259.

Vilhjalmson, R. (1993). Life stress, social support and clinical depression: A reanalysis of the literature. *Social Science Medicine, 37*, 331–342.

Virués-Ortega, J., & Buela-Casal, G. (2006). Psychophysiological effects of human–animal interaction: Theoretical issues and long-term interaction effects. *Journal of Nervous and Mental Disease, 194*, 52–57.

CHAPTER 2

Community Benefits of Human–Animal Interactions... the Ripple Effect

LISA JANE WOOD

The bulk of evidence to date on the benefits of human–animal interaction in the community relates to individual-level benefits between humans and companion animals. Anecdotes around the world about the benefits of owning or interacting with companion animals are corroborated by research studies that associate pet ownership with a diversity of therapeutic, psychological, physiological, and psychosocial benefits (Wood, Giles-Corti, & Bulsara, 2005). Yet the domain of a companion animal's influence can extend beyond its human companions, creating a ripple effect through the broader community.

This chapter explores the potential role of pets as facilitators of social interactions and social capital within neighborhoods and communities, among both those who own companion animals and those who live in the broader community. Social capital has been associated with a range of health and well-being outcomes and has been recognized in the child development literature (Ainsworth, 2002; Brooks-Gunn, Duncan, Klebanov, & Sealand, 1993; Coleman, 1988; Goddard, 2003; Runyan et al., 1998). According to Runyan et al.,

> Those interested in the healthy development of children, particularly children most at risk for poor developmental outcomes, must search for new and creative ways of supporting interpersonal relationships and

strengthening the communities in which families carry out the daily
activities of their lives (1998, p. 12).

Pets have often been described as a bridge between humans and
nature (Podberscek, 2000). Now there is an emerging, albeit scattered,
body of evidence that companion animals can also act as a social bridge
between people and, further, can contribute to the "ties that bind" communities together as a civil society. This chapter draws on relevant literature to date and on findings from qualitative and quantitative research
undertaken since 2003 at the University of Western Australia.

SOCIAL CAPITAL

Social capital is a popular buzzword that has been defined and used in
various ways. The idea of social capital has engendered increasing
political and social policy attention and has appeared in a proliferation
of literature across a range of disciplines, including sociology, psychology, economics, political sciences, education, and health. Some of the
seeds of social capital theory grew from Coleman's sociological interest
in factors influencing child development and learning (Coleman, 1988),
evolving also from the work of Bourdieu (1986) and Putnam (1995) in
the social and political sciences, respectively. The breadth of disciplines
that take an interest in social capital is one of its conceptual strengths,
but this variety has spawned a number of definitions and approaches
to social capital measurement. At the simplest end of the spectrum of
definitions, social capital has been described as the "glue" that holds
society together (Lang & Hornburg, 1998) and as the raw material of
civil society that is created from the everyday interactions between
people (Onyx & Bullen, 1997). Robert Putnam, one of the earliest and
most prominent thinkers on social capital, defines it as the "connections among individuals, social networks and the norms of reciprocity
and trustworthiness that arise from them" (2000, p. 19). Among the
various definitions, there is reasonable convergence regarding the key
elements of the social capital construct, depicted in Figure 2.1.

Despite its current popularity, social capital is not a totally new or
unique concept. It encapsulates social processes, such as trust and participation, that have long been of interest to humanity and particularly
to scholars. As articulated by Sartorius, "Since the dawn of time, the
survival of human beings has depended on the level of their integration into one or more mutually helpful communities. Those with social
support and links with others live better than those who remain
isolated" (2003, p. S105).

One of the reasons for social capital's rapid rise to conceptual popularity seems to be that it imputes a "capital," or calculable, value to

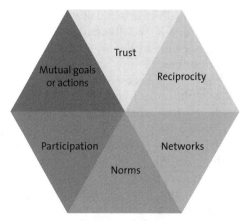

Figure 2.1.   Key conceptual elements of social capital.

human aspects of community, organizations, policies and family life that are sometimes overlooked but that nonetheless are vital to individual and collective well-being (Baum, 1999; Hawe & Shiell, 2000). The capital analogy also yields an opportunity to promote the development of social capital as an investment, rather than a cost (Vimpani, 2000), a useful line to take in a world that is often dominated by economic rationalism (Dasgupta & Serageldin, 1999; Sobel, 2002).

Although one of the strands of social capital research relates to child development, the primary focus to date has been on the nexus between social capital and educational attainment (Ainsworth, 2002; Goddard, 2003). Social capital can benefit children educationally: Children who grow up in communities that are richer in social capital are more likely to be exposed to helpful social networks and to adults who provide access to information, resources, and opportunities that may be educationally beneficial (Ainsworth, 2002). Social capital within the family has also been linked to educational success, through mechanisms such as familial norms and sanctions that relate to school participation and knowledge of who to contact for information, advice, and support (Fullan, Watson, & Leithwood, 2003). It has been argued that social capital may be more crucial for families that have fewer financial and educational resources; it is strongly associated with positive developmental and behavioral outcomes in high-risk preschool children (Runyan et al., 1998).

Social Capital and Companion Animals

Only a few of the companion animal studies to date have explicitly considered the interface among pets, pet owners, and broader community interactions. However, studies that relate to companion animals and concepts such as loneliness, social isolation, and social support hint that companion animals and their interactions and roles in the lives of humans are relevant to the way in which people view and engage in local communities.

The potential nexus between pets and social capital was included as a secondary and exploratory hypothesis in a social capital survey undertaken in Perth, Western Australia, in 2002 (Wood, 2006). A number of pet-related questions were added to the survey instrument, which already included items measuring social capital, sense of community, self-reported mental health, and perceptions and attitudes toward the physical neighborhood environment. The survey was part of a broader study that focused on the relationship between neighborhood design and social capital and mental health, with the goal of identifying aspects of community that facilitate or hinder social capital creation. The overall social capital scale was developed through factor analysis and included subscales that measured levels of trust, reciprocity, civic engagement, perceived suburb friendliness, and social networks.

In a multivariate analysis using ordinal logistic regression, pet owners scored significantly higher on an overall social capital scale after controlling for various demographics, compared with those who did not own pets. Specifically, pet owners were 74% more likely to have a high social capital score than were nonowners. The finding held for respondents who owned various types of pets; there was no significant difference on the social capital scale when the data were analyzed specifically by dog ownership (Wood et al., 2005). In addition, further analysis and focus group data that also were collected as part of the broader social capital study suggested that companion animals may have a ripple effect that extends beyond their owners to nonowners and the broader community.

So what explains this observed association between social capital and companion animals? Because social capital is a complex construct without simple cause and effect pathways, the relationship with companion animals is unlikely to be direct. Rather, human interactions with companion animals may mediate some of the elements of social capital or may be linked to other social and environmental factors that potentially influence the formation of social capital in local communities (Wood et al., 2005). The remainder of the chapter, therefore, will attempt to shed light on some of the mechanisms that may underlie the nexus between companion animals and social capital.

Morris et al. (2001) have conceptualized seven potential opportunities or benefits that pets can bring to their human companions: the opportunities to appreciate nature and wildlife; feel inspired and learn; be childlike and playful; be altruistic and engage in nurturing; experience companionship, caring, and comfort; be a parent; and strengthen bonds with other humans. This final "opportunity" begins to touch on the community-related outcomes of human–animal interactions, whereas the others are circumscribed (intentionally) within the immediate human–pet relationship.

As we as researchers reflect on the ripple effect of companion animals for human–human interactions and the broader community, it is feasible to describe these interactions as similar potential "opportunities" that can accrue. Drawing from the literature to date and research undertaken with colleagues in Western Australia, we, the authors of this chapter, propose eight mechanisms through which companion animals might contribute to social capital. These mechanisms are depicted in the Figure 2.2 and expounded in the sections that follow.

Facilitation of Interactions and Relationships with Others

Social contact and interaction with others is one of the cornerstones of human civilization, yet there are concerns that the "harried isolating nature of modern life appears to be minimizing our capacity for human contact" (Walljasper, 2007, p. 10). There is considerable evidence surrounding the benefits of more consolidated interaction in the form of social ties, social networks, and social support (Berkman & Glass, 2000), but incidental and informal social interaction is also important and can be the precipitant for further social relationships. It has been described by Albery (2001) as psychologically nourishing for humans to feel connected to neighbors; he argues that these relationships need not be close friendships in order to bring benefits, but may be merely relationships with acquaintances and people within our proximity with whom we can enjoy a chat.

Although the role of animals in facilitating social contact has been intermittently investigated since the mid-1980s, it has not surged ahead as quickly as has research on the therapeutic or physical health benefits associated with animals. Nonetheless, the anecdotes of many a pet owner are corroborated by research that finds that dogs are a conversation trigger between strangers or casual acquaintances (Messent, 1983; Robins, Sanders, & Cahill, 1991; Rogers, Hart, & Boltz, 1993). One experimental design compared people walking alone or with a dog and found that dog walkers were far more likely to experience social contact and conversation than are solitary walkers (McNicholas & Collis, 2000; Messent, 1983). Robins goes so far as to describe dogs as an antidote for

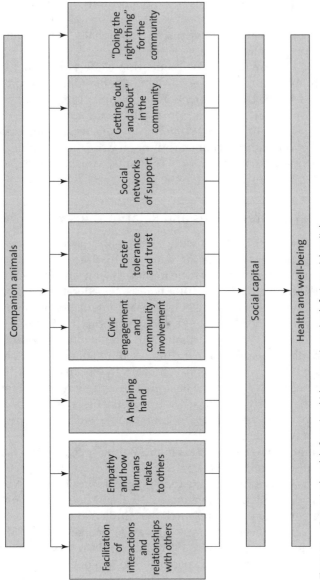

Figure 2.2. Conceptual model of way in which companion animals foster social capital.

the human anonymity of contemporary society's public places (Robins et al., 1991).

Within the variety of species that make up today's pets, dogs are most likely to venture with their owners into the broader community and hence have the greatest capacity to facilitate social interaction and contact. However, this social contagion effect is not limited to dogs: One study indicates that small animals such as rabbits and turtles can also lead to contact and conversation between strangers when their owners take them to a park (Hunt, Hart, & Gomulkiewicz, 1992). Another example is a case study of a park in New York City where older men from the local Chinese community gather with their songbirds (called Hua mei birds), illustrating how companion animals can bring people together socially in the public realm (Walljasper, 2007).

The icebreaker role of animals has been poignantly and also empirically observed in the social experiences of people with disabilities (Hart & Hart, 1987). When such people are accompanied by an animal, "the presence of a pet seems to 'normalize' social situations, getting everyone through the ice-breaker stage to the point where they can risk directly engaging with the unfamiliar person" (Newby, 1997, p. 180).

Although most of these studies view social contact from the perspective of the pet owner, recent Australian research suggests that even people who do not own a companion animal themselves view pets as a social icebreaker; for example, in situations such as talking to dog walkers passing by their house, meeting or talking to a neighbor with a pet, or chatting to dog owners down at the local park (Wood, Giles-Corti, Bulsara, & Bosch, 2007), as reflected in the following quotes from qualitative research (Wood, 2006):

> I like to see them as they come past walking their dogs . . . . there is always somebody out walking the dog and if you're out they always speak to you.

> . . . people walk through there all the time with their dogs and I get to know them. I've probably met hundreds of people who go through there who speak to me every morning and every evening and I've made some quite good friends amongst some on the street.

Animals, of course, are not the sole conversational icebreakers on sidewalks and parks: Babies and young children often have a similar effect. In many countries, however, there are now more households with pets than with children; as noted by Newby (1997), not everyone can have a baby, and even for those who do, the "baby" years that invite spontaneous interaction from strangers are far fewer than the potential life years of owning a companion animal.

Empathy and How Humans Relate to Others

In the preceding discussion of companion animals as facilitators of social contact, the animals' roles are primarily that of "social bridge" between people, but their effect on our social lives may go much deeper than that by influencing the way in which humans relate to others (Newby, 1997). This is one of the aspects of companion animals that has been most studied in relation to child development. Animals are credited with contributing to the development of a range of life skills, helping children develop empathy, learn to care and nurture, take on responsibility, and deal with grief and death (Serpell, 1999; Thompson & Guillone, 2003).

The capacity for cooperation, social trust, and shared objectives lies at the heart of many definitions of social capital (Cox, 1995; Putnam, 1995), and that capacity plausibly can be helped or hindered by the way in which humans view and relate to others and how well people are able to see the world from another's perspective. Without stretching the potential link between pets and children too far, one can observe that companion animals provide an opportunity and context for children to develop some of the relational skills and awareness that contribute to community social capital. A companion animal gives a child practice in relating to someone different from him- or herself, gives the child an opportunity to show empathy, and teaches the child how to accommodate the needs of another. Relevant to how humans relate to others, for example, is evidence that associates children's pet ownership and bonding with their pets with higher levels of empathy and more prosocial behaviors (Thompson & Guillone, 2003).

Companion animals are a great leveler, transcending racial, cultural, geographic, age, and socioeconomic boundaries in terms of their ownership and impact. This effect is evident in the exchanges between dog owners of diverse backgrounds at a local park or in therapeutic settings where an animal serves as the catalyst for communication between timid patients and health professionals (Wood, 2009). The formative childhood years play a critical role in shaping beliefs about the extent to which others are similar or different from oneself, and pets can provide a common bond among children in this regard.

A Helping Hand

Reciprocity is generally recognized as one of the core dimensions of social capital and has been measured in a number of studies. This measurement ranges from single items about perceived willingness to help others as a social capital proxy (Kawachi, Kennedy, & Glass, 1999;

Subramanian, Lochner, & Kawachi, 2003) to multiple questions about favor exchanges (reciprocity) and volunteering that are embedded within a series of social capital items (Onyx & Bullen, 2000; Saguaro Seminar: Civic Engagement in America, 2000). The rubric of social capital covers both informal helpfulness (e.g., lending a household item or a sympathetic ear to a neighbor) and more formal or structured experiences such as organized volunteering. Some people argue that doing things for others is less common these days, that community spirit is flagging, and that the busyness of life has eroded volunteering. However, recent examples, such as the willingness of employees affected by the global financial crisis to accept pay freezes rather than see colleagues laid off and the flood of practical and financial donations and support to victims of the devastating Victorian bushfires in Australia, are reminders of the capacity of humans to help one another in times of need.

So how are companion animals related to people helping one another out? Qualitative research undertaken in Western Australia suggests that pets often precipitate the exchange of favors between people and that pet-related favors can be particularly symbolic of trust because of the love and attachment vested by people in their pets (Wood et al., 2007). Favors relating to feeding or minding a companion animal can apply to the full spectrum of pets: goldfish, rabbits, birds, cats, dogs, and horses.

The provision of pet-related favors appears also to have a potential spill-over effect onto neighborhood goodwill and trust, as reflected in some of the following comments (Wood, 2006):

> We mind [i.e., care for] everybody's pet because my husband is a pet lover and everybody comes to us to watch their dog if they're going on holiday or anything and they all come and borrow things. (Wood et al., 2007, p. 49)

> Our fence blew down a few weeks ago and someone from up the road brought our dog back and I find it a very good place to live and I think everyone gets on well. (Wood et al., 2007, p. 49)

Congruent with the notion of the indirect ripple effect of companion animals, however, the favors were not limited to pet care. The social capital study found that significantly more pet owners than nonowners reported giving and receiving neighborly favors (e.g., collecting mail, loaning a household item, minding a child), only one of which related to pets themselves (Wood et al., 2005).

Growing up in a community where people help one another out contributes to the process by which children's values and attitudes are laid down. More directly, companion animals provide one of the early opportunities for children to take at least partial responsibility for another being: Feeding pets, walking the dog, or minding animals for a neighbor are all formative experiences in this regard. The act of caring for an animal encourages children to think empathetically and identify with the needs of another.

Civic Engagement and Community Involvement

The notion of a civil society is often referred to in social capital discourse (Cox, 1995; Putnam, 1996), as is civic engagement, which relates to the capacity of individuals to be concerned and active within the community. Such engagement in turn creates the "capital" from which others can benefit. Civic engagement also contributes to the building of trust and networks. It might be surmised that people with companion animals have an active interest and involvement in aspects of community that directly affect them, such as access to parks and open space for walking animals or regulations about pet ownership. However, the civic engagement scale included in the social capital study did not include any animal-related questions. Instead, it asked respondents about responses to 10 possible actions taken on local issues, such as attending a local action meeting, writing to a newspaper or politician about a local issue, or signing a petition. Pet owners were 57% more likely to be civically engaged than were nonowners on this civic engagement scale (Wood et al., 2005).

There are also other forms of civic engagement or community involvement that are directly related to companion animals. Dog walkers have a vested interest, for example, in making local parks and open space available and keeping them maintained, so they add their voices to the broader imperative for access to parks, open space, and opportunities to come into contact with nature. Volunteering is a form of community involvement that is often included as a measure of social capital (Baum et al., 1999), and companion animals are associated with volunteering in a number of forms. Some types of volunteering benefit owners of companion animals (e.g., services to assist older people to care for their pets), other types bring people into therapeutic contact with companion animals (e.g., hospital visitation programs, animal-assisted therapy), and some types benefit the animals themselves (e.g., rescue programs, foster-home programs for neglected pets).

As well as the obvious benefits that volunteer services provide to recipients, the very act of volunteering itself can bring mental health and well-being benefits to the volunteer (Fernandez & James, 2007). The direct benefits of volunteering flow into indirect benefits such as greater levels of community trust and civic engagement (Putnam, 1993) and help to build community goodwill and community mindedness.

Fostering Tolerance and Trust

Trust is a distinct hallmark of social capital that is seen as essential to collective and individual well-being. Conversely, the absence of trust can constrain human relationships and breed fear and intolerance to differences. It is perhaps not mere coincidence that interest in the notion of social capital has grown in parallel with concerns about the decline of trust and tolerance in modern society. As articulated by Eva Cox in a seminal public lecture series on civil society,

> Trust is essential for our social well-being. Without trusting the goodwill of others, we retreat into bureaucracy, rules, and demands for more law and order. Trust is based on positive experiences with other people and it grows with use. We need to trust that others are going to be basically reasonable human beings. (1995, p. 9)

So how do companion animals affect trust between humans? The fact that pets often appear to trust their owners and other humans, whether this attitude is warranted or not, is admirable, but it is not the link to trust that is of interest to this chapter. Rather, we as researchers are interested in the spill-over effect that companion animals might have on trust between people. When companion animals bring residents or neighbors together and help them chat with one another, it is not merely a social nicety. Such interactions can help to break down barriers and stereotypes and can thereby play an important role in building trust and sense of community at the neighborhood level. Qualitative research suggests that companion animal owners are predisposed to gauge others as being "like-minded" by virtue of a shared love of animals (Wood, 2009; Wood et al., 2007). Newby (1997) contends that everyone, even people who do not have a companion animal of their own, can tell a tale of a pet, be it past, present, or someone else's, if the topic arises in a social conversation setting; she suggests that there are very few other topics that are common to all people. Distrust of others can dissipate when people feel a connection or common bond through pet ownership.

The social capital study found that pet owners were more likely to agree that most people can be trusted generally, although the finding was not statistically significant (Wood et al., 2005), it merits further investigation. Notions of trust are also embedded in other core dimensions of social capital and are not necessarily captured by overt questions about trust alone. For instance, the exchange of pet-related favors may exemplify an outworking of trust, given that there is, after all, less emotional investment in borrowing a cup of sugar than in entrusting one's much-loved pet to the care of a neighbor. Similarly, it could be hypothesized that the higher levels of civic engagement observed among pet owners in part relates to their "trust" that some good will arise from their involvement and that is not futile to make the effort.

Social Networks of Support

There is growing research interest in the role that social networks and social support play in health. The strongest associations between social support and health relate to psychological well-being (Berkman & Glass, 2000), but poor social support and social isolation have gained some credence as risk factors for cardiovascular disease (Bunker et al., 2003). Companion animal research to date has largely considered social support from the perspective of the animals as a direct source of social support to their human companions (Garrity & Stallones, 1998). Of interest to this chapter, however, is the suggestion that companion animals may enhance health by acting as a catalyst for increased or strengthened social networks, which can in turn provide social support.

The anecdotes of many a dog walker are corroborated by qualitative research accounts of dog walkers regularly meeting to walk together, meeting at the park, inviting one another to Christmas get-togethers, and sharing other social activities with people that they met through their companion animal (Wood, 2009; Wood et al., 2007). In terms of empirical evidence, in an Australian survey conducted in 1995, 58% of pet owners indicated that they had gotten to know people and made friends through having pets (McHarg, Baldock, Headey, & Robinson, 1995). In the social capital study, 40.5% of pet owners overall and 50% of dog owners indicated that they had gotten to know other people in their neighborhood through their pet, and 84% of owners who walked their dogs reported that they talked to other pet owners during these walks (Wood et al., 1995). Another Western Australian study on park usage in a cluster of suburbs found that residents with dogs generally had higher levels of social interaction with other residents at parks than did nonowners of dogs. For example, 84.5% of dog owners had conversations with other people in parks, compared with 65.2% of nonowners, and 37.9% of dog owners had made friends at a park, compared with 26.5% of nonowners (Wood et al., 2008).

It is pertinent to note, however, that not all research supports the notion that contacts through companion animals translate into tangible social networks or support. In a study in the United Kingdom, pet ownership did not have a significant effect on the size or composition of participants' social networks. The authors concluded that casual interactions facilitated by dogs do not necessarily enhance social networks or social support (Collis, McNicholas, & Harker, 2003). Without negating the validity of this empirical finding, it can be argued that further studies are warranted. For example, recent qualitative research (Wood, 2009) suggests that, whether they occur in statistically significant numbers in all communities or not, there are some significant social networks of support forged through companion animals, as reflected in the following case study excerpts.

> I came to Perth not knowing anyone. Luckily, I chose a suburb very close to the dog park where I met a very interesting, friendly, and eclectic bunch of dog owners that saved my sanity. . . . Some days I thought I would die of loneliness and boredom and the only thing that would get me through was knowing that from 4–5 I could go to the park and talk to real adults that had an interest in me as a person and that interest had started because of our mutual love of dogs. Thank goodness for the dogs, they were my ice-breakers and gave me a bond with total strangers who I soon called my friends. (Wood, 2009, p. 11)

> When I was coping with a family crisis to do with ageing parents, I was offered help to look after Dino [my dog], legal and medical advice, insights from other's similar experiences, and just generally people prepared to listen . . . the dog mafia is extensive and certainly kept me sane. (Wood, 2009, p. 11)

Getting "Out and About" in the Community

Walking is one of the most accessible and affordable forms of physical activity, and it can yield a range of physical and mental health benefits. In addition to the benefits for walkers themselves, however, there are broader, neighborhood-level benefits of people being "out and about." The customary evening stroll that is entrenched in the culture of a number of Mediterranean countries, for example, contributes to the social vitality of communities and brings people into contact with one another and their surroundings (Walljasper, 2007). The exchange of a wave or hello, as well as the incidental contact that people have with others when they are out walking, is thought to be part of what helps to build sense of community.

The motivation and impetus that dogs provide for people to be out walking is reflected in higher levels of walking and overall physical activity among dog owners (Cutt, Giles-Corti, Knuiman, Timperio, & Bull, 2008). As well as the health and well-being benefits of walking itself for both adults and children (and, indeed, their dogs), it can also be argued that the visible presence of people walking dogs and the impetus that dogs provide for people to be out walking contribute to increased feelings of collective safety and have a positive effect on a generalized sense of community (Wood et al., 2007). Conversely, fear of crime can deter people from becoming involved in their communities or making generalized overtures of friendliness to their neighbors and can impede the development of trust and sense of community (Perkins, Mekks, & Taylor, 1992; Sooman & Macintyre, 1995). If people are fearful, they may also be less likely to go out of their homes, use local facilities, attend clubs or functions, or interact with strangers or people they meet in the street, particularly at night (Wood, 2006).

Residents' perceptions of crime and safety are influenced by many things, irrespective of actual crime rates or experiences (Hale, 1996; Wilson-Doenges, 2000). Fear of crime and not feeling safe can sometimes be as detrimental in a community as actual crime. In the qualitative research of the authors of this chapter, the visible presence of people "out and about"—for example, walking dogs—emerged as a positive marker of community safety. Conversely, deserted streets and parks conveyed negative impressions about safety, crime, and general sense of community. Among dog owners who walked their dogs ($N = 99$) in the social capital study (Wood, 2009), 63.6% indicated that owning a dog helped them to feel safer when they were out walking. Again the spill-over effect was present, with community "out and aboutness" and its influence on perceptions of safety benefiting people with or without companion animals themselves. One study participant said,

> If you don't see anyone walking around the street or walking their dog or anything or only occasionally you might see someone walking their dog down the street . . . it's like what is going on here? (Wood, 2009, p. 51)

The preceding observations resonate with Jane Jacob's notion of "eyes on the street," in which she argued that a well-used city street is apt to be far safer than a deserted one (Jacobs, 1961). Dog walking and even interactions with companion animals in front yards and on porches can contribute positively to "eyes on the street" and in turn perceptions of community safety.

"Doing the Right Thing" for the Community

The role of social norms in facilitating cooperation and mutual benefit for community members is one of the cornerstones of social capital (Putnam, 1995). "Doing the right thing" by each other and the community can apply to a range of issues, including the ways in which humans respond to climate change, resolve disputes with neighbors, care for those who are disadvantaged, or cooperate in the sharing of public spaces (Wood, 2009). Sometimes communities default to regulatory or policy measures to prohibit certain behaviors or protect vulnerable groups (including children) in order to bring about the desired result, but there is some loss of community goodwill when desirable behaviors are promoted by punishing noncompliance.

The negative community consequences of companion animals sometimes dominate public discourse and media attention (e.g., zoonoses, stray cats, the noise of barking dogs, dog bites) and precipitate regulatory measures to curb the consequences of irresponsible pet ownership (Newby, 1997). A series of case studies recently compiled in Australia, however, highlights the way in which people who engage with their communities to solve animal-related issues can produce creative lateral solutions underpinned by community cooperation and support (Wood, 2009). In essence, these solutions are about normalizing responsible pet ownership and relying on collective goodwill and informal affirmations and sanctions that reinforce "doing the right thing." Designated off-leash areas for dogs, away from children's playgrounds, and the provision of bags and friendly reminders to collect pets' feces are practical examples of such solutions in action (Wood, 2009).

IMPLICATIONS FOR PROMOTING HEALTH

So how can the ripple effect of companion animals on community life through the mechanism of social capital be further developed and applied to improving the health and well-being of children and others?

Through the lens of social capital, a community that is welcoming to companion animals can be beneficial for human residents, too, independently of whether they have a companion animals of their own. Clearly not everyone can, wants to, or is able to own a pet, but accumulating evidence suggests that some collective benefits that extend beyond the owners themselves may accrue to communities through the presence of companion animals. Moreover, social capital theory suggests that people can benefit from a community that is rich in social capital, regardless of their own level of contribution to that social fabric (Cannuscio, Block, & Kawachi, 2003; Kawachi, Kennedy, Lochner, & Prothrowstith, 1997). In other words, it is a form of capital that can benefit even people who have not invested in it personally (Kawachi et al., 1997).

It can also be argued that companion animals are in some ways an "indicator species" for desirable community life and that the type of neighborhood and community that is good for companion animals is also good for children (and vice versa). As articulated by Newby, "If we can't even find the space to take the dog for a walk, are we sure there is enough there to meet human needs?" (1997, p. 263). Walljasper similarly observes that in communities where pets thrive, people thrive, too, and that neighborhoods that are congenial to companion animals benefit all people, whether or not they have an animal of their own (Walljasper, 2007). He says, "When you create a neighborhood that's friendly to dogs, it's friendly to people, too. The traffic is not speeding and dangerous. There are green places to hang out and walk" (as cited in Hage, 2007).

Many public health interventions struggle to sustain their presence and impact in the community. Companion animals represent an underutilized opportunity, as they are often a long-term, well-integrated, and much-loved component of people's lives. Recent physical activity advertisements in Australia featuring dogs as motivators and companions for walking are a pertinent example of tapping into the companion-animal angle within public health interventions and strategies. There may be similar scope to build on this angle within strategies and programs that target social isolation, sense of community, and neighborhood safety, to name a few issues. Moreover, there are synergies between interventions promoting dog walking as a conduit for physical activity, for example, and social capital benefits associated with companion animals. Volunteer involvement in animal-assisted therapy programs with children is another example of an existing intervention that has synergies with social capital. One could also consider incorporation of a companion animal dimension in some of the health interventions that target children in community settings, such as walk-to-school initiatives or campaigns to promote active play over sedentary time that is spent on screen-based activities.

Many of the factors that most influence health and well-being lie outside of the health sector, a fact that is well recognized in the social determinants of health literature (Wilkinson & Marmot, 2003) and in ecological models and theories of health (Nutbeam & Harris, 2004). Access to healthy food, quality education, walkable environments, clean air, and opportunities to socialize and forge social support networks are among the factors that are vital to health and that are embedded within the broader community settings in which people work, live, and play.

In the real world of policy and decision making and program planning in sectors outside of health, the health rationale for doing something does not always carry the weight that experts in public health hope it will. Hence there is pragmatic merit in finding other angles and complementary benefits to health-promoting actions to engage the interest and commitment of people whose core business is not health. In this regard, companion animals and their ripple effect on social capital can provide another "in" or angle for raising issues in the media, engaging with neighborhood organizations, and reaching planners and urban designers. A recent resource for local government in Australia (http://www.petnet.com.au/living-well-together-handbook) provides some relevant case studies that illustrate this point (Wood, 2009).

The capacity to identify other tangible ways of building on the social capital and companion animal nexus to promote children's (and adults') health and well-being could be strengthened by further research in a number of areas. Potential areas for future research include the following:

- *The inclusion of questions about companion animals (e.g., pet ownership, social interactions facilitated by companion animals) in other studies of social capital and sense of community (both qualitative and quantitative):* Such studies ideally include the large-scale surveys of social capital that are ongoing in a number of countries, such as the United States, the United Kingdom, Canada, and Australia. Similarly, this perspective should be included in broader studies of children's health and well-being, particularly in the context of community settings or relating to psychosocial processes.

- *The inclusion of social capital and social interaction in other areas of companion animal research—for example, studies investigating psychological and psychosocial benefits associated with companion animals:* The community ripple effect may be present even from seemingly one-to-one human–animal interactions.

- *A consideration of social capital in current or future research that looks at the nexus between companion animals and child health and well-being:* for example, the recent research relating to the links between children's physical activity, obesity, and pets (Timperio, Salmon, Chu, & Andrianopoulos, 2008) and research on the role that dogs play in getting people out and about and walking within their local communities (Cutt, Giles-Corti, et al., 2008; Cutt, Knuiman, & Giles-Corti, 2008).

- *Collaboration with researchers in areas relating to neighborhood and community environments:* There is accumulating evidence that the built environment affects both physical and mental health, a finding that has garnered interest among researchers, practitioners, and policy makers not only in public health, but in urban design and planning disciplines.

CONCLUSION

Viewing the impact and benefits of companion animals in society through a social capital lens draws attention to the ripple effect that companion animals can have on human–human interactions and the social fabric of communities. Children stand to benefit from communities that generally have strong social capital, as well as from the social dividends that are associated with companion animals.

REFERENCES

Ainsworth, J.W. (2002). Why does it take a village? The mediation of neighbourhood effects on educational achievement. *Social Forces, 81*(1), 117–152.

Albery, N. (2001). *The world's greatest ideas: An encyclopedia of social inventions.* New Society Publishers: Gabriola Island, BC, Canada.

Baum, F. (1999). Social capital: Is it good for your health? Issues for a public health agenda. *Journal of Epidemiology and Community Health, 53*(4), 195–196.

Baum, F., Modra, C., Bush, R., Cox, E., Cooke, R., & Potter, R. (1999). Volunteering and social capital: An Adelaide study. *Volunteer Journal of Australia, 4*(1), 13–22.

Berkman, L., & Glass, T. (2000). Social integration, social networks, social support, and health. In L. Berkman & I. Kawachi (Eds.), *Social Epidemiology.* New York: Oxford University Press.

Bourdieu, P. (1986). The forms of capital. In J. Richardson (Ed.), *Handbook of theory and research for the sociology of education.* New York: Greenwood Press.

Brooks-Gunn, J., Duncan, G.J., Klebanov, P.K., & Sealand, N. (1993, September). Do neighbourhoods influence child and adolescent development? *American Journal of Sociology, 2,* 353–395.

Bunker, S., Colquhoun, D., Esler, M., Hickie, I., Hunt, D., Jelinek, V., et al. (2003, March 17). "Stress" and coronary heart disease: Psychosocial risk factors. *Medical Journal of Australia, 178,* 272–276.

Cannuscio, C., Block, J., & Kawachi, I. (2003). Social capital and successful aging: The role of senior housing. *Annals of Internal Medicine, 139*(5, Pt. 2), 395.

Coleman, J.S. (1988). Social capital in the creation of human capital. *American Journal of Sociology, 94*(Suppl.), S95–S120.

Collis, G., McNicholas, J., & Harker, R. (2003). *Could enhanced social networks explain the association between pet ownership and health?* Unpublished manuscript, Department of Psychology, University of Warwick, United Kingdom.

Cox, E. (1995). *A truly civil society: 1995 Boyer lectures.* Sydney, Australia: Australian Broadcasting Corporation.

Cutt, H., Giles-Corti, B., Knuiman, M., Timperio, A., & Bull, F. (2008). Understanding dog owners' increased levels of physical activity: Results from RESIDE. *American Journal of Public Health, 98,* 66–69.

Cutt, H., Knuiman, M., & Giles-Corti, B. (2008). Does getting a dog increase recreational walking? *International Journal of Behavioral Nutrition and Physical Activity, 5*(1), 17–27.

Dasgupta, P., & Serageldin, I. (Eds.). (1999). *Social capital: A multifaceted perspective.* Washington, DC: World Bank.

Fernandez, S., & James, R. (2007, September). Volunteering for happiness and health. *Australian Health Promotion Association Update.*

Fullan, M., Watson, N., & Leithwood, K. (2003). What should be the boundaries of the schools we need? *Education Canada, 43*(1), 12.

Garrity, T., & Stallones, L. (1998). Effects of pet contact on human well-being. In C.C. Wilson & D.C. Turner (Eds.), *Companion animals in human health* (pp. 3–22). Thousand Oaks, CA: SAGE Publications, Inc.

Goddard, R.D. (2003). Relational networks, social trust, and norms: A social capital perspective on students' chances of academic success. *Educational Evaluation and Policy Analysis, 25*(1), 59–74.

Hage, D. (2007, November 10). A simple path to strong neighborhoods. *Star Tribune.* Retrieved April 20, 2010, from http://www.startribune.com/opinion/commentary/11764191.html

Hale, C. (1996). Fear of crime: A review of the literature. *International Review of Victimology, 4,* 79–150.

Hart, L., & Hart, B.L. (1987). Socializing effects of service dogs for people with disabilities. *Anthrozoos, 1,* 41–44.

Hawe, P., & Shiell, A. (2000). Social capital and health promotion: A review. *Social Science & Medicine, 51,* 871–885.

Hunt, S., Hart, L., & Gomulkiewicz, R. (1992). Role of small animals in social interactions between strangers. *Journal of Social Psychology, 132,* 245–256.

Jacobs, J. (1961). *The death and life of the great American cities.* New York: Random House.

Kawachi, I., Kennedy, B., & Glass, R. (1999). Social capital and self-rated health: A contextual analysis. *American Journal of Public Health, 89*(8), 1187–1193.

Kawachi, I., Kennedy, B., Lochner, K., & Prothrowstith, D. (1997). Social capital, income inequality, and mortality. *American Journal of Public Health, 87*(9), 1491–1498.

Lang, R., & Hornburg, S. (1998). What is social capital and why is it important to public policy? *Housing Policy Debate, 9*(1), 1–16.

McHarg, M., Baldock, C., Headey, B., & Robinson, A. (1995). *National people and pets survey.* Urban Animal Management Coalition, Sydney, Australia.

McNicholas, J., & Collis, G. (2000). Dogs as catalysts for social interactions: Robustness of the effect. *British Journal of Psychology, 91*(Pt 1), 61–70.

Messent, P. (1983). Social facilitation of contact with other people by pet dogs. In *New perspectives on our lives with companion animals,* edited by A. Katcher and A. Beck, pp. 37–46. Philadelphia: University of Pennsylvania Press.

Morris, M., Stephens, D.L., Day, E., Holbrook, S.M., & Strazar, G. (2001). A collective stereographic photo essay on key aspects of animal companionship: The truth about dogs and cats. *AMS Review, 1.*

Newby, J. (1997). *The pact for survival: Humans and their companions.* Sydney, Australia: ABC Books.

Nutbeam, D., & Harris, E. (Eds.). (2004). *Theory in a nutshell: A guide to health promotion theory* (2nd ed.). Sydney, Australia: McGraw Hill.

Onyx, J., & Bullen, P. (1997). *Measuring social capital in five communities in NSW: An analysis.* Sydney: University of Technology.

Onyx, J., & Bullen, P. (2000). Measuring social capital in five communities. *The Journal of Applied Behavioural Science, 36*(1), 23–42.

Perkins, D.D., Mekks, J.W., & Taylor, R.B. (1992). The physical environment of street blocks and resident perception of crime and disorder: Implications for theory and measurement. *Journal of Environmental Psychology, 12,* 21–23.

Podberscek, A.L. (2000). *The relationships between people and pets.* Cambridge, MA: Cambridge University Press.

Potapchuk, W.R., Crocker, J.P., & Schechter, W.H. (1997). Building community with social capital: Chits and chums or chats with change. *National Civic Review, 86*(2), 129–139.

Putnam, R. (1993, Spring). The prosperous community: Social capital and public life. *The American Prospect, 13,* 35–42.

Putnam, R. (1996). The strange disappearance of civic America. *The American Prospect, 7,* 1–18.

Putnam, R. (2000). *Bowling alone: The collapse and revival of American community.* Cambridge, MA: Harvard University Press.

Putnam, R.D. (1995, January). Bowling alone: America's declining social capital. *Journal of Democracy, 1,* 65–78.

Robins, D., Sanders, C., & Cahill, S. (1991). Dogs and their people: Pet-facilitated interaction in a public setting. *Journal of Contemporary Ethnography, 20*(1), 3–25.

Rogers, J., Hart, L.A., & Boltz, R.P. (1993). The role of pet dogs in casual conversations of elderly adults. *The Journal of Social Psychology, 133,* 265–277.

Runyan, D.K., Hunter, W.M., Socolar, R.R.S., Amaya-Jackson, L., English, D., Landsverk, J., et al. (1998). Children who prosper in unfavourable environments: The relationship to social capital. *Pediatrics, 101*(1, Pt. 1), 12–18.

Saguaro Seminar: Civic Engagement in America. (2000). *Social capital community benchmark survey.* Cambridge, MA: John F. Kennedy School of Government, Harvard University.

Sartorius, N. (2003). Social capital and mental health. *Current Opinion in Psychiatry, 16*(Suppl. 2), S101–S105.

Serpell, J. (1999). Guest editor's introduction: Animals in children's lives. *Society and Animals, 7,* 87–94.

Sobel, J. (2002). Can we trust social capital? *Journal of Economic Literature, 40*(1), 139.

Sooman, A., & Macintyre, S. (1995). Health and perceptions of the local environment in socially contrasting neighbourhoods in Glasgow. *Health and Place, 1*(1), 15–26.

Subramanian, S., Lochner, K., & Kawachi, I. (2003). Neighbourhood differences in social capital: A compositional artefact or a contextual construct? *Health and Place, 9*(1), 33–44.

Thompson, K.L., & Guillone, E. (2003). Promotion of empathy and prosocial behaviour in children through humane education. *Australian Psychologist, 38.*

Timperio, A., Salmon, J., Chu, B., & Andrianopoulos, N. (2008). Is dog ownership or dog walking associated with weight status in children and their parents? *Health Promotion Journal of Australia, 19*(1), 60–63.

Vimpani, G. (2000). Child development and the civil society: Does social capital matter? *Developmental and Behavioral Pediatrics, 21*(1), 44–47.

Walljasper, J. (2007). *The great neighborhood book.* New Society Publishers: Gabriola Islands, BC, Canada.

Wilkinson, S., & Marmot, R. (Eds.). (2003). *Social determinants of health: The solid facts* (2nd ed.). Geneva: World Health Organization.

Wilson-Doenges, G. (2000). An exploration of sense of community and fear of crime in gated communities. *Environment and Behaviour, 32*(5), 597–611.

Wood, L. (2006). *Social capital, mental health and the environments in which people live.* Unpublished doctoral dissertation. The University of Western Australia, Perth.

Wood, L. (Ed.). (2009). *Living well together: How companion animals can help strengthen social fabric.* Melbourne, Australia: Petcare Information and Advisory Service and Centre for the Built Environment and Health, School of Population Health, The University of Western Australia.

Wood, L., Giles-Corti, B., & Bulsara, M. (2005). The pet connection: Pets as a conduit for social capital? *Social Science & Medicine, 61*(6), 1159–1173.

Wood, L., Walker, N., I'Anson, K., Ivery, P., French, S., & Giles-Corti, B. (2008). *PARKS: Parks and reserves Kwinana study: The use and role of parks within the Town of Kwinana.* Kwinana, Australia: Centre for the Built Environment and Health, The University of Western Australia, Perth.

Wood, L.J., Giles-Corti, B., Bulsara, M.K., & Bosch, D. (2007). More than a furry companion: The ripple effect of companion animals on neighborhood interactions and sense of community. *Society and Animals, 15*(1), 43–56.

CHAPTER 3

Animals and Child Health and Development

ALAN M. BECK

Animals are common in the lives of Americans; some 62% of all U.S. households have pets, according to the American Pet Products Association's 2009–2010 National Pet Owners Survey. A vast majority of pet owners (76%) are found in traditional families (and within that context, owners may be parents, older adults, or children), and 62% of owners are married. More than 38% of pet-owning families have at least one child under age 18, with some differences depending on the kind of pet; of these families, 41% own dogs, 37% own cats, 37% own birds, 56% own fish, 59% own reptiles, 66% own small pets, and 43% own horses (American Pet Products Association, 2009).

By the time they reach preschool, children appropriately identify dogs, cats, puppies, and kittens; they know that adult animals are caregivers for babies. Young boys' interest in caring for human infants reportedly decreases as they grow, but their interest in the care of animals does not decline, perhaps because pet care is not associated with gender, unlike care of human infants (Melson & Fogel, 1989). Among elementary school children, there is no significant difference between males and females in the level of attachment to animals (Stevens, 1990).

Animals are more than a common part of the real lives of young people; they also occupy a major role in children's imaginary lives. Animal characters appear in 75% of a random sample of children's books published from 1916 to 1950 (Lystad, 1980). Most bestselling children's stories feature animal protagonists (Melson, 2001). Unlike human characters, animals in fairy tales and children's stories impart the essence of the issue without the baggage of age, ethnicity, or gender; animals can teach children values without the association of value judgments.

School is where children work, and there, too, animal contact is relatively common. In Indiana, more than 26% of elementary school classrooms have animals, including 21.3% of schools in large cities, 37.5% of schools in towns, and 38.7% of rural schools. The classroom animals play many roles, including encouraging students to pay attention to their lessons, making subject matter more interesting, and rewarding children for good work (Rud & Beck, 2003). Classroom dogs also appear to encourage improved motor skills (Gee, Sherlock, Bennett, & Harris, 2009; see also Chapter 7). Children read about what is interesting to them, so it is noteworthy that "Dog" and "Cat" are, respectively, the most common and second most common articles that children look up in encyclopedias (Findsen, 1990). Urban areas provide less routine contact with animals. Indeed, urban schools are less likely to have animals in the classroom than are rural schools; however, some studies have found that urban children are slightly more attached to animals than are rural children (Stevens, 1990).

In the family setting, pets, as with other family members, can be triangulated into a family system to relieve an uncomfortable emotional system between two people, such as parent and child. For example, a child might say things to the pet instead of to the parent, but the parent gets the message (Cain, 1983; Levinson, 1969, 1972). Children frequently turn to their pets as a way of mitigating life's stresses, such as starting school for the first time (Melson, Schwarz, & Beck, 1997). In addition, a child's interest in animals can improve family dynamics. In one study, families with young children (7–12 years old) were given a bird feeder and an initial supply of birdseed. The parents reported that family involvement was a particularly beneficial aspect of the program, and 90% of the families that participated were still feeding birds a year after the program had ended (Beck, Melson, da Costa, & Liu, 2001).

IMPACT OF ANIMALS ON CHILDREN

The pervasiveness of animal contact may have profound effects on child development, and animals play many roles in such development. There is a widespread belief that pets are good for children and teach them responsibility. Although there are no specific data to validate the belief, it is interesting to note that "teaches responsibility" was listed as a benefit of pet ownership by 37% of dog owners and 55% of owners of small pets (American Pet Products Association, 2009). Perhaps parents assume that the small pet can encourage responsible conduct. Many small pets are dependent for their care on a child who is the caregiving "parent": Pets are our children's children (Beck & Katcher, 1996).

Another way that companion animals may benefit children is by improving their social skills. Pet-owning children, presumably from watching their animals, demonstrate improved sensitivity to subtle nuances of nonverbal communication and a willingness to establish social contacts (Guttmann, Predovic, & Zemanek, 1985; Millot, Filiatre, Gagnon, Eckerlin, & Montagner, 1986). Playing with pets and providing care to pets were observed to influence the behavior of second- and fifth-grade children with pets in the home. Among these children, involvement with animals was positively associated with constructive nonschool endeavors, including playing with computers, doing art, reading, being read to, and getting involved in organized group activities (Melson, 1988).

A major role that pets play is being a child's best friend (Melson, 2001; Melson et al., 2009). Whereas nearly half of adults confide in a pet, more than 70% of young people do so (Katcher & Beck, 1986, 1987). A child can talk to and share with a pet without worrying about confidentiality, reprisal, or judgment, and without needing to meet any expectations (Melson, 2001). A pet dog, especially, can play a role of reflected appraisal similar to that of a best friend and therefore can be an important and positive figure in the child's social environment (Davis, 1987).

> The values of pet ownership in promoting normal child development may be summarized as follows: A child who is exposed to the emotional experiences inherent in playing with a pet is given many learning opportunities that are essential to wholesome personality development. His play with the pet will express his view of the world, its animals, and its human beings, including his parents and peers. Further, through play with the pet, the child may learn to resolve some of the problems of relating to his peers and of achieving a wholesome balance of dependence and independence with regard to his family. (Levinson, 1972, p. 78)

Animals in Therapeutic Settings

Most animal-assisted therapy (AAT) programs for children are based in institutions and use resident animals, such as fish and birds, or visiting animals, usually dogs. There also are many programs that require the child to visit the animal, as in therapeutic horseback riding or programs that utilize dolphins.

The therapeutic use of animal contact to enhance physical and mental health began long before there was any scientific evidence for its effectiveness. Much of the early literature documents fortuitous interactions with animals that happened to be present in a therapeutic setting (McCulloch, 1983). The animals were intended to provide a diversion or the joys traditionally associated with interacting with pet animals. These expectations are reasonable, as often the best medicines are appropriate concentrations of what is generally beneficial (Beck & Katcher, 1984). The accumulating evidence that animals can provide positive enrichment, if not actual therapy, encourages the use of animals in a variety of institutional settings (Beck & Katcher, 2003; National Institutes of Health, 1987). AAT studies have common problems, however, including small sample sizes, unavoidable nonrandom assignment of treatments, necessary nonblinding of the intervention, and outcomes that may be subtle, transitory, or delayed (Beck & Katcher, 1984).

With the increasing popularity of AAT comes increased scrutiny and expectations that researchers will develop a clear hypothesis and improved experimental design related to the therapeutic use of animals. Although the literature on the impact of animal contact in general includes some reasonably large epidemiologic studies, studies addressing AAT are more commonly descriptive, small studies (Barker & Wolen, 2008). Nevertheless, AAT has demonstrated a modest positive impact on autism spectrum symptoms, some medical difficulties, behavioral problems, and emotional well-being (Nimer & Lundahl, 2007). Most AAT studies with children tend to focus on clinical populations (Barker & Wolen, 2008); many such studies address attempts to mitigate anxiety or pain in the hospital setting (Braun, Stangler, Narveson, & Pettingell, 2009; Havener et al., 2001; Kaminski, Pellino, & Wish, 2002; Nagengast, Baun, Megel, & Leibowitz, 1997; Sobo, Eng, & Kassity-Krich, 2006). Just as the use of animals in nursing homes is increasing, so is the use of animals in children's hospitals.

BIOMEDICAL ETHICAL ISSUES IN PUBLIC HEALTH RESEARCH

There are risks associated with any therapeutic intervention. Therapy using animals poses some special problems that may involve the patients, staff, or visitors. Animal bites, allergies, zoonoses, and falls caused by the animals or their excreta are the most common causes of concern (see also Chapter 4). Nevertheless, there is little indication that animal programs are particularly dangerous, and there are few reports of adverse effects (Schantz, 1990; Walter-Toews, 1993). Although AAT has a good safety record, the potential for problems increases as programs involve more people and more animals (Beck, 2000, Katcher, & Beck, 2010). There are guidelines for institutions on how to safely introduce and maintain animals in therapeutic or school settings (Lefebvre, Golab,

Christensen, et al., 2008; Centers for Disease Control and Prevention, 2007; Lee, Zeglen, Ryan, & Hines, 1983). There are even guidelines for animal contact with individuals who have special needs, including people with suppressed immune function (American Veterinary Medical Association, 1995, 2007). But it is time to move beyond the fragmentation of existing information to develop an overarching set of recognized guidelines that protect both patients and animals in therapeutic settings. These guidelines should, at the very least, provide for the selection of appropriate animals, creation of animal care protocols, surveillance of negative incidents, and development of emergency handing procedures. One of the most troublesome issues associated with animals in the home and in therapeutic settings is the belief that animal allergies will be a problem for children. Contact with dogs slightly increases the risk of asthma (Takkouche, González-Barcala, Etminan, & FitzGerald, 2008), and dog-owning children with asthma may experience worsened symptoms when they are exposed to air pollutants (McConnell et al., 2006).

However, there is evidence that dog and cat contact early in a child's life protects the young person from allergy in the future. Exposure to dogs in infancy, especially at time of birth, is associated with reductions in wheezing and atopy (Bufford et al., 2008) and exposure to pets reduces the risk of developing atopy-related diseases in early childhood (Nafstad, Magnus, Gaarder, & Jaakkola, 2001). Indeed, exposure to two or more dogs or cats in the first year of life may reduce the subsequent risk of allergic sensitization to multiple allergens during childhood (Ownby, Johnson, & Peterson, 2002). There is even evidence that early exposure can protect a person from non-Hodgkin's lymphoma (Tranah, Bracci, & Holly, 2008). According to physician allergists, the suggestion that a family get rid of their pet is met with considerable resistance—more than 70% of patients resist or do not comply. Before passing judgment on parents or patients for wanting to protect the animal, one should know that pet ownership among allergists is about the same as in the general population and whereas 36% of allergists who do not own pets recommend the removal of pets, only 19% of pet-owning allergists do so. Allergists who owned pets as children are also significantly less likely to recommend removal of the pet from the family (Baker & McCulloch, 1983). Indeed, it may be useful to remember that pets are often viewed as members of the family and that there is a great deal of evidence regarding the benefits of human–human contact (social support theory) that can be applied to these situations (Hawkley & Cacioppo, 2007; Hupcey, 1998; Lynch 1977, 2000; Schone & Weinick, 1998).

To justify any risk associated with animal contact, it must be demonstrated that the animal has value to the patient (by performing a risk/benefit assessment). The most common criticism of animal-facilitated therapy programs is that they are not goal oriented, and even when goals are identified, evaluation of the program's outcome often is inconclusive (Beck, 2000; Beck & Katcher, 1984; Draper, Gerber, & Layng, 1990; Hundley, 1991). To justify any risk, the benefits have to be clearly and realistically identified through interdisciplinary approaches and multisite studies.

In the past, health care institutions welcomed visits with animals from animal shelters and humane societies. This policy allowed animals with unknown health histories to interact with patients whose immune systems could have been compromised. In addition, because humane societies tended to bring the most attractive and best behaved animals, these same animals were not available to potential adopters at the shelter and sometimes were never adopted. It is now more common for volunteers or institutional staff to bring their own animals. Often owner–pet pairs have had some experience as animal visitors or even have certification (e.g., by the Delta Society, which requires owners to meet minimum standards for awareness of institutional expectations and animal health and behavior). Owned or certified animals usually appreciate being with their owners and soon appear to enjoy the experience, whereas the visits seem to be stressful for some shelter animals. Therapeutic horseback riding has standards for animal use (Iannuzzi & Rowan, 1991), but most small-animal programs just use common sense.

We as researchers also must assess the risks to the animals that are employed, not only to honor our society's ethical commitment to animals, but to improve the quality of the research and therapeutic outcomes for humans as well as animals. Animal fatigue, overwork, and burnout can occur with therapy animals. Another major ethical problem is the use of exotic (nondomesticated) animals. There are few standards of care or use for these animals, and less is known about assessing their stress. Dolphin-assisted therapy programs attract much media coverage and many donors, but an extensive review showed that outcome data are flawed and not compelling for this practice as a therapy (Marino & Lilienfeld, 2007). A subsequent study found that the use of dolphins was beneficial, but the study failed to convincingly argue that dolphins were significantly better than farm animals (Breitenbach, Stumpf, Fersen, & Ebert, 2009). It can only be concluded that it is unethical to use dolphins when they have been associated with questionable therapeutic outcomes, are very expensive to maintain, are less available to patients, and may be stressed by the experience, and also when proven outcomes have been achieved with dogs and farm animals.

Objective assessment of physiological stress and a better understanding of captive animal behavior may provide new insights into the human–animal bond and the management of captive animals. There is a growing body of literature on how to define and measure stress in animals (Moberg, 1985), but more work in this area is needed. Assessing the most ethical and safest way to include visiting and residential animals in any setting should be an area of continuing study (Beck, 2000; Katcher & Beck, 2010). "Reconciling the risks to the animals with their rehabilitation value is neither simple nor easy unless one follows the dictum that animals absolutely should not be used as means to an end" (Iannuzzi & Rowan, 1991, p. 159). A therapeutic session should benefit not only the patient but also the therapist, staff, and animal.

Lastly, it is important to identify the children for whom, or situations in which, contact with animals is potentially problematic or inappropriate for either the people or the animals. Some people do not want animal contact and their concerns must be recognized. Understanding the reasons that people, especially children, do not want animal contact may be of scientific value and may provide insights that could benefit them.

In sum, there has been an increasing trend to permit, and even encourage, animal contact with children in a variety of institutional settings. To that end, institutions have allowed various approaches, including visits with animals and making mascot or resident animals available for contact. In general, the animals have proven to be of benefit. It should be rememberd that animals are just one way to enrich the environment for people in institutional settings.

REFERENCES

American Pet Products Association. (2009). *2009–2010 national pet owners survey*. Greenwich, CT: Author.
American Veterinary Medical Association. (1995). AVMA guidelines for responding to clients with special needs. *Journal of the American Veterinary Medical Association, 206*, 961–976.
American Veterinary Medical Association. (2007). *Guidelines for animal-assisted activity, animal-assisted therapy and resident animal programs*. Retrieved December 14, 2009, from http://www.avma.org/issues/policy/animal_assisted_guidelines.asp
Baker, E., & McCulloch, M.J. (1983). Allergy to pets: Problems for the allergist and the pet owner. In A.H. Katcher & A.M. Beck (Eds.), *New perspectives on our lives with companion animals* (pp. 341–345). Philadelphia: University of Pennsylvania Press.
Barker, S.B., & Wolen, A.R. (2008). The benefits of human–companion animal interaction: A review. *Journal of Veterinary Medical Education, 35*, 487–495.
Beck, A.M. (2000). The use of animals to benefit humans, animal-assisted therapy. In A.H. Fine (Ed.), *The handbook on animal assisted therapy: Theoretical foundations and guidelines for practice* (pp. 21–40). New York: Academic Press.
Beck, A.M., & Katcher, A.H. (1984). A new look at pet-facilitated therapy. *Journal of the American Veterinary Medicine Association, 184*, 414–421.

Beck, A.M., & Katcher, A.H. (1996). *Between pets and people: The importance of animal companionship.* West Lafayette, IN: Purdue University Press.

Beck, A.M., & Katcher, A.H. (2003). Future directions in human–animal bond research. *American Behavioral Scientist, 47*(1), 79–93.

Beck, A.M., Melson, G.F., da Costa, P.L., & Liu, T. (2001). The educational benefits of a ten-week home-based wild bird feeding program for children. *Anthrozoös, 14,* 19–28.

Braun, C., Stangler, T., Narveson, J., & Pettingell, S. (2009). Animal-assisted therapy as a pain relief intervention for children. *Complementary Therapies in Clinical Practice, 15,* 105–109.

Breitenbach, E., Stumpf, E., Fersen, L.V., & Ebert, H. (2009). Dolphin-assisted therapy: Changes in interaction and communication between children with severe disabilities and their caregivers. *Anthrozoös, 22,* 277–289.

Bufford, J.D., Reardon, C.L., Li, Z., Roberg, K.A., DaSilva, D., Eggleston, P.A., et al. (2008). Effects of dog ownership in early childhood on immune development and atopic diseases. *Clinical and Experimental Allergy, 38,* 1635–1643.

Cain, A.O. (1983). A study of pets in the family system. In A.H. Katcher & A.M. Beck (Eds), *New perspectives on our lives with companion animals* (pp. 72–81). Philadelphia: University of Pennsylvania Press.

Centers for Disease Control and Prevention. (2007, July 6). Guidelines for animals in school settings. *Morbidity and Mortality Weekly Report, 56*(RR05), 18–19. Retrieved December 14, 2009, from http://www.cdc.gov/mmwr/preview/mmwrhtml/ rr5605a5.htm

Davis, J.H. (1987). Preadolescent self-concept development and pet ownership. *Anthrozoös, 1,* 90–94.

Draper, R.J., Gerber, G.J., & Layng, E.M. (1990). Defining the role of pet animals in psychotherapy. *Psychiatric Journal University of Ottawa, 15*(3), 169–172.

Findsen, O. (1990, March 15). The ABCs of encyclopedias. *Journal and Courier,* pp. D1, D6.

Gee, N.R., Sherlock, T.R., Bennett, E.A., & Harris, S.L. (2009). Preschoolers' adherence to instructions as a function of presence of a dog and motor skills task. *Anthrozoös, 22,* 267–276.

Guttmann, G., Predovic, M., & Zemanek, M. (1985). The influence of pet ownership on non-verbal communication and social competence in children. In *Proceedings of the International Symposium on the Occasion of the 80th Birthday of Nobel prizewinner Prof. Dr. Konrad Lorenz* (pp. 58–63). Vienna: Institute for Interdisciplinary Research on the Human–Pet Relationship.

Havener, L., Gentes, L., Thaler, B., Baun, M.M., Driscoll, F.A., Beiraghi, S., et al. (2001). The effects of a companion animal on distress in children undergoing dental procedures. *Issues in Comprehensive Pediatric Nursing, 24,* 137–152.

Hawkley, L.C., & Cacioppo, J.T. (2007). Aging and loneliness: Downhill quickly? *Current Directions in Psychological Science, 16,* 187–191.

Hundley, J. (1991). Pet project: The use of pet facilitated therapy among the chronically mentally ill. *Journal Psychosocial Nursing, 29*(6), 23–26.

Hupcey, J.E. (1998). Clarifying the social support theory–research linkage. *Journal of Advanced Nursing, 27*(6), 1231–1241.

Iannuzzi, D., & Rowan, A.N. (1991). Ethical issues in animal-assisted therapy programs. *Anthrozoös, 4,* 154–163.

Kaminski, M., Pellino, T., & Wish, J. (2002). Play and pets: The physical and emotional impact of child-life and pet therapy on hospitalized children. *Children's Health Care, 31*(4), 321–335.

Katcher, A.H., & Beck, A.M. (1986). *Dialogue with animals. Transactions & studies of the College of Physicians of Philadelphia, 8,* 105–112.

Katcher. A.H., & Beck, A.M. (1987). Health and caring for living things. *Anthrozoös, 1,* 175–183.

Katcher, A.H., & Beck, A.M. (2010). Newer and older perspectives on the therapeutic effects of animals and nature. In A.H. Fine (Ed.), *The handbook on animal assisted therapy and Interventions* (pp. 49–58). New York: Academic Press.

Lee, R.L., Zeglen, M.E., Ryan, T. & Hines, L.M. (1983). Guidelines: Animals in nursing homes. *California Veterinarian* (Suppl. 3), 1–42.

Lefebvre, S.L., Golab, G.C., Christensen, E., Castrodale, L., Aureden, K., Bialachowski, A., et al., *American Journal of Infection Control*. (2008). Guidelines for animal-assisted interventions in health care facilities. *American Journal of Infection Control, 36*, 78–85.

Levinson, B.M. (1969). *Pet-oriented child psychotherapy.* Springfield, IL: Charles C Thomas.

Levinson, B.M. (1972). *Pets and human development.* Springfield, IL: Charles C Thomas.

Lynch, J.J. (1977). *The broken heart: The medical consequences of loneliness.* New York: Basic Books.

Lynch, J.J. (2000). *A cry unheard: New insights into the medical consequences of loneliness.* Baltimore: Bancroft Press.

Lystad, M. (1980). *From Dr. Mather to Dr. Seuss: 200 years of American books for children.* Boston: G.K. Hall.

Marino, L., & Lilienfeld, S.O. (2007). Dolphin-assisted therapy: More flawed data and more flawed conclusions. *Anthrozoös, 20*, 239–249.

McConnell, R., Berhane, K., Molitor, J., Gilliland, F., Künzili, N., Thorne, P.S., et al. (2006). Dog ownership enhances symptomatic responses to air pollution in children with asthma. *Environmental Health Perspectives, 114*, 1910–1915.

McCulloch, M.J. (1983). Animal-facilitated therapy: Overview and future directions. In A.H. Katcher & A.M. Beck (Eds.), *New perspectives on our lives with companion animals* (pp. 410–430). Philadelphia: University of Pennsylvania Press.

Melson, G.F. (1988). Availability of and involvement with pets by children: Determinants and correlates. *Anthrozoös, 2*, 45–52.

Melson, G.F. (2001). *Why the wild things are: Animals in the lives of children.* Cambridge, MA: Harvard University Press.

Melson, G.F., & Fogel, A. (1989). Children's ideas about animal young and their care: A reassessment of gender differences in the development of nurturance. *Anthrozoös, 2*, 265–273.

Melson, G.F., Peter, H., Kahn, P.H., Jr., Beck, A.M., Friedman, B., Roberts, T., et al. (2009). Children's behavior toward and understanding of robotic and living dogs. *Journal of Applied Developmental Psychology, 30*, 92–102.

Melson, G.F., Schwarz, R.L., & Beck, A.M. (1997). Importance of companion animals in children's lives: Implications for veterinary practice. *Journal of the American Veterinary Medical Association, 211*(12), 1512–1518.

Millot, J.L., Filiatre, J.C., Gagnon, A.C., Eckerlin, A., & Montagner, H. (1986). Children and their dogs: An ethological study of communication. In *Living together: People, animals, and the environment* (p. 126). Boston: Delta Society International Conference.

Moberg, G.P. (Ed.). (1985). *Animal stress.* Bethesda, MD: American Physiological Society.

Nafstad, P., Magnus, P., Gaarder, P.I., & Jaakkola, J.J. (2001). Exposure to pets and atopy-related diseases in the first 4 years of life. *Allergy, 56*, 267–269.

Nagengast, S.L., Baun, M.M., Megel, M., & Leibowitz, J.M. (1997). The effects of the presence of a companion animal on physiological arousal and behavioral distress in children during a physical examination. *Journal of Pediatric Nursing, 12*, 323–330.

National Institutes of Health. (1987, September 10–11). *The health benefits of pets. Workshop summary.* Bethesda, MD: Office of Medical Applications of Research, Technology Assessment Workshop.

Nimer, J., & Lundahl, B. (2007). Animal-assisted therapy: A meta-analysis. *Anthrozoös, 20*, 225–238.

Ownby, D.R., Johnson, C.C., & Peterson, E.L. (2002). Exposure to dogs and cats during the first year of life and the risk of allergic sensitivity at six to seven years of age. *Journal of the American Medical Association, 288*, 963–972.

Rud, A.G., Jr., & Beck, A.M. (2003). Companion animals in Indiana elementary schools. *Anthrozoös, 16,* 241–251.

Schantz, P.M. (1990). Preventing potential health hazards incidental to the use of pets in therapy. *Anthrozoös, 4,* 14–23.

Schone, B.S., & Weinick, R.M. (1998). Health-related behaviors and the benefits of marriage for elderly persons. *The Gerontologist, 38,* 618–627.

Sobo, E.J., Eng, B., & Kassity-Krich, N. (2006). Canine visitation (pet) therapy. *Journal of Holistic Nursing, 24*(1), 51–57.

Stevens, L.T. (1990). Attachment of pets among eighth graders. *Anthrozoös, 3,* 177–183.

Takkouche, B., González-Barcala, F.-J., Etminan, M., & FitzGerald, M. (2008). Exposure to furry pets and the risk of asthma and allergic rhinitis: a meta-analysis. *Allergy, 63,* 857–864.

Tranah, G.J., Bracci, P.M., & Holly, E.A. (2008). Domestic and farm-animal exposures and risk of non-Hodgkin's lymphoma in a population-based study in the San Francisco Bay area. *Cancer Epidemiology, Biomarkers and Prevention, 17*(9), 2382–2387.

Walter-Toews, D. (1993). Zoonotic disease concerns in animal assisted therapy and animal visitation programs. *Canadian Veterinary Journal, 34,* 549–551.

Samantha and the Happy Couple

Sally and Tim had been high school sweethearts. Shortly after they got married, they moved to an apartment in a large city. They had lived in a rural area and were used to having family pets. They decided that it would be easier to have a cat than a dog, and got a kitten whom they named Samantha. After a couple years, they decided to start a family, and Sally became pregnant. When she announced to her friends that she and Tim were becoming parents, one of her girlfriends suggested that she "get rid of" Samantha, because it was very dangerous to have a cat in the house during pregnancy. She seemed so sure of her facts that Sally was really worried. She talked to Tim, they searched the Internet, and they were confused and frightened by some of the information they saw there. What to believe? Whom to ask? They decided on two sources: the nurse practitioner at Sally's doctor's office and their veterinarian.

On her next visit to her obstetrician, Sally sat down with the nurse practitioner who was her primary point of care. She liked this capable, gentle man who always seemed to have answers or know where to get them. When she asked him her question, the nurse practitioner instantly smiled and nodded.

"Oh, we get this question a lot. I can give you some things to read, but the keys are these. Toxoplasmosis, which actually most cats do carry, is dangerous if you get it while pregnant. We strongly recommend that Tim take over cat litter duty and that you steer clear of the kitty litter throughout your pregnancy. You should keep up with normal healthy hygiene, of course, and keeping the cat clean and doing lots of hand washing are always good ideas anyway. You should be fine."

The veterinarian was equally positive. She, too, said she got that question a lot. She gave Sally a pamphlet on toxoplasmosis and pregnancy, provided information similar to what the nurse practitioner had told her, and updated all of Samantha's immunizations. Armed with this information, Sally and Tim decided that they could relax and enjoy their growing family, which included and would continue to include Samantha!

CHAPTER 4

Public Health Implications of Pets

Our Own Animals and Those of Others

LYNNE HAVERKOS, KARYL J. HURLEY,
SANDRA McCUNE, AND PEGGY McCARDLE

This chapter outlines the ways in which pets can influence child development and health. There is mounting evidence that pets such as dogs and cats and other companion animals such as horses can promote psychological and physical health benefits in their owners. Pets may also play a "therapist" role in clinical settings. Preceding chapters have described the therapeutic role that pets may play in a wide range of conditions, including psychiatric and psychological conditions, physical and mental disabilities, and mood disorders. Some evidence suggests that pets can serve as sentinels of certain chronic conditions such as cancer (Pickel, Manucy, Walker, Hall, & Walker, 2004; Willis et al., 2004), epilepsy (Strong, Brown, & Walker, 1999), and hypoglycemia (low blood sugar) (O'Connor, O'Connor, & Walsh, 2008).

The hope of these benefits needs to be balanced by the potential costs of pet ownership and the burdens that can be associated with the pet-keeping experience. Pets and children should be adequately prepared for each other and appropriately matched, and a proper choice of animal should be made, including the breed, nutrition, training, and veterinary care. Responsible pet ownership can minimize many, if not all, of the potential burdens and risks, and allow full appreciation of the benefits, of owning an animal.

The chapter begins with a summary of the scale of pet keeping, followed by a brief overview of some of the demonstrated and potential benefits and negative health effects (e.g., allergies, falls, bites, zoonoses) of human–animal interactions on health and development. The chapter closes with guidance on the selection of an appropriate pet for an individual or family with a child.

PET OWNERSHIP IN WESTERN HOUSEHOLDS

Americans have a love affair with pets—62% of American households (71.1 million) own one or more pets (American Pet Products Association, n.d.). According to the National Pet Owners Survey conducted by the American Pet Products Association (2009), Americans own 171.1 million freshwater fish, 93.6 million cats, 77.5 million dogs, 15.9 million small animals, 15 million birds, 13.6 million reptiles, 13.3 million horses, and 11.2 million saltwater fish. A similar phenomenon is found in other Western countries. In Britain, 43% of households have pets, including 9 million cats and 6 million dogs (Pet Food Manufacturers Association, 2004). In Australia, 63% of the 6.6 million households own a pet, and 53% of all households own a cat or dog (Australian Companion Animal Council, 2007).

Children are exposed to domesticated animals not only in their homes but also in public places, such as community parks and neighborhoods, zoos, farms, petting farms, and fairs. Although most pets are domestic animals, birds, and fish, there has been a 75% increase in the number of exotic animals in the United States since 1992 (American Pet Products Association, n.d.).

Pet ownership and human–animal interactions offer numerous psychological and health advantages, but they also generate public health concerns regarding animal-related injuries, animal-transmitted diseases, and animals' impact on certain health conditions. Concerns about allergies and zoonotic infections are sometimes cited as reasons for giving up family pets, yet Ownby, Johnson, and Peterson (2002) found that daily hygiene and pet care can reduce allergic reactions by up to 95%.

HEALTH AND QUALITY-OF-LIFE EFFECTS FOR PET OWNERS

It has long been suspected that pet ownership provides certain health benefits, but the evidence has been inconsistent. Some conclusions are based on cross sectional studies that are incapable of demonstrating causality, whereas others are based on studies of varying quality or studies that included small numbers of participants. Nonetheless, there are studies that have shown benefits of pet ownership, such as reduced risk of cardiovascular disease (Anderson, Reid, & Jennings, 1992), higher survival rates following myocardial infarction (Friedmann, Katcher, Lynch, & Thomas, 1980), significantly lower use of practitioners' services (Headey, 1999), reduced risk of asthma and allergic rhinitis in children who were exposed to pet allergens in the first year of life (Nafsted, Magnus, Gaader, & Jaakola, 2001; Ownby et al., 2002), and better physical and psychological well-being in older individuals who were living independently (Raina, Waltner-Toews, Bonnett, Woodward, & Abernathy, 1999). Investigators conducting longitudinal studies in Germany and Australia found that the healthiest population groups in both of those countries, defined as those who made the fewest doctor visits, were pet owners of medium- to long-term duration. The researchers concluded that pet ownership was correlated with improved medium-term health (Headey & Grabka, 2007).

Clearly, more data are needed to confirm such conclusions. For example, some recent studies have failed to replicate the finding that pet ownership is associated with reduced cardiovascular disease and reduced use of general practitioner services (Parslow & Jorm, 2003), or the psychological or physical benefits on health for community-dwelling older people (Parslow, Jorm, Christensen, Rodgers, & Jacomb, 2005). Such conflicting data indicate that these questions have not been definitively answered; the reasons for these different findings must be determined and rigorous studies designed to address them.

Researchers have examined the mechanisms by which pet ownership seems to positively affect mental and physiologic health. The major effects appear to be reduced distress and anxiety, decreased loneliness and depression, and increased exercise (Friedmann & Tsai, 2006). Although Wells (2009) did not find a statistically significant association between pet ownership and self-reported health in people with chronic fatigue syndrome, the pet owners believed that their pets were enhancing the owners' quality of life. Thus, both the physiologic and the psychological outcomes must be examined when considering the health effects of animals on their owners.

Allergies

According to the American College of Allergy, Asthma, and Immunology, an estimated 10% of the U.S. population experiences allergies to dogs and cats, with rates as high as 20%–30% among individuals with asthma (n.d.). Allergens in the forms of proteins in animal dander, fur, feathers, body waste, saliva, and fleas can trigger the human immune system to produce a specific type of antibody, immunoglobulin E (IgE), which can cause an inflammatory response. Allergies may present as allergic rhinitis, asthma, or contact hypersensitivity (hives). There are mixed findings in the literature regarding the relationship between early exposure to pets and childhood allergy (Simpson & Custovic, 2005).

Heinrich et al. (2002) found a positive correlation between pet allergen levels in the home and infants' levels of IgE at birth, suggesting that exposure to pets during pregnancy may influence fetal immune development in a protective manner. Aichbhaumik et al. (2008) also found that women who were exposed to cats or dogs during pregnancy delivered infants with lower cord blood levels of IgE than did women who were not exposed to pets. However, not all studies corroborate these findings; for example, Schönberger et al. (2005) did not find a positive correlation between prenatal exposure to pet allergens and total serum IgE at birth in high-risk children.

Animal-related Falls

Falls are the leading cause of nonfatal injury in Americans. In 2006, about 8 million Americans were seen in emergency departments for fall injuries, with approximately 1% associated with dogs and cats (Centers for Disease Control and Prevention [CDC], 2001; Schroeder & Ault, 2001). The CDC estimates that approximately 30 out of every 100,000 Americans experienced a pet-related fall each year from 2001 to 2006 (CDC, 2009b), with dog-related fall injuries occurring 7.5 times more often than cat-related injuries. The number of falls equated to an incidence of only 0.03%. Although the number of injuries is small, it is interesting to note that more than half of the falls associated with dogs occurred from tripping or falling over the dog while walking it, or from being pushed or pulled by the dog. Over 80% of cat-related falls (which are far less frequent) were from tripping over cats (CDC, 2009b).

Animal Bites

Globally, animal bites represent a serious public health concern and children are disproportionately affected (Ozanne-Smith, Ashby, & Stathakis, 2001). It has been estimated that between 3 and 6 million people, or 1%–2% of the population, are bitten by animals each year in the United States (Gilchrist, Sacks, White, & Kresnow, 2008). The majority of bites requiring medical attention are received from dogs (85%–90%), cats (5%–10%), and rodents (2%–3%), with the balance received from other small animals (rabbits, ferrets), farm animals (horses, cattle, pigs), monkeys, reptiles, and other animals (Hodge & Tecklenburg, 2006).

Dog bites account for 1% of emergency department visits, and a very small proportion of these require hospitalization (CDC, 2001; Weiss, Friedman, & Coben, 1998). Fatal dog bites are extremely rare and cause an average 19 deaths per year (Langley, 2009), but this number appears to be increasing along with increases in human and canine populations. Sacks, Sinclair, Gilchrist, Golab, & Lockwood (2000) calculated that 0.0002% of all dog bites between 1979 and 1998 were fatal. Dog bites can cause lacerations and crush-type wounds, which can be followed by infections, and disfiguring injuries that require reconstructive surgery and hospitalizations. People who experience severe or multiple animal bites may develop posttraumatic stress disorder (Peters, Sottiaux, Appelboom, & Kahn, 2004) and may need psychological evaluation and psychological treatment, especially if they suffer mutilating injuries (Rusch, Grunert, Sanger, Dzwierzynski, & Matloub, 2000). Despite their relative infrequency, dog bites represent a significant cost to society, with direct annual costs of emergency room treatment estimated at $102.4 million and for hospitalizations at $62.5 million (Quinlan & Sacks, 1999; Weiss et al., 1998).

There is no national tracking system for animal bites in the United States, but some telephone surveys and emergency department data have been used to estimate national rates. Telephone surveys conducted by the CDC in 1994 (Sacks, Kresnow, & Houston, 1996) and in 2001–2003 (Gilchrist et al., 2008) revealed similar estimated numbers of annual dog bites (4.7 and 4.5 million, respectively). The later survey showed a significant decrease (47%) in the rate of dog bites for children age 14 and younger from the rate in the earlier survey and a decline in the rate of medical care sought for children following dog bites. Although the rate of medical care required by children decreased, children were still more likely to be treated for a dog bite than were adults. The most impressive declines in bite rates occurred in children from birth to 4 years of age and in boys.

Two surveys using emergency department data (CDC, 2003, and Weiss et al., 1998) showed similar numbers of patients (333,000 and 370,000, respectively) being treated in emergency departments for dog bites. The injury rate was highest for children ages 5–9 years and decreased with increasing age (CDC, 2003). Children 5 years and younger were at increased risk of injury due to their small size and behavior. Approximately 42% of dog bites occurred in children who were 14 years or younger, and the rates were significantly higher for boys than girls. A seasonal increase in bites occurred from April to

September, with a peak in July. Head and neck injuries were most common in children from birth through 4 years of age, and bites to the extremities were most common in children who were over age 15.

Males are more likely to be bitten by dogs than are females. Other risk factors for dog bites include being in a multidog household (Gershman, Sacks, & Wright, 1994), interacting with dogs of certain breeds (Schalamon, Ainoedhofer, & Singer, 2006), and interacting with dogs that are male, unneutered, or leashed or chained (Gershman et al., 1994). Dire, Hogan, and Riggs (1994) reported that a majority of dog bites were provoked. One retrospective review of animal bites to the hand revealed that attempting to separate fighting animals and attempting to aid an injured animal increased the likelihood of being bitten (Benson, Edwards, Schiff, Williams, & Visotsky, 2006). Less information is known about environmental determinants such as socioeconomic status of owners, type of housing, number of people living in the home, and neighborhood conditions.

In a study of 804 dog owners, Reisner and Shofer (2008) found that owners had limited knowledge of dog behavior and factors that increased the risk of bites to infants and children (i.e., body language, social signals, and resource-guarding and self-defense situations). In order to gain insight into child-directed canine aggression, investigators at a university veterinary hospital examined the records of 111 children who had been bitten by dogs. Records revealed that most of the children were bitten by dogs that had no history of biting children, and that resource guarding and discipline measures were the most common stimuli for aggression. The offending dogs had a high rate of behavioral abnormalities including aggression and anxiety, and about half had or were suspected of having potentially contributing medical conditions. Strategies such as neutering and training, which are typically used to calm dogs, were not routinely effective in deterring dog bites among this population of dogs (Reisner, Shofer, & Nance, 2007).

Cat bites are less frequent than dog bites, but they are of concern because secondary infection occurs earlier and more often (Dire, 1991; Freer, 2007). In the United States, cat bites represent 3%–15% of all animal bites; the majority of them are superficial and mild and are probably provoked (Palacio, Leon-Artozqui, Pastor-Villalba, Carrera-Martin, & Garcia-Belenguer, 2007). Women suffer cat bites more often than men, and the bites are usually located on their hands. Cat bites to the head and neck regions are more common among children (Patrick & O'Rourke, 1998).

The rate of infection following dog bites is estimated to be 4%–25% (Abrahamian, 2000; Talan, Citron, Abrahamian, Moran, & Goldstein, 1999; Taplitz, 2004; Weber & Hansen, 1991; and Westling et al., 2006) and infection following cat bites is 30%–50% (Kannikeswaran & Kamat, 2009; Smith, Meadowcroft, & May, 2000). The infectious organisms usually originate in the mouth of the biting animal or on the skin of the victim. The higher infection rate following cat bites is due to the puncturing nature of the wounds and the higher incidence of the bacterium *Pasturella multocida* in cats' mouths. The most common organisms isolated from infected dog and cat bites are *Staphylococcus aureus*, *Pasteurella multocida*, and *Pasteurella canis* (Kannikeswaran & Kamat, 2009) but other organisms include *Streptococcus*, *Fusobacterium*, and *Capnocytophaga* (Oehler, Velez, Mizrachi, Lamarche, & Gompf, 2009). Local infection and cellulitis are leading causes of illness following dog and cat bites. Sepsis can be a serious complication of animal bites, especially due to infection with *Pasteurella multocida* or *Capnocytophaga canimorsus*, a bacterium that causes a rare infection most commonly seen in persons who have a predisposing condition such as splenectomy, alcohol abuse, or immune dysfunction.

Zoonoses

Zoonoses are diseases that are transmitted from animals to humans under natural conditions. They are estimated to account for 75% of today's emerging infectious diseases (Souza, 2009; Taylor, Latham, & Woolhouse, 2001). Of the 1,415 known human pathogens, 61% are zoonotic in origin (Pickering, Marano, Bocchini, Angulo, & the Committee on Infectious Diseases, 2008), and pathogens that can exist within multiple host species are twice as likely to be associated with an emerging infectious disease as are pathogens that rely on a single host species. Animal-related infections can be caused by a variety of viruses, bacteria, parasites, and fungi. Animals can be important vectors of human illness, and humans can become accidental hosts when they have direct contact with the urine or tissues of affected animals or when they have indirect contact via contaminated water or soil. Table 4.1 summarizes the notable viral zoonoses.

Viruses

Viruses can be transmitted from animals to humans, but very few of them actually are transmitted this way.

Avian Influenza A

Avian or "bird flu" outbreaks among poultry occur intermittently on a global scale and range in severity from mild to severe. They are highly

Table 4.1. Symptoms, sources and precautions for well-known zoonotic viruses

Viral diseases	Symptoms	Frequency	Source of infection	Precautions
Avian Influenza A (bird flu)	Fever, cough, sore throat, muscle aches, conjunctivitis, pneumonia	Sporadic cases globally	Infected poultry	Wash hands, avoid contaminated meat
H1N1 (swine flu)	Fever, cough, sore throat, muscle aches, chills, respiratory infections	Pandemic in 2009	Person to person, not animal to person	Wash hands, disinfect surfaces, avoid people with flu
Rabies	Fever, headache, confusion	6,841 cases in animals and 2 cases in humans in United States in 2008	Raccoons, skunks, bats, foxes, coyotes, dogs, cats, cows, horses	Fatal if untreated; vaccinate dogs, cats, and horses and avoid contact with unfamiliar and ill animals

Source: Centers for Disease Control and Prevention (2010b).

contagious and have caused illness and deaths in humans in Asia, Africa, Europe, the Pacific, and the Near East. Transmission can occur from infected poultry to humans (CDC, 2010a). Confirmed human cases of avian influenza A/H5NI can be found on the World Health Organization (WHO) Avian influenza web site http://www.who.int/csr/disease/avian_influenza/en/.

H1N1 Infection

In June 2009, the World Health Organization declared a global pandemic of novel influenza A (H1N1, or "swine flu"; CDC, 2009a). It was the first global influenza pandemic in 41 years. Swine, turkey, ferrets, cats, and dogs contracted H1N1 infections in 2009, with evidence suggesting transmission to animals from ill humans. People were not infected by eating contaminated pork.

Rabies

Prior to the control of canine rabies in the United States in the 1940s and 1950s, about 50 cases of human rabies were reported each year. These cases were due mainly to bites by rabid dogs (Held, Tierkel, & Steele, 1967). In 2008, dogs and cats accounted for 5.1% of all cases of rabid animals reported to the CDC (Blanton, Robertson, Palmer, & Rupprecht, 2009). In developing nations, domestic dogs remain the most frequently reported rabid animals, and globally dogs are the main source of rabies transmission to humans, causing over 55,000 human deaths per year, mainly in Africa and Asia (World Rabies Day Mission, 2009). Thanks to vaccinations of dogs, canine rabies is no longer the threat to human life in the United States that it once was.

Bacteria

Several notable types of bacteria are transmissible from animals to humans, although they are more frequently transmitted through contaminated food or water. Table 4.2 summarizes some notable bacterial zoonoses.

Brucellosis

Brucella bacteria can be transmitted through abrasions in the hands of workers handling infected animals, but is more commonly spread by ingesting infected unpasteurized milk or dairy products. Brucellosis is reportable to local health departments and has an incidence of fewer than 0.5 cases per 100,000 population (CDC, 2010b).

Campylobacteriosis

Campylobacter bacteria can be transmitted from farm animals, cats, and dogs (especially puppies) to children via fecal-oral transmission. It is very important to wash hands well, especially after cleaning up animals' stools or playing with pets, in order to avoid infection (CDC, 2010b).

Cat-Scratch Fever

The bacterium *Bartonella henselae*, transmitted through cat scratches or bites, causes about 24,000 cases of cat scratch fever per year, with severity of symptoms ranging from mild to more severe, with fever and tender, enlarged lymph nodes (CDC, 2010b). About 50% of 8-month-old kittens will have antibody evidence of prior infection to *Bartonella* and 24% will have Bartonella bacteria in the blood (Guptill et al., 2004).

Leptospirosis

The uncommon bacterial disease leptospirosis is spread by contact with contaminated urine, blood, or tissues of infected animals. On rare occasions, it can cause life-threatening infections in humans (CDC, 2010b).

Lyme Disease

Deer ticks carry *Borrelia* bacteria, which cause Lyme disease, which may present with fever and flu-like illness, with or without a "bulls-eye"

Table 4.2. Bacterial diseases and agents

Bacterial diseases	Symptoms	Frequency	Source of infection	Precautions
Brucellosis (*Brucella*)	Flu-like symptoms	100 cases per year in United States	Infected dairy products, rarely from dogs	Wash hands, avoid unpasteurized milk
Campylobacteriosis (*Campylobacter*)	Diarrhea, fever, abdominal pain	13 cases per 100,000, estimated >2.4 million cases per year in United States	Infected poultry, milk or water, dogs, cats, farm animals	Wash hands, avoid undercooked meat
Cat-scratch Fever (*Bartonella*)	Red papule at site of bite or scratch, swollen lymph nodes, fever, headache, fatigue	Estimated at 9.3 per 100,000 or 24,000 cases annually in United States	Infected kittens and cats, organism transmitted between cats by fleas	Avoid cat scratches, clean wounds with soap and water
Leptospirosis (*Leptospira*)	High fever, severe headache, chills, muscle aches, vomiting, may include jaundice, red eyes, abdominal pain, diarrhea, or rash	100–200 cases per year in United States	Cattle, pigs, horses, dogs, rodents, wild animals, and contaminated water	Wash hands after handling pet and pet excrement, vaccinate pet
Lyme disease (*Borrelia*)	Fever, headache, muscle or joint pain, rash	19,931 cases in United States in 2006	Deer and ticks	Use insect repellent, remove ticks promptly and clean bite site
Psittacosis (parrot fever) (*Chlamydia psittaci*)	Fever, chills, headache, muscle aches and dry cough	Fewer than 50 confirmed cases per year in United States	Dried secretions from infected pet birds and poultry	Control disease in birds
Rocky mountain Spotted fever (*Rickettsia*)	Fever, rash, pain in joints and stomach	250–1200 cases per year in United States	Dogs and dog ticks	Can be fatal; remove ticks promptly and clean bite site

Table 4.2.   *(continued)*

Bacterial diseases	Symptoms	Frequency	Source of infection	Precautions
Salmonellosis (*Salmonella*)	Diarrhea, fever, and abdominal pain	40,000 cases reported per year in United States	Lizards, snakes, and turtles, baby chicks, ducklings (more contagious) dogs, cats, birds (wild and pet), horses, and farm animals (less contagious)	Wash hands, handle food properly, avoid contact with infected animals or food
Staphylococcus aureus Methicillin-resistant (MRSA)	Skin infections, pneumonia and other infections	Estimates of 94,360 cases of health care–associated invasive MRSA infections in United States in 2005	Companion animals and humans rarely share the same strain of bacteria	Wash hands, disinfect household surfaces

Source: Centers for Disease Control and Prevention (2010b).

rash. The disease can be treated with antibiotics; left untreated, the disease can spread to joints, the heart, and the central nervous system (CDC, 2010b).

Psittacosis

This relatively rare bacterial zoonotic infection, also called parrot fever, occurs in fewer than 50 cases per year in the United States. It presents with flu-like symptoms and is transmitted by airborne, dried secretions from infected birds such as parrots, parakeets, macaws, cockatiels, turkeys, and ducks (CDC, 2010b).

Rocky Mountain Spotted Fever

The bacterium *Rickettsia rickettsii* causes this infection, which can progress to a very serious illness requiring hospitalization (CDC, 2010b).

Salmonellosis

The bacteria *Salmonella* can be transmitted to people from contaminated chicken or eggs or from contaminated reptiles, baby chicks, ducklings, dogs, cats, pet birds, horses, and farm animals. Infants, young children, and immunosuppressed individuals are at elevated risk of infection (CDC, 2010b).

Staphylococcus Aureus Infection

There has been a worldwide increase in the incidence of methicillin-resistant *Staphylococcus aureus* (MRSA) infections in humans, accompanied by an increase in new strains of MRSA in the animal kingdom. One recent small study found that the presence of a cat in the home was a strong predictor for the isolation of methicillin-resistant *Staphylococcus aureus* from environmental surfaces in the home (Scott, Duty, & McCue, 2009). MRSA can be found in 4% of healthy dogs and 0%–4% of healthy cats. Pets and humans rarely share the same strain of MRSA, but pets may serve as potential reservoirs or vectors for human MRSA (Kottler, 2010; Loeffler, 2010). There is evidence that new strains of MRSA are emerging from pigs and are causing human infection (Morgan, 2008).

Parasites

Several parasitic infections associated with animals are also worth noting. Table 4.3 summarizes notable parasitic zoonoses.

Cryptosporidiosis

Cryptosporidiosis is one of the most common causes of waterborne disease in humans in the United States, and people who are immunocompromised as a result of undergoing treatment for cancer, organ transplant, or HIV/AIDS are at increased risk of contracting this gastrointestinal infection (CDC, 2010b). Good handwashing and the avoidance of potentially contaminated water or food can help prevent the spread of this disease.

Giardiasis

Individuals who drink untreated or insufficiently treated water, international travelers, and children in child care are at increased risk of developing this illness (CDC, 2010b). The *Giardia* parasite can be found in soil, water, or food that has been contaminated by the feces of infected people, cats, dogs, cattle, deer, or beavers.

Hookworm and Tapeworm Infections

Hookworm is a parasitic infection of the skin and intestinal tract, and tapeworm may cause very few symptoms in mild cases (CDC, 2010b).

Table 4.3. Symptoms, sources and precautions for parasitic zoonoses

Parasitic diseases	Symptoms	Frequency	Source of infection	Precautions
Cryptosporidiosis (*Cryptosporidium*)	Watery diarrhea, fever, abdominal cramps, nausea, and vomiting	One of the most common causes of waterborne diseases in United States; 300,000 cases per year in United States	Puppies, cats, and farm animals; contaminated food and water	Wash hands, avoid drinking or using potentially contaminated water
Giardiasis (*Giardia*)	Diarrhea with stomach or abdominal cramps	Approximately 20,000 cases in the United States in 2005	Dogs, cats, cattle, deer, and beaver, contaminated water	Wash hands, avoid drinking or using potentially contaminated water
Hookworm (*Ancylostoma* and *Uncinaria*)	Painful, itchy skin condition, abdominal pain	730 million people in developing countries but rare in United States	Skin contact with soil contaminated with eggs in feces of hookworm-infected animals	Avoid going barefoot in contaminated soil; have pets checked and treated for worms
Tapeworm (*Dipylidium*)	No or few symptoms in people	Rarely reported in medical literature, may be misdiagnosed as pinworms	Spread when dog, cat, or human swallows a flea infected with tapeworm larvae	Treat dogs and cats to prevent fleas
Toxocariasis (*Toxocara*)	Ocular larva migrans (eye disease), visceral larva migrans (swelling of body organs)	14% of population in United States infected and more than 700 people experience permanent partial loss of vision yearly due to *Toxocara*	Dogs and cats	Wash hands; children should avoid eating contaminated soil; de-worm dogs and cats
Toxoplasmosis (*Toxoplasma*)	Flu-like illness in healthy people; eye disease; miscarriage, stillbirth, or congenital infection in pregnant women; fever, confusion, headache, seizures, nausea, and poor coordination in immunosuppressed individuals	Third leading cause of death attributed to food-borne illness in the United States; evidence of prior exposure in 24% of population in United States	Infected cat stools and contaminated soil	Wash vegetables, avoid undercooked meat, wash hands especially after changing kitty litter

Source: Centers for Disease Control and Prevention (2010b).

Toxocariasis

Children and adults can contract this parasitic infection through exposure to the *Toxocara* eggs in feces of cats or dogs carrying roundworms in their intestines. Ocular larva migrans can lead to permanent partial loss of vision, and visceral larva migrans can lead to swelling of the body's organs or central nervous system. Severe cases are rare, but are more likely to occur in young children who eat contaminated soil (CDC, 2010b).

Toxoplasmosis

One of the most serious parasitic diseases, toxoplasmosis is the third-leading cause of death attributable to foodborne illness in the United States. Infants and young children, organ transplant patients, people with HIV/AIDS, and people who are being treated for cancer are at elevated risk. Good handwashing is very important after gardening or after coming in contact with cat stools (CDC, 2010b).

Fungi

Fungal infections can also be transmitted between animals and humans. Table 4.4 summarizes notable fungal zoonoses.

Cryptococcosis   These infections are the most common zoonotic fungal diseases. Cryptococcosis may be spread to humans by the inhalation of airborne fungi found in contaminated bird droppings (CDC, 2010b).

Dermatophytes (Ringworm)   Two types of dermatophyte infections are athlete's foot and jock itch (CDC, 2010b).

Histoplasmosis   People become infected by breathing airborne spores of *Histoplasma* found in soil contaminated with bird droppings. The CDC (2010b) advises that infants, young children, and older persons (especially those with chronic lung disease) are at increased risk for severe disease. Widespread disease is seen more commonly in people with cancer, AIDS, and other forms of immunosuppression.

Prevention of Zoonoses

Hemsworth and Pizer (2006) reviewed the literature on pet ownership in immunocompromised children and concluded that the majority of pet species that carry zoonoses do not appear to pose a major risk to immunocompromised children. The CDC noted that a person's immune system is affected by his or her age and health status and that children under age 5, organ transplant patients, people with HIV/AIDS, and people being treated for cancer are at elevated risk of zoonotic infections. Additional information on animal-related diseases among high-risk people is available at http://cdc.gov/healthypets/extra_risk.htm.

Table 4.4.   Symptoms, sources and precautions for fungal zoonoses

Fungal diseases	Symptoms	Frequency	Source of infection	Precautions
Cryptococcosis (*Cryptococcus*)	Cough, fever, headaches, dizziness, sleepiness, confusion	Occurs in immunocompromised individuals, rarely in healthy people	Pigeon droppings	Avoid pigeon droppings
Dermatophytes (*Microsporum*, *Trichophyton*)	Skin, scalp, and nail disease with itchy, red, raised, scaly patches or bald patches	Widespread in world and in United States	Direct contact with skin of infected dogs, cats, horses, and farm animals	Wear sandals or shoes at gym, pool, and locker room; avoid touching bald spots on animals; avoid sharing personal care items
Histoplasmosis (*Histoplasma*)	Fever, chest pain, cough	Skin tests are positive in 80% of population in endemic areas (central and eastern United States)	Soil contaminated with bird or bat droppings	Avoid areas with accumulation of bird or bat droppings

Source: Centers for Disease Control and Prevention (2010b).

Young children and infants are at increased risk of contracting zoonoses because they touch surfaces that could be contaminated with animal stools or contaminated foods and they tend to put objects, including their hands, into their mouths. Young children require supervision when they interact with animals to prevent them from engaging in overly aggressive play or from kissing animals. They need to be reminded to wash their hands after interacting with pets and other animals.

According to the CDC (2010c), individuals at elevated risk do not have to give up pets, but precautions should be taken to safeguard their health. Some of the precautions that individuals who are at elevated risk should take regarding interaction with animals include the following:

- Always wash your hands with soap and water after playing with or caring for an animal, especially before eating or handling food.
- Do not feed pets raw or undercooked meats, poultry, or eggs, or allow them to eat animal droppings or drink from toilet bowls.
- Avoid handling pets that have diarrhea; seek veterinary care if a pet's diarrhea lasts more than 1–2 days.
- Do not touch stray animals or adopt unhealthy or wild pets.

- Avoid touching the stools of any animals.

- Pregnant women should avoid contact with cats' litter boxes. If another person cannot clean the litter box, the woman should wear gloves when she changes the litter.

- Individuals who are at elevated risk should avoid reptiles (lizards, snakes, and turtles), baby chicks and ducklings, and exotic pets, including monkeys.

PREVENTION OF ANIMAL-RELATED INJURIES

People's risks of being injured by animals are elevated when people fail to understand animal behavior, ignore risk factors that are associated with bites and other injuries (Reisner & Shofer, 2008), or fail to take the necessary precautions to reduce injuries. In addition, the risks of infection are increased when children and adults do not understand routes and mechanisms of disease transmission or fail to take precautions to reduce the spread of diseases. The quality of human–animal interactions can be improved by educating people about optimal pet selection, animal behavior, and proper pet care. Enhanced surveillance of animal-related injuries and zoonotic diseases also can improve the quality of human–animal interactions by providing data that can inform education efforts.

There are many ways for pet owners to reduce their risk of injury. For example, to reduce the risk of animal-related falls in the house, people can move pets' toys, bowls, and other items out of the way and participate in obedience training for their dogs (CDC, 2009b). It is helpful for prospective dog owners to obtain breed-specific information before they select a dog, as some breeds (e.g., German shepherds, pit bulls, Dobermans) are considered to be more aggressive than others (e.g., Labrador retrievers, Dalmatians, golden retrievers) (Presutti, 2001; Schalamon, Ainoedhofer, & Singer, 2006). Male and unneutered dogs are more likely to be aggressive than are neutered and female dogs (Gershman et al., 1994).

CHOOSING A PET

It is important for people to choose the right pet for their family. Although pets can provide many benefits and promote the healthy development of children, not all pets are suitable for all children. Some of the factors that people should consider in order to ensure the best and safest fit for a pet within their family unit are the age, number, and health of the children in the household, existing allergies to pets, the time and expense that will be required to care for the pet, the available space in the home, and the species or breed that best fits the family's activities and lifestyle. The key to a harmonious relationship with pets and children is mutual care and respect. A pet should not be acquired solely "for the kids" or as a temporary diversion, but rather should be considered a lifelong family member that requires socialization and training in order to be a gentle, loving companion.

Which Pet Is Best?

Pets, as with humans, have individual personalities and quirks that make them unique and distinctive to their caregivers. However, some generalizations about common pet species and breeds can help people decide which pet best fits their lifestyle. Dogs and cats are the most common and traditional pet species in American households today, with over 77.5 million dogs and 93.6 million cats in homes. However, there are many different pet species, and a responsible pet owner must understand the specialized needs and appropriate care for every pet in their home. Table 4.5 provides some generalizations about common pet species, including temperament, time and care commitments, degree of attachment, and suitability as a pet for a child.

Pet cats and dogs require a good amount of space, depending on their size and activity levels. They also demand a higher degree of care and human interaction than most other pets. Cats can be wonderful companions for children. They are traditionally self-reliant, solitary creatures that seek attention when *they* deem it necessary. Cat temperaments can range from mischievous, affectionate, and playful to aloof, shy, or even apparently unsociable. No two cats are alike, so it is best to observe a potential pet with others or spend time stroking and playing with the cat to assess a level of connection and personality prior to adopting the animal as a pet. There are many breeds of cats with variable personality traits, but the most common ones are domestic short- or long-haired cats. The best pet cats are well socialized and trained by positive reinforcement methods.

Cats are best kept indoors with space to hide, run, scratch, and climb. Indoor cats that do not have access to these various surfaces and activities may become stressed and fall ill, or they may become bored and destructive. Cats may be allowed outdoors in areas with fewer predators, less traffic, and fewer other cats; however, the risk of accidents, infections, and disappearances can be traumatic and expensive if health care is needed. They also pose significant harm to wildlife. An excellent resource on keeping cats happy and healthy indoors is The Indoor Cat Initiative at The Ohio State University (http://www.vet.ohio-state.edu/indoorcat).

Table 4.5. General guidelines in choosing a species of pet for children

Pet species	Lifestyle/ temperament	Care required/ expense	Level of attachment	Risk/life spans	Recommendation
Small furries: hamster, gerbil, rabbits, guinea pigs	May be a good starter pet.	Easy to care for; food and water, bedding, and cage. Not very expensive as a pet, but require frequent cage cleanings.	Low to medium. They may recognize human contact but do not typically seek it or like to be held for extended periods.	Low to medium. They can occasionally bite.[a] Short life span: 1–2 years for small rodents and up to 5–12 years for rabbits and guinea pigs.	Good for young children ages 5–12 years; older children tend to lose interest.
Fish	Good for all lifestyles.	Appropriate tank and filter, heating, food. Can be expensive, depending on setup. Care is minimal for feeding, but tank must be routinely cleaned.	None to minimal. These pets are good for teaching responsibility and care of others.	Low to none. Short life spans: 1–2 years for common aquarium fish.	All ages.
Reptiles; snakes, turtles, lizards	Not as affectionate or as interactive as mammals	Must have tank, heaters, appropriate foods with balanced calcium and minerals. Food is often live mice or crickets.	None to minimal.	Medium; may bite[a] or carry harmful bacteria.	Not recommended for young children. May be okay for teens and adults well educated in their care.
Birds	Require training and socialization to be appropriate pets. May be noisy	Needs: cage, toys, perches, balanced foods, regular wing clipping. A relatively inexpensive pet, but most are not toilet trained and seeds can be messy.	Small birds such as parakeets can be either affectionate or detached, depending upon training and socialization. Large birds tend to be attached to one adult, so they may not be best pet for children.	Medium; may bite.[a] Longer life spans: 10 years for parakeets to several decades for parrots.	Small birds; children ages 5 to adult. Hand-reared birds make the best pets. Larger parrots are for adults only.

Cats	Can range from aloof to very social and affectionate	Food and water, housing and enriched environments if indoors, such as play toys, perches, hiding spots, scratching posts, and routine veterinary care.[b] Most do like and seek human companionship.	Medium to high. When treated with respect for their space and individuality, cats can be wonderful pets for children.	Low to medium. Bites and scratches are not uncommon if mishandled or poorly socialized.[a] Allergies to cats may be an issue. Cats can live 15–20+ years.	Ages 5+: Breeds are not as variable in temperament as dogs, and size is relatively constant. Indoor cats live longer and carry less risk of zoonotic diseases.
Dogs	Wide variety of breeds, sizes, temperaments, and behaviors	Food and water, socialization, shelter, exercise, toys, preventative medical care.[b] Dogs need space to exercise and attention to thrive. Many, if not most pet dogs become very attached to their families and are considered and treated as a "pet child."	Medium to high. A dog can be a child's "best friend" and help the child learn empathy, loyalty, respect, and responsibility.	Low to medium. All dogs can bite when provoked or in fear.[a] Life span is 9–16 years, with small dogs living longer than large dogs. Dogs with "hypoallergenic" coats[c] may be best for allergic children.	Ages 5+: Well-socialized and well-trained dogs can be wonderful family members. Many different breeds and sizes of pet dogs to match available space and lifestyle.
Exotic/wild animals (monkeys, big cats, other)	Wide variety of wild and exotic animals. Most live in zoos and sanctuaries. Few are pets or legal in private residences.	Large spaces must be provided along with individualized care, depending on the species. Little is known about exact nutritional or exercise requirements. Human contact should be minimal.	Great caution must be exercised with any contact with exotic pets. One-to-one contact with a child is dangerous and never recommended.	High. Not enough is known about exotic species' temperaments, behaviors, and diseases. They are unpredictable by definition.	Exotic species are not recommended as pets for children.

[a] Every pet, as with every human, can bite or scratch. Children must be taught how to handle them properly and when to give them their space.

[b] Routine medical care includes neutering, vaccinations, deworming, dental cleanings, and annual checkups.

[c] Hypoallergenic breeds are those with short wiry haircoats that shed less than others (e.g., poodles and their crosses, Airedale terriers, Portuguese water dogs).

73

Cats can be left alone for long stretches of time, as they do not need to be let out or walked for their exercise or to relieve themselves; however, their litter boxes need daily cleaning. Kittens may not be the best choice of pets for children, because they may scratch; in addition, many kittens are easily frightened by loud noises and may grow up to be fearful.

Dogs are the most variable species on earth (Sutter et al., 2007). They range in size from the smallest Chihuahua to the tallest Great Dane. Their coats can be long, short, wiry, curly, or silky, with all sorts of color combinations and grooming requirements. Dogs have earned the title of "man's best friend" because they can and often do provide love and companionship 24-7. Available space and time are important considerations for a family that is selecting a breed or size of dog, but perhaps the most important consideration for a family pet is temperament. There are many popular breeds known for their affable and affectionate nature that are well suited to living with children: golden retrievers, Labrador retrievers, beagles, pugs, and boxers, to name a few (Gershman et al., 1994). There are several studies and websites that discuss various breeds and individual dogs' temperaments (e.g., http://vetapps.vet.upenn.edu/cbarq). However, dog temperaments can vary even within breeds, so it is important for a family with children to spend time with a potential pet, observing its behavior around other people or children if possible. The prospective owners should seek input from the shelter behavioral counselors, breeders, veterinarians, or others who have raised or looked after the dog. If possible, they should observe the parent dogs' temperament and behavior because there is likely a genetic influence. The best pet dogs, as with the best pet cats, have been well socialized, handled frequently when young and introduced to new situations so that they do not become fearful, well trained by means of positive reinforcement techniques, and appropriately cared for.

Dogs do take more time and care than other pet species. They need to be walked several times a day for exercise and to relieve themselves. The cost of a dog can vary from a nominal shelter donation to thousands of dollars for a purebred animal. In addition, dogs need a collar, a leash, a bed, toys, food, a crate, treats, grooming supplies, and routine medical care. Proper veterinary care includes vaccinations, neutering, grooming, regular health checks, and dental cleaning to keep animals healthy and prevent disease transmission to humans. The prospective owners must understand the level of commitment and agree to it before they obtain any pet; sadly, shelters are already overcrowded with abandoned animals.

Smaller pets, such as fish, gerbils, rabbits, and hamsters, have shorter life spans and may not be as interactive or as responsive to human touch as a cat or dog, but they can make excellent pets for inquisitive children. These pet species are best kept as "observed pets" rather than as interactive or frequently handled pets because their capacity for attachment to humans is relatively low, they can be readily injured by a child, and they may be easily stressed. Although they require little space and are inexpensive to keep, it is just as important for someone in the household to commit to spending the necessary time on their care as it is to commit to caring for a dog or cat. It is essential for these animals to have a clean environment and fresh food and water daily.

Small hand-raised birds such as parakeets or cockatiels can be good companions for children, but parents and teachers should know that these birds may also be noisy, messy feeders and are not commonly toilet trained. The expense for their care is moderate: They require cages, seed, toys, routine care, and feather clipping to prevent them from flying away. Parakeets can live more than 10 years and cockatiels can live more than 20 years. It is important to consider all these factors before committing to keeping a bird as a pet.

Horses and farm animals such as sheep and goats are not the traditional house pets covered in this chapter, but they can be great sources of companionship for some older children and teenagers. Due to the size and strength of these animals, adults must always be present when children are interacting with them, and extra care must be taken to ensure the children's safety.

Species that are not appropriate pets for children require quite specialized or time-intensive care, or are unpredictable, fearful, undomesticated, or dangerous to a child. Reptiles are not great first pets for children for these reasons, and exotic or wild animals should never be children's pets.

It is beyond the scope of this chapter to address the choice of an animal for use in animal-assisted therapy. However, many resources address this topic. See, for example, the Delta Society (http://www.deltasociety.org), Therapy Dogs International (http://www.tdi-dog.org), and Fredrickson-MacNamara and Butler, 2006.

Age of Pet Ownership

By the age of 5, most children understand kindness and the word "no," can exhibit self-control, and can be taught to interact safely with animals. Several researchers have studied the phenomenon of *biophilia*, a seemingly innate attraction to animals, in children. Children must be taught to respect the space and needs of pets. They must learn how to interpret the signals, such as posture and warning sounds, that an animal exhibits in order to avoid negative interactions. An essential rule of thumb is to engage children in interactions with pets only under adult supervision. There are several programs and references available for parents and teachers to use in introducing children to dogs, and many of the lessons can also be applied to other species. Good resources include the Blue Dog Parent Guide and CD (http://www.avma.org/bluedog), intended to help 3- to 6-year-olds avoid dog bites, and The Canine Commandments (Shepherd, 2007), a set of rules to help children and their parents interact with dogs in a nonthreatening, understanding, and educational manner. The American Humane Society's "KIDS: Kids Interacting with Dogs Safely consists of an educational curriculum and coloring books for 4 to 7-year-olds (http://www.americanhumane.org/human-animal-bond/programs/humane-education/kids-education-project.html). The curriculum teaches children about safety around dogs through fun lessons and helps to build character in children.

Ensuring a Safe Child–Pet Interaction

The welfare of both child *and* pet must be a focus of attention during all interactions. Small children should never be left unattended with pets—even trusted family dogs. One tragic example described a previously well-behaved 7-year-old Labrador that had bitten a toddler. The toddler required emergency medical care and stitches, and the dog was euthanized. Sadly, a postmortem examination revealed a pencil stub pushed into the dog's ear canal that had punctured the eardrum. Fortunately, such stories are rare and preventable. A child's behavior around dogs depends entirely on what the child is taught, consciously or not.

The DOs and DON'Ts for Children Interacting with Pets (Shepherd, 2007) presents a few guidelines to teach children how to interact safely and considerately with pets:

DOs

- Be gentle, speak softly, and respect the pet's need to be alone sometimes and to sleep and eat without interruption.

- Always ask permission from your parent and the pet owner before touching any pet.

- Touch carefully. As with people, animals feel pain and do not like to have their ears or hair pulled.

- Understand and heed the warning signs that animals may make (hissing, growling, retreating, snarling) and know when to leave them alone.

- If a pet looks fearful or is backing away, so should you.

- Always wash your hands after interacting with a pet.

DON'Ts

- Never approach a pet that you do not know.

- Do not chase or corner a pet; let it come to you.

- Avoid direct eye contact with dogs, which can be threatening to some of them.

- Never tease a dog or pull a toy or food away from it.

- Do not feed a pet table food—particularly chocolate, grapes, or certain gums to dogs—because these items may be toxic to them.

- Never slap, kick, shout at, or act in a threatening way toward any animal.

These as DOs and DON'Ts are presented here for adults to teach to children. Children should be carefully taught how to approach animals and how to read animals' warning signs. All animals, as with humans, can bite and scratch when they are provoked. Children must learn how to interact safely with animals not only to protect themselves, but also to protect the safety and health of the animal. For example, it is important not to feed chocolate to dogs because it is toxic to them, but even foods that are not toxic should be limited; the extra calories distributed by well-meaning children can predispose pet cats and dogs to obesity, unbalanced diets, and poor health. Children who have been educated to behave in a humane and understanding way toward pets will have a distinct advantage in their interactions with all living beings. They also are far less likely to be bitten. Pets are not for all children. Children who harm pets through carelessness, because of a lack of education, or because of a mental health disturbance should not be allowed to interact with animals for their own welfare and that of the animals.

SUMMARY

Pets can provide comfort and social support, can lessen anxiety, and can teach children responsibility, loyalty, empathy, and friendship. Further research should investigate the role of pets in healthy child development in order to provide an evidence base for best practices within the home and clinical settings.

The potential benefits of pet interaction with children need to be balanced by the potential costs, including the risk of injuries and illness. Many of the dangers can be prevented or minimized. The choice of pet for any child must be carefully planned to suit the needs of the pet, the personality and preferences of the child, the family lifestyle, and the available space, time, and other resources. Armed with the information presented here, people of all ages, including children, can have safe, valuable, and fulfilling interactions with their own pets and those of others.

REFERENCES

Abrahamian, F.M. (2000). Dog bites: Bacteriology, management, and prevention. *Current Infectious Disease Report, 2*(5), 446–453.

Aichbhaumik, N., Zoratti, E.M., Strickler, R., Wegienka, G., Ownby, D.R., & Havstad, S. (2008). Prenatal exposure to household pets influences fetal immunoglobulin E production. *Clinical and Experimental Allergy, 38*(11), 1787–1794.

American College of Allergy, Asthma & Immunology. (n.d.). *Indoor allergens 101.* Retrieved December 11, 2009, from http://www.acaai.org/public/Home/Allergens_101.htm

American Pet Products Association. (n.d.). *Industry statistics and trends.* Retrieved December 11, 2009, from http://americanpetproducts.org/press_industrytrends.asp

Anderson, W.P., Reid, CM., & Jennings, G.L. (1992). Pet ownership and risk factors for cardiovascular disease. *The Medical Journal of Australia, 157*(5), 298–301.

Australian Companion Animal Council. (2007). *Pet ownership statistics.* Retrieved November 29, 2009, from http://www.acac.org.au/pet_care.html

Benson, L.S., Edwards, S.L., Schiff, A.P., Williams, C.S., & Visotsky, J.L. (2006). Dog and cat bites to the hand: Treatment and cost assessment. *The Journal of Hand Therapy, 31*(3), 468–473.

Blanton, J.D., Robertson, K., Palmer, D., & Rupprecht, C.E. (2009). Rabies surveillance in the United States during 2008. *Journal of the American Veterinary Medical Association, 235*(6), 676–689.

Centers for Disease Control and Prevention. (2001). *WISQARS nonfatal injury reports.* Retrieved November 29, 2009, from webappa.cdc.gov/sasweb/ncipc/nfirates2001.html

Centers for Disease Control and Prevention. (2003). Nonfatal dog bite-related injuries treated in hospital emergency departments—United States, 2001. *Morbidity and Mortality Weekly Report, 52*(26), 605–610.

Centers for Disease Control and Prevention. (2009a). *H1N1 flu.* Retrieved May 4, 2010, from http://www.cdc.gov/h1n1flu/qa.htm

Centers for Disease Control and Prevention. (2009b). Nonfatal fall-related injuries associated with dogs and cats—United States, 2001–2006. *Morbidity and Mortality Weekly Report, 58*(11), 277–281.

Centers for Disease Control and Prevention. (2010a). *Avian influenza.* Retrieved May 4, 2010, from http://www.cdc.gov/flu/avian/outbreaks/current.htm

Centers for Disease Control and Prevention. (2010b). *Browse by disease.* Retrieved May 5, 2010, from http://www.cdc.gov/healthypets/browse_by_diseases.htm

Centers for Disease Control and Prevention. (2010c). *Healthy pets, healthy people.* Retrieved May 5, 2010, from http://www.cdc.gov/healthypets/extra_risk.htm

Dire, D.J. (1991). Cat bite wounds: Risk factors for infection. *Annals of Emergency Medicine, 20*(9), 973–979.

Dire, D.J., Hogan, D.E., & Riggs, M.S. (1994). A prospective evaluation of risk factors for infection from dog-bite wounds. *Academic Emergency Medicine, 1,* 258–266.

Fredrickson-MacNamara, M., & Butler, K. (2006). The art of animal selection for animal-assisted activity and therapy programs. In A. Fine (Ed.), *Handbook on animal-assisted therapy: Theoretical foundations and guidelines for practice* (2nd ed., pp. 121–148). San Diego: Academic Press.

Freer, L. (2007). Bites and injuries inflicted by wild and domestic animals. In P.S. Auerbach (Ed.), *Wilderness medicine* (5th ed., pp. 133–155). St. Louis: Mosby.

Friedmann, E., Katcher, A.H., Lynch, J.J., & Thomas, S.A. (1980). Animal companions and one-year survival of patients after discharge from a coronary care unit. *Public Health Reports, 95*(4), 307–312.

Friedmann, E., & Tsai, C.-C. (2006). The animal–human bond: Health and wellness. In Fine, A.H. (Ed.), *Handbook on animal assisted therapy: Theoretical foundations and guidelines for practice* (pp. 95–117). San Diego: Academic Press.

Gershman, K.A., Sacks, J.J., & Wright, J.C. (1994). Which dogs bite? A case-control study of risk factors. *Pediatrics, 93,* 913–917.

Gilchrist, J., Sacks, J.J., White, D., & Kresnow, M.J. (2008). Dog bites: Still a problem? *Injury Prevention, 14*(5), 296–301.

Guptill, L., Wu, C., HogenEsch, H., Slater, L., Glickman, N., Dunham, A., et al. (2004). Prevalence, risk factors and genetic diversity of *Bartonella henselae* infection in pet cats in four regions of the United States. *Journal of Clinical Microbiology, 42,* 652–659.

Headey, B. (1999). Health benefits and health cost savings due to pets: Preliminary results from an Australian national survey. *Social Indicators Research, 47,* 233–243.

Headey, B., & Grabka, M. (2007). Pets and human health in Germany and Australia: National longitudinal results. *Social Indicators Research, 80,* 297–311.

Heinrich, J., Bolte, G., Holscher, B., Douwes, J., Lehmann, I., Fahlbusch, B., et al. (2002). Allergens and endotoxin on mothers' mattresses and total immunoglobulin E in cord blood of neonates. *European Respiratory Journal, 20,* 617–623.

Held, J.R., Tierkel, E.S., & Steele, J.H. (1967). Rabies in man and animal in the United States, 1946–65. *Public Health Reports, 82,* 1009–1018.

Hemsworth, S., & Pizer, B. (2006). Pet ownership in immunocompromised children—a review of the literature and survey of existing guidelines. *European Journal of Oncology Nursing, 10,* 117–127.

Hodge, D., & Tecklenburg, F.W. (2006). Bites and stings. In G.R. Fleischer, S. Ludwig, & F.M. Henretig (Eds.), *Textbook of pediatric emergency medicine* (5th ed., p. 1045). Philadelphia: Lippincott Williams & Wilkins.

Jones, J.L., Kruszon-Moran, D., Won, K., Wilson, M., & Schantz, P.M. (2008). *Toxoplasma gondii* and *Toxocara spp.* co-infection. *American Journal of Tropical Medicine and Hygiene, 78*(1), 35–39.

Kottler, S., Middleton, J.R., Perry, J., Weese, J.S., & Cohn, L.A. (2010). Prevalence of *Staphylococcus aureus* and methicillin-resistant *Staphylococcus aureus* carriage in three populations. *Journal of Veterinary Medicine, 24*(1), 132–139.

Langley, R.L. (2009). Human fatalities resulting from dog attacks in the United States, 1979–2005. *Wilderness and Environmental Medicine, 20,* 19–25.

Loeffler, A., & Lloyd, D.H. (2010). Companion animals: A reservoir for methi-cillin-resistant *Staphylococcus aureus* in the community? *Epidemiology and Infection, 138*(5), 595–605.

Loukas, A., Bethany, J.M., Mendez, S., Fujiwara, R.T., Goud, G.N., Ranjit, N., et al. (2005). Vaccination with recombinant aspartic heoglobinase reduces parasite load and blood loss after hookworm infection in dogs. *PLoS Medicine, 2*(10), e295.

Massei, F., Gori, L., Macchia, P., & Maggiore, G. (2005). The Expanded Spectrum of Bartonellosis in Children. *Infectious Disease Clinics of North America, 19,* 691–711.

Morgan, M. (2008). Methicillin-resistant *Staphylococcus aureus* and animals: Zoonosis or humanosis? The *Journal of Antimicrobial Chemotherapy, 62*(6), 1181–1187.

Nafsted, P., Magnus, P., Gaader, P.I., & Jaakola, J.J.K. (2001). Exposure to pets and atopy-related diseases in the first 4 years of life. *Allergy, 56,* 307–312.

O'Connor, M.B., O'Connor, C., & Walsh, C.H. (2008). A dog's detection of low blood sugar: A case report. *Irish Journal of Medical Science, 177*(2), 155–157.

Oehler, R.L., Velez, A.P., Mizrachi, M., Lamarche, J., & Gompf, S. (2009). Bite-related and septic syndromes caused by cats and dogs. *The Lancet Infectious Diseases, 9*(7), 439–447.

Ownby, D.R., Johnson, C.C., & Peterson, E.L. (2002). Exposure to dogs and cats in the first year of life and risk of allergic sensitization at 6 to 7 years of age. *The Journal of the American Medical Association, 288,* 963–972.

Ozanne-Smith, J., Ashby, K., & Stathakis, V.Z. (2001). Dog bite and injury pre-vention: Analysis, critical review, and research agenda. *Injury Prevention, 7,* 321–326.

Palacio, J., Leon-Artozqui, M., Pastor-Villalba, E., Carrera-Martin, F., & Garcia-Belenguer, S. (2007). Incidence of and risk factors for cat bites: a first step in prevention and treatment of feline aggression. *The Journal of Feline Medicine and Surgery, 9*(3), 188–195.

Parslow, R.A., & Jorm, A.F. (2003). Pet ownership and risk factors for cardiovas-cular disease: Another look. *Medical Journal of Australia, 179,* 466–468.

Parslow, R.A., Jorm, A.F., Christensen, H., Rodgers, B., & Jacomb, P. (2005). Pet ownership and health in older adults: Findings from a survey of 2551 com-munity based Australians aged 60–64. *Gerontology, 51,* 40–47.

Patrick, G.R., & O'Rourke, K.M. (1998). Dog and cat bites: Epidemiologic analy-ses suggest different prevention strategies. *Public Health Reports, 113,* 252–257.

Pet Food Manufacturers Association. (2004). *Profile 2004.* London: Author.

Peters, V., Sottiaux, M., Appelboom, J., & Kahn, A. (2004). Posttraumatic stress disorder after dog bites in children. *The Journal of Pediatrics, 144,* 121–122.

Pickel, D., Manucy, G.P., Walker, D.B., Hall, S.B., & Walker, J.C. (2004). Evidence for canine olfactory detection of melanoma. *Applied Animal Behaviour Science, 89,* 107–116.

Pickering, L.K., Marano, N., Bocchini, J.A., Angulo, F.J., & the Committee on Infectious Diseases. (2008). Exposure to nontraditional pets at home and to animals in public settings: Risks to children. *Pediatrics, 122*(4), 876–886.

Presutti, J.R. (2001). Prevention and treatment of dog bites. *American Family Physician, 63,* 1567–1572.

Quinlan, K.P., & Sacks, J.J. (1999). Hospitalizations for dog bite injuries: Letter to the editor. *The Journal of the American Medical Association, 281,* 232–233.

Raina, P., Waltner-Toews, D., Bonnett, B., Woodward, C., & Abernathy, T. (1999). Influence of companion animals on the physical and psychological health of older people: An analysis of a one-year longitudinal study. *The Journal of the American Geriatric Society, 47,* 323–329.

Reisner, I.R., & Shofer, F.S. (2008). Effects of gender and parental status on knowledge and attitudes of dog owners regarding dog aggression toward children. *The Journal of the American Veterinary Medical Association, 233,* 1412–1419.

Reisner, I.R., Shofer, F.S., & Nance, M.L. (2007). Behavioral assessment of child-directed canine aggression. *Injury Prevention, 13*(5), 348–351.

Rusch, M.D., Grunert, B.K., Sanger, J.R., Dzwierzynski, W.W., & Matloub, H.S. (2000). Psychological adjustment in children after traumatic disfiguring injuries: A 12-month follow-up. *Plastic and Reconstructive Surgery, 106,* 1451–1458.

Sacks, J.J., Kresnow, M., & Houston, B. (1996). Dog bites: How big a problem? *Injury Prevention, 2,* 52–54.

Sacks, J.J., Sinclair, L., Gilchrist, J., Golab, G.C., & Lockwood, R. (2000). Breeds of dogs involved in fatal human attacks in the United States between 1979 and 1998. *The Journal of the American Veterinary Medical Association, 217,* 836–840.

Schalamon, J., Ainoedhofer, H., & Singer, G. (2006). Analysis of dog bites in children who are younger than 17 years. *Pediatrics, 117*(3), e374–e379.

Schönberger, H.J., Dompeling, E., Knottnerus, J.A., Kuiper, S., van Weel, C., & Schayck, C.P. (2005). Prenatal exposure to mite and pet allergens and total serum IgE at birth in high-risk children. *Pediatric Allergy and Immunology, 16,* 27–31.

Schroeder, T., & Ault, K. (2001). *National Electronic Injury Surveillance System All Injury Program: Sample design and implementation.* Bethesda, MD: U.S. Consumer Product Safety Commission.

Scott, E., Duty, S., & McCue, K. (2009). A critical evaluation of methicillin-resistant *Staphylococcus aureus* and other bacteria of medical interest on commonly touched household surfaces in relation to household demographics. *American Journal of Infection Control, 37*(6), 447–453.

Shepherd, K. (2007). *The canine commandments.* Bristol, United Kingdom: Broadcast Books.

Simpson, A., & Custovic, A. (2005). Pets and the development of allergic sensitization. *Current Allergy and Asthma Reports, 5,* 212–220.

Smith, P.F., Meadowcroft, A.M., & May, D.B. (2000). Treating mammalian bite wounds. *The Journal of Clinical Pharmacy and Therapeutics, 25*(2), 85–99.

Souza, M.J. (2009). Bacterial and parasitic zoonoses of exotic pets. *The Veterinary Clinics of North America: Exotic Animal Practice, 12*(3), 401–415.

Strong V., Brown, S.W., & Walker, R. (1999). Seizure-alert dogs: Fact or fiction? *Seizure, 8*(1), 62–65.

Sutter, N.B., Bustamante, C.D., Chase, K., Gray, M.M., Zhao, K., Zhu, L., et al. (2007). A single IGF1 allele is a major determinant of small size in dogs. *Science, 316*(5821), 112–115.

Talan, D.A., Citron, D.M., Abrahamian, F.M., Moran, G.J., & Goldstein, E.J. (1999). Bacteriologic analysis of infected dog and cat bites. *New England Journal of Medicine, 340*(2), 85–92.

Taplitz, R.A. (2004). Managing bite wounds: Currently recommended antibiotics for treatment and prophylaxis. *Postgraduate Medicine, 116*(2), 49–52, 55–56, 59.

Taylor, L.H., Latham, S.M., & Woolhouse, M.E. (2001). Risk factors for human disease emergence. *Philosophical transactions of the Royal Society of London: Series B, Biological sciences, 356,* 983–989.

Weber, D.J., & Hansen, A.R. (1991). Infections resulting from animal bites. *Infectious Disease Clinics of North America, 5,* 663–680.

Weiss, H.B., Friedman, D.I., & Coben, J.H. (1998). Incidence of dog bite injuries treated in emergency departments. *The Journal of the American Medical Association, 279*(1), 51–53.

Wells, D.L. (2009). Associations between pet ownership and self-reported health status in people suffering from chronic fatigue syndrome. *The Journal of Alternative and Complementary Medicine, 15*(4), 407–413.

Westling, K., Farra, A., Cars, B., Ekblom, A.G., Sandstedt, K., Settergren, B., et al. (2006). Cat bite wound infection: A prospective clinical and microbiological study at three emergency wards in Stockholm, Sweden. *The Journal of Infection, 53*(6), 403–407.

Willis, C.M., Church, S.M., Guest, C.M., Cook, W.A., McCarthy, N., Bransbury, A.J., et al. (2004). Olfactory detection of human bladder cancer by dogs: proof of principle study [with commentary by T. Cole]. *British Medical Journal, 329*, 712–715.

World Rabies Day Mission. (2009). Retrieved December 15, 2009, from http://www.worldrabiesday.org/EN/World_Rabies_Day_Mission.html

Yoder, J.S., & Beach, M.J. (2007). *Giardiasis Surveillance—United States, 2003–2005.* Division of Parasitic Diseases, National Center for Zoonotic, Vector-Borne, and Enteric Diseases, CDC 56 (SS07): 11–18. Retrieved May 5, 2010, from http://www.cdc.gov/mmwr/preview/mmwrhtml/ss5607a2.htm

CHAPTER 5

Parents as Armchair Ethologists

Decreasing the Risks of Child–Dog Interactions

PATRICIA B. McCONNELL

Although there are many benefits of including dogs in a family—such as opportunities to teach patience and compassion, a greater connection to the natural world for children, and health benefits associated with close contact with animals—dog ownership is not without its costs. Dog trainers, behaviorists, and veterinarians are well aware that the combination of dogs and children is not always a safe or happy one. Owners frequently contact these professionals for advice about the relationship between their children and the family dog. Problems between these interspecific family members can range from relatively minor problems (the dog's barking wakes the baby) to serious ones (the dog has bitten the toddler).

In 2001, approximately 155,000 dog bites to children under the age of 14 were treated in emergency rooms (Centers for Disease Control and Prevention [CDC], 2003). Research on emergency room visits for dog bites suggests that children are the most common recipients of bites from domestic dogs (CDC, 2003; Weiss, Friedman, & Coben, 1998). From 1992 to 1994, boys ages 5–9 years had the highest rate of bites requiring an emergency room visit (Weiss et al., 1998).

However, a more recent report (Gilchrist, Sacks, White, & Kresnow, 2008) found a 47% decline in bites to children, especially those to boys and those from birth to 4 years of age. It is also important to note that of the dog bites treated in emergency rooms, 99% of them were defined as Level 1 injuries (fast healing, no lasting impairment)—the lowest rank on the Injury Severity Scale (Bradley, 2005). Indeed, 98.2% of the dog-bite patients treated in emergency rooms in 2001 were treated and released immediately (CDC, 2003). Nonetheless, injuries from animal bites continue to be a public health problem, affecting 1.5% of the population annually (Gilchrist et al., 2008).

Dog bites are not the only serious problem related to dogs and children. Practicing animal behaviorists see dozens or hundreds of cases each year in which a bite never occurred, but in which the dog, the child, or both suffered from problems relating to their interaction. In some cases, the dogs are placed in new homes (rehomed) or surrendered to shelters, which can cause tremendous emotional suffering to all involved. This is often a profoundly difficult decision for responsible dog owners and one that can cause great emotional pain for any family member bonded to the dog. The dog may not find a new home, and if it does, it may not be an appropriate one. In other cases, the dog is relegated to a small kennel in the backyard, where it may suffer from isolation and boredom. Even if the dog is retained in the home, children and dogs may live in a state of chronic tension that is resolved only when the dog dies or the child grows up.

Many of these problems could be prevented if some simple, easily taught principles became common knowledge. This chapter describes the ethological basis of preventable miscommunications between children and dogs and provides practical, straightforward suggestions to increase the benefits, and decrease the problems, of a multispecies household.

THE NATURE OF THE PROBLEM: DIFFERENCES IN SOCIAL SIGNALING

Although people and dogs share a significant number of social signals (e.g., facial expressions of fear), several human expressions, postures, and species-typical actions differ from those of dogs. Each species interprets the behavior of the other through its own genetic and cultural filter, which is often at odds with the motivation behind the signal sender.

Hugging

There is no better example of communication differences between people and dogs than the action of hugging. Hugging, known by primatologists as *ventral-ventral contact*, is a common display of affection and source of solace in both human and many nonhuman primates.

Chimpanzees are famous for embracing or hugging when they are excited, nervous, or greeting long-lost social partners (Goodall, 1971; de Waal, 1989). Gorillas and baboons engage in hugs less frequently than chimps and humans but will nonetheless wrap their arms around each other in peaceful, affiliative contexts.

Although there is clearly a cultural component to the frequency of hugging, hugging is a common behavior in humans in predictable contexts. It is used to affectionately greet another person, to provide or obtain solace in times of distress (think of all the images in the news of people hugging one another after 9/11), and to express affection to a loved one. Hugging continues the closeness and warmth that are provided by mammals when they nurse their young on their ventera, with both individuals in chest-to-chest contact. Thus, humans are, at minimum, classically conditioned to obtain this kind of contact in social intimacy, and perhaps even genetically predisposed to seek it out.

This predisposition seems obvious in the behavior of young children. Young children, beginning as early as 18 months of age, spontaneously hug others to express affection or sympathy (Bates, Benigni, Bretherton, Camaioni, & Volterra, 1979). Indeed, one of the first signs that a young child is cognizant of others' feelings is when the child understands that another person feels pain from an injury and responds empathetically by hugging the person.

However, domestic dogs do not express or receive affection through ventral-ventral contact. In contrast with humans, canids such as domestic dogs do not nurse in ventral-ventral contact. They perceive constriction around the upper back and chest as an uncomfortable confinement at best and a display of social status at worst. Analyzing the behavior from an ethological perspective, dogs circle their forelegs around the torsos of other dogs only when they perform "standing over." In this action, one dog drapes and sometimes clasps its forelegs around the back and chest of another dog to express social dominance (Hetts & Estep, 2000; McConnell, 2007).

How, then, are dogs to perceive pressure around their chests from "forelegs" wrapped around their bodies by a young child? Although it is popular among some circles to talk about "getting dominance" over the dog, it is not well known how dogs perceive humans as social partners. Regardless of peoples' understanding of a dog's perception of the social message that is inherent in hugs, it is clear from their behavior that most dogs find hugs uncomfortable. The most common response to a hug, even from a familiar person, is a closed mouth, a tongue flick, and a turning away of the head with whites showing on the side of the eyes. All of these behaviors are believed by trainers and behaviorists to be associated with stress and anxiety in domestic dogs. Although owners often believe that their dogs love to be hugged, they rarely see the dog's actual facial expression when it is being hugged and are often unaware of signs of discomfort that are subtler than growling or snapping.

Kissing

Face kissing is another potential miscommunication between people and dogs. Direct eye-to-eye contact is considered friendly and affiliative in human discourse, even between strangers. Indeed, Rheingold suggested that "visual contact is the basis of human sociality" (quoted in Robson, 1961, p. 14). Gazing between familiar people increases social bonding, and eye contact between mother and child is an important step in the development of healthy social relationships (Robson, 1967). In addition to face-to-face encounters, humans in North America express affection by kissing, either lip to cheek or lip to lip. Along with hugging, children begin kissing others before they are 2 years of age (Bates et al., 1979) and often have to be inhibited from restraining the heads of family pets and kissing them somewhere on the face. Dogs never press the anterior portion of their muzzles together, although they do commonly lick the faces of other individuals, but from the side, not head-to-head.

Dogs and humans are similar in that familiarity plays a role in the comfort level of face-to-face contact: Many dogs will tolerate close eye contact and even face kissing from a familiar person but are less comfortable when a stranger performs similar actions. Thus, kissing and face-to-face contact is especially problematic in interactions between children and unfamiliar dogs. Polite dogs avoid direct face-to-face approaches and eye-to-eye contact when they greet unfamiliar individuals. Standard greeting behavior between two unfamiliar dogs involves lateral rather than head-on approaches and the avoidance of direct stares.

Tail Wagging

Social signals from dogs are also misinterpreted by the species at the other end of the leash. The majority of the American public believes that a tail wag is an indication of a "happy" or a "friendly" dog, but that is not the case. A moving tail can be associated with many different internal affects and with a range of potential behaviors. A dog that greets a child with a stiff body; rounded, fixed eyes; a closed mouth; and a slow wag from the distal portion of the tail is indicating the potential for offensive aggression. On the other hand, a dog that approaches a child with a loose body, open mouth, squinted eyes, and tail wag that engages the entire hindquarters is accurately judged to be a relaxed dog that poses little threat to the child.

Tail wags in dogs are similar to smiles in humans in that they can be performed in a variety of contexts and can signal a variety of internal affects. Human smiles are usually associated with a friendly and happy emotional state, but everyone has experienced a "cold" smile from someone who was using a smile for social capital to cover an internal state of anger. True smiles ("Duchenne" smiles) can be observed when the orbicularis oculi muscles around the eyes are contracted (Ekman, 2004), just as a wag can be determined to be friendly when muscles outside of the tail are affected and the dog's body is loose and relaxed.

Fear as a Factor in Child–Dog Interactions and Child Safety

Behaviorists and trainers commonly see dogs that are comfortable around both familiar and unfamiliar adults but not around children. There are several probable explanations for this, although little research has been done on the canine perceptions of human children versus adults. First, the movements of young children are less predictable than that of adults. Children stop and start faster, move faster, and move in less predictable ways. They move their limbs in ways that adults rarely do. In addition, children modulate their voices considerably less than do adults. They tend to be louder (think how often parents have to ask children to use their "inside voice") and emit vocalizations with instant high-amplitude onsets, moving from silence to full power in very little time. This "wall of sound" can be distressing, especially for dogs of sound-sensitive breeds such as Border collies and Shetland sheepdogs.

Because children are small in stature, their faces are inherently closer to the ground and thus closer to direct eye contact with dogs. It is perhaps no accident that so many bites from dogs to children under the age of 12 are bites to the face, given that the teeth of dogs and the faces of children are often in the same horizontal plane and that direct eye contact is likely to occur.

A particularly difficult time for dogs (and for parents) is the transition when a child learns to crawl. Many a parent has been lulled by their dog's acceptance of a child when the infant was relatively sessile and then blindsided by their dog's reaction when the child became able to crawl. Not surprisingly, dogs tend to be more fearful of stimuli moving toward them than they are of stimuli that remain in place and that can be approached or avoided at will. This differential response between approaching and being approached is common in many mammalian species (Grandin, 2009).

Arousal

Overarousal and a lack of emotional control during play is a behavior problem shared by both people and dogs. The joke "I went to a fight and a hockey game broke out" is funny because it reflects the common experience of emotionally aroused sports players or fans losing control and becoming aggressive. Indeed, on occasion this lack of control results in serious injury and fatalities (Donahue & Wann, 2009).

Dogs too can change from playful to aggressive if they become overly aroused. All good "puppy kindergarten" instructors are aware of the importance of monitoring arousal levels and interrupting play between puppies if one of the dyad is becoming overly aroused. Well-socialized adult dogs appear to manage arousal levels in part by inter-mixing active play with pauses (London & McConnell, 2008). Indeed, London and McConnell suggest that *play bows,* in which one individual of a play dyad interrupts the action by depressing the forequarters to the ground in a "bow," may function as much as "time outs" as they do as metacommunication signals to indicate that the actions that follow should not be construed as aggressive or predatory (Beckoff, 1995). Given that much of play behavior consists of actions that are also seen in fighting and predation, these are important signals.

However, just as in humans, not all play partners are skilled at managing their own arousal levels, and professional trainers know to monitor these dogs just as children are monitored on playgrounds. Children and dogs are especially susceptible to overarousal when they are playing together. Children have no equivalent of a play bow in their repertoire and are more likely to continue to ramp up a dog's emotional excitement than is a canine play partner.

In addition, many responsible parents are not aware of the need to watch for signs of overarousal in the family dog. It is far beyond the skill level of young children to look for subtle signs of increasing excite-ment in individuals of any species, and no one could credibly expect the family dog to take on that role.

Predatory Behavior

Problems can arise not only from overarousal but from stimulation of the predatory nature of domestic dogs during play with children. Young children, with their erratic movements and high voices, may be more likely to stimulate predatory behavior than are adults. In both humans and dogs, a common component of play is running and chas-ing (Ward, Bauer, & Smuts, 2008). As cursorial (chasing) predators, domestic dogs are predisposed to advance from chasing to nipping or biting; individuals of herding breeds are especially predisposed to using their mouths to stop the forward motion of a moving play partner. Undoubtedly, one of the reasons for the universal popularity of breeds such as golden retrievers and Labrador retrievers is their lack of a predatory response to running children.

Expressions

The facial expressions of basic emotions such as fear, anger, and happiness are expressed in similar ways by both people and dogs (McConnell, 2007). For example, in humans, fear is characterized in part by retracted commissures (corners of the mouth), elevated eyelids, and a backward retraction of the head (Ekman, 2004). Similar changes can be seen on the faces of dogs in contexts in which the environment and the dog's behavior are consistent with a fearful internal affect. Retracted commissures forming a V at the corners of the mouth, rounded eyes with elevated eyelids, and a retraction of the head are commonly used by trainers and behaviorists to classify a dog's behavior as being motivated by fear (McConnell, 2007).

In contrast, following the principle of antithesis of Darwin, expressions that signal the potential of offensive aggression and that are most closely related to the primal emotion of anger are characterized in both species by a closed mouth with forward commissures, depressed eyebrows and eyelids, and a forward movement of the head (Darwin, 1889/1998; Ekman, 2004; McConnell, 2007).

Despite the similarities in the species' expressions of fear, even adults who have grown up around dogs often are not able to translate expressions of low-level fear or the potential of offensive aggression on the faces of their dogs. People tend to focus on two aspects of a dog's behavior as predictors of aggressive behavior: whether it is barking and whether it is showing its teeth. Dogs that are doing neither in the presence of children are often described as "fine" by their owners or others, whereas professionals might see a stiff-bodied dog that is attempting to get away, that has commissures retracted in fear, or that is tongue flicking as a potentially dangerous animal (Handelman, 2008; McConnell, 2007; Pelar, 2009).

KEEPING CHILDREN AND DOGS SAFE

A tremendous amount can be done to decrease the likelihood of injury or emotional trauma when children and dogs share a home and when assistance animals participate in therapeutic interventions. Professionals in a variety of fields are in an excellent position to increase the potential of beneficial interactions and decrease the probability of negative ones.

Educate the Parents

First and foremost, parents must be better educated as to how to keep children and dogs safe and happy in the same household. Shelters, public health services, dog training classes, and veterinary clinics can all play a role in helping parents understand how to decrease the risks of raising children with a predator, albeit a domesticated one.

The suggestions that follow are designed to decrease the risk of injury and trauma in an interspecific family and to increase the positive health benefits provided by dogs in so many households. The overwhelming consensus among trainers and behaviorists is that the general public is unable to correctly interpret canine visual signals that indicate discomfort, fear, or the potential of offensive aggression. If parents had the same knowledge as professionals they would be motivated to intervene long before the potential for injury intensified. As stated earlier, most members of the general public focus on barks, growls, or tooth displays as warning signs of potential dog-related injuries. They interpret tail wags as a sign of friendliness, when that is not necessarily the case. As a consequence, they tend to assume that a dog is "fine" if it is not growling or barking aggressively. In contrast, professionals in the field attend to other postures and facial expressions as indicators of a dog's internal state and predictors of potential actions in the near future. Following is a list of four expressions and postures that parents should correctly interpret, and act upon. This list could be posted in schools, animal shelters, public health services clinics, and veterinarians' offices in a collaborative public education effort.

Open Mouth/Closed Mouth

Calm, affiliative dogs exhibit relaxed lower jaws, which create a clear visual signal of a partially open mouth. Their commissures are often slightly raised, replicating the iconic half circle of a human smile. Most people are able to correctly interpret a partially opened mouth and relaxed jaw as signs of a friendly dog, but not everyone does. A prominent magazine rejected an image of the author's Great Pyrenees as looking aggressive, when, to a professional, her relaxed lower jaw and squinting eyes indicated a positive internal affect. They chose, instead, a photo of the dog in which her mouth was tightly closed and her head was turned away from the lens. Dogs close their mouths when they are concentrating (perhaps she heard a squirrel?) and when they are nervous or uncomfortable in some way—thus, the image printed was

Compare the open mouth and "squinted" eyes of the child, exhibiting a positive internal affect, with the closed mouth and rounded eyes of the dog, whose expression suggests a level of discomfort about the interaction. From McConnell, P.B. (2007). *For the love of a dog: Understanding emotion in you and your best friend*. New York: Ballantine; reprinted by permission.

one that looked friendly to the editors and nervous and uncomfortable to trainers and behaviorists.

Professionals use the open mouth/closed mouth distinction as an indicator of internal affect on a daily basis. Indeed, Pelar in *Kids and Dogs* (2009) argues that if only one important signal could be taught to parents, this one would have the most effect. Luckily, it is an easy visual signal to observe and to teach. If parents understood that a dog which goes from open mouth to closed mouth when it is approached by a child is not necessarily "fine," a significant amount of suffering could be avoided.

Relaxed Body/Stiff Body

The other universally important signal that every trainer, behaviorist, and medical professional knows is the change from a relaxed, fluid body to a stiff and immobile one. A friendly dog is relaxed enough that as its tail wags, the entire hindquarters move, a gesture called a body wag. The change from this state of relaxation to a stiff body usually accompanies a change from open mouth to closed mouth and is an obvious indicator of a dog's discomfort in the presence of a child (or any other context). This signal is slightly less obvious than an open versus closed mouth, but once people are educated of its importance they find it easy to spot. A stiff body and a closed mouth is a red flag to

A perfect example the similarity of facial expressions in mammals, in which the humans and the dog all illustrate the relaxed muscles and slightly open mouth of comfortable and stress-free individuals. From McConnell, P.B. (2007). *For the love of a dog: Understanding emotion in you and your best friend*. New York: Ballantine; reprinted by permission.

professionals—its occurrence in reaction to an action of that by a person should cause that person to change behavior. If parents were aware of its importance, a great deal of hardship could be avoided. Parents can learn to intervene when a dog is sending its first signals of discomfort, rather than waiting for signals such as growls that indicate an increasing intensity of discomfort and a higher likelihood of injurious actions.

Tongue Flicks

Tongue flicks are given either as appeasement signals or as expressions of low-level anxiety, and those contexts may overlap (Handelman, 2008;

Hetts & Estep, 2000). In this behavior, the tongue is extruded directly forward from the muzzle (not laterally out the side of the mouth, as when a dog is salivating). Professionals are quick to note the occurrence of tongue flicks and change their behavior if a dog does so in response to their behavior or to the behavior of someone else. Dogs that are uncomfortable in the presence of children often use tongue flicks, especially when they are being hugged or restrained. Tongue flicks are extremely easy to observe, once the significance of the signal has been identified.

Tail Wags

Earlier, it was noted that a wagging tail is not a reliable indicator of a relaxed and affiliative dog. It does not always indicate a friendly demeanor, nor does it guarantee that a dog will not become aggressive. However, this information is not generally known; indeed, most people appear to believe the opposite. Every behaviorist has dozens, if not hundreds, of cases in which someone said "Why did he bite me when he was wagging his tail?" It should be easy to disseminate the correct information to the general public: A wagging tail is *not* necessarily an indicator of friendliness.

Open mouths, relaxed bodies, tongue flicks, and body wags are all relatively simple signals that anyone can learn. There are, of course, many more ethologically relevant signals that professionals use to predict the future behavior of a dog, but learning to correctly interpret the four signals previously discussed could significantly increase the ability of the general public to avoid dog-related injuries to their children.

The following messages must be conveyed clearly: 1) dogs can be uncomfortable when they interact with children and 2) parents must

Everything about this dog suggests an intense level of tension and the potential of aggression. Note the dog's closed mouth, stiff body, and direct stare toward the face of the handler, in contrast to the tail tucked flat against the hindquarters. From McConnell, P.B. (2007). *For the love of a dog: Understanding emotion in you and your best friend.* New York: Ballantine; reprinted by permission.

protect their dogs from the inadvertent actions of children, just as they protect their children from potentially injurious actions of dogs. The consensus of trainers and behaviorists is that if parents do not protect dogs from the actions of children, then the dogs will be forced to protect themselves. Even the most well-meaning children can cause accidental harm or trauma to a dog. Children cannot be expected to read the signals of discomfort that are generated by a dog, nor are they aware, without training and maturity, that their actions might be frightening or aversive to the family pet. It is the responsibility of parents to correctly evaluate their dog's responses to their child's action and to intervene long before the dog feels it necessary to protect itself. It is the responsibility of professionals in a variety of fields to help parents do that.

"But He's Always Been Fine!"

Parents also need to be aware that, as with other people as well, young dogs will tolerate behavior that they perceive to be aversive, but once they mature they will no longer tolerate it. "But he's always allowed the children to dress him up," or some such variant, is a common statement made after a dog snaps at, nips, or bites a child in a context that previously seemed safe. One would think, given the human tendency for anthropomorphism, that parents would relate to a dog's changes in tolerance as it ages—but this rarely happens. As professionals, we must go out of our way to educate parents that dogs are less likely to tolerate behavior that they find aversive as they age. Mature dogs that are "object possessive" will use threats and aggression to maintain exclusive access to treasures around the house. Mature, status-seeking dogs may use threats or bites to discipline what they perceive to be inappropriate behavior from subordinates, even though when they were young dogs they sent only subtle signals of objection. Elderly dogs may be in pain, may be experiencing discomfort, or simply may be more easily tired and irritable. Overall, a dog's behavior as an adolescent or young adult does not necessarily predict how it will behave once it is mature or elderly. Many injuries and heartaches could be prevented if that understanding were common knowledge among parents and dog owners.

Physical Presence Is Not Enough

Parents are often shocked at how fast a situation between dog and child can become problematic. "But I was *right there*!" is an exclamation heard thousands of times a year by trainers, vets, and behaviorists, as part of the history of a bite to a child. Simply being in the same room with a child and a dog is not enough to prevent a bite. This is partly due to the general public's lack of ability to read visual signals from uncomfortable canines and may also be due to what is believed to be a faster reaction time in dogs than in people. It is imperative to educate parents that it is not enough for them to be present, unless they are actively monitoring the behavior and expressions of both the dog and the child.

Not All Dogs Can Be Lassie

There is universal agreement among behaviorists and trainers that some dogs will never be suited to living in a home with children. In some cases, the dog's reactivity and quickness to use its mouth to solve conflicts makes the dog unsafe around children. In other cases, the dog might never be at risk for causing injury but may be living in a state of chronic fear or anxiety. Behaviorists and trainers commonly see both situations. In either case, the welfare of the child, the dog, or both can be significantly compromised. Behaviorists, veterinary behaviorists, trainers, and health care providers need to find ways to educate the general public that not all dogs can safely tolerate living with young children—it is neither safe for the child nor kind to the dog. Rehoming a beloved pet is one of the hardest choices that a responsible dog owner will face; experienced professionals need to consult with families to evaluate the situation and facilitate and support appropriate rehoming if no other means of behavior modification is feasible. They must help parents understand that responsible rehoming is not abandonment; instead, it is a choice in the best interests of all involved.

SELECT AND CONDITION THE DOG

Another important aspect of preventing problems between children and dogs is to look at the dogs themselves. Although educated parents can do much to decrease the potential for problems, it is better to breed and raise dogs that are comfortable around the typical behavior of children.

The Importance of Nature

The evidence is overwhelming that genetics have a profound effect on the behavior of the domestic dog. For example, as in humans, dogs that are ambidextrous (a behavior primarily affected by nature, not nurture) have higher levels of anxiety-related behavioral problems (Branson &

Rogers, 2006). Shyness, or the fear of unfamiliar things, appears to be genetically mediated in both species (Goddard & Beilharz, 1985; Panskepp, 1998; Suomi, 1998). Problems with anger management and aggression are common in individuals of many species who are born with overly active amygdalas and lower levels of oxytocin receptors (Panskepp, 1998; Windle et al., 2004). An acknowledgment of the importance of genetics has allowed Guide Dogs for the Blind to significantly increase the number of dogs that successfully complete its guide dog program. By carefully selecting for relatively passive, nonreactive dogs that are yet still motivated to learn new tasks and bond with individual owners, the program has substantially improved the success rate of its puppies.

Although more good research on the genetic basis of behavior in the domestic dog is desperately needed, it seems overwhelmingly clear to professionals in the field that the trait often labeled as docility has a heritable basis (Nicholls, 2009). However, breeders of purebred dogs are more often rewarded for selecting dams and sires for traits that are related to success in the conformation ring or for working ability. Large sums of money are paid for champion bloodlines of winning field retrievers or schutzhund dogs. Stud fees, silver chalices, and blue ribbons are awarded to winners of conformation shows, but there are few or no external rewards for breeding docile dogs that will tolerate the behavior of a typical 3-year-old child. Although many responsible breeders do indeed select for docile dogs that are likely to be reliable around growing children, there are few rewards for their effort. Indeed, truly responsible breeders, who select for both behavioral and physical health and who guarantee to take back any of the dogs they have bred and provide them with good homes, are often castigated for breeding at all. Given that the American market for puppies will never collapse and that most surrenders to shelters are adolescent dogs who could not be returned to a breeder, surely it is important to educate the public of the importance of obtaining dogs from either 1) shelters that use credible behavioral assessments to evaluate the potential of a good match and agree to take dogs back if there is a problem or 2) responsible breeders who guarantee good homes for the puppies and also guarantee a good home to any dog that is not able to safely or humanely live in the family with which it was placed.

Behavioral Assessments

Although it is impossible to predict any individual's behavior from one context to another, *temperament tests,* more accurately termed *behavioral assessments,* are an important addition to the placement decisions of progressive shelters. The American Society for the Prevention of Cruelty to Animals has adopted the SAFER program and has found significantly reduced returns of animals after the program was implemented. An increase in funding and support for shelters, as well as additional research, could do much to increase the likelihood of successful adoptions into families with children. It is true that no one test will ever be completely predictive of any animal's future behavior, but procedures that decrease the potential of trauma due to child–dog interactions should all be welcome.

Nurture

As described earlier, an understanding of canine ethology can do much to enhance the benefits of mixing children and dogs. If parents understood that being hugged by a child is at best aversive and at worst threatening to a dog, they could both discourage their children from hugging the family dog and condition a newly acquired dog to associate the action with something positive. Basic principles of *counter classical conditioning* are used commonly by behaviorists and trainers to change a dog's response to a particular action or context (McConnell, 2005). They can be taught in parenting classes, dog training classes, and veterinary clinics. For example, a young puppy can be conditioned to associate an arm around its back or a hug from a child with a favorite food treat or playtime with a special toy. Thus, pressure on top of the shoulders becomes a predictor of something about which the dog feels happy anticipation, stimulating the production of dopamine and oxytocin versus the hypothalamic–pituitary–adrenal axis of fear and aggression.

SCIENCE-BASED TRAINING

As researchers, we must expand efforts to educate parents to use training methods that are humane, safe, and based on credible science. "Getting dominance over the dog" is an oft-abused and misunderstood concept that is not only ineffective in many contexts, but that can put both adults and children at risk. *Dominance* is used by biologists to indicate a relationship between two individuals that predicts who will obtain ownership of a limited, highly valued resource. An expert in wolf behavior summarizes it as "social freedom" (Zimen, 1983). It has nothing to do with a dog's coming when it is called or the way that the dog behaves toward another dog, nor is it necessarily enforced or obtained with physical force or threats (Smith, 2006).

Moreover, using social status and/or physical force to influence a dog's behavior increases the risk for smaller, weaker children. Certainly, the use of force and intimidation can have a profound effect on behavior, but it is not a successful strategy to employ around young children. As highly social mammals that are well attuned to pack dynamics, dogs that are raised with force and intimidation might learn (not necessarily consciously) that these tactics succeed against any smaller or weaker family member.

Of particular concern is the commonly touted advice to physically correct a dog for growling at a child. Such an action sets up the worst of all possible scenarios: No attempt is made to determine the context of the warning and how to prevent it from happening in the future, and worse, the dog is punished for providing a warning that it might be about to snap or bite. Behaviorists and progressive trainers strongly advise against inhibiting a dog's warning system, because doing so often leads to a bite that, according to the owner, "comes out of the blue."

Decades of research on learning make it clear that positive reinforcement is the most successful method of influencing the behavior of any individual, regardless of species (Reid, 1996). The more parents learn to *reinforce correct behavior* instead of *punishing incorrect behavior*, the better behaved pet dogs will be and the less likely they will be to strike out toward a smaller and weaker individual.

Encourage Parents to Manage

Parents should be encouraged to manage the family environment as much as possible. As long as a dog is not spending excessive amounts of time in a crate, there is nothing wrong with putting the dog in a safe place when, for example, several 4-year-olds come over to play. Animal trainers are far more likely than the general public to successfully manage potentially problematic situations by putting their dog into a place that is safe (for all involved) as a matter of course. Because they are better able to read dogs' body language and because they have years of experience hearing about serious incidents, trainers are attuned to contexts that are most likely to lead to problems—overarousal at doorways, excitement or possessiveness over food, and overarousal during excited, noisy play—all are contexts in which even "good dogs" can end up in trouble. Obedience classes would do well to emphasize *environmental management* as much as *training* in their beginning curriculum; veterinarians and public health officials should do the same.

Teach Children How to Respond to Unfamiliar Dogs

Programs that teach children to "be a tree" to reduce the risk of a dog bite are an important addition to public health and safety (e.g., the Be a Tree Program). However, one important addition might be to instruct children to keep their bodies relaxed and their breathing normal while they stand still. In canine communication, a stiff and immobile posture implies that aggressive behavior is a potential in the near future. Thus, children should be safer if they avoid a tense posture when standing still. In my experience, people who are asked to stand still often unconsciously close their mouths and hold their breath—exactly the wrong signal to send if the goal is to relax an unfamiliar dog.

Living with Familiar Dogs

Programs that instruct children how to behave around unfamiliar dogs have great value, but most dog bites to children are received from the family dog (Weiss et al., 1998). This is not surprising, given the higher frequency of interaction between children and dogs that live together, but it does suggest that efforts to improve child safety should include instructing children how to behave around the dogs that share their homes, not just unfamiliar dogs on the street.

Two excellent sources of information from professional trainers about appropriate child–dog interactions are *Raising Puppies and Kids Together* (Silvani & Eckhardt, 2005) and *Kids and Dogs: A Professional's Guide to Helping Families* (Pelar, 2009). These authors concur with the vast majority of trainers and behaviorists who suggest that, in order to create safe and humane interactions between children and dogs, parents should 1) inhibit any behavior of children that is aversive to dogs and that can result in defensive aggression and 2) encourage the children to engage in safe and humane behavior that significantly decreases the risk of injury or the need to rehome the dog.

Both publications stress the importance of teaching children to approach the family dog quietly, without chasing or grabbing at the dog. Children also need to learn not to pick the dog up—an action that is often aversive or seriously frightening for the dog and that can result in defensive aggression. Many children seem compelled to pick up small dogs, so parents need to be extra attentive to this behavior as a problem. As mentioned earlier, hugging is a strong behavioral predisposition of children, and it is often interpreted by dogs as threatening or uncomfortable. Rough-and-tumble wrestling play between children and dogs, another behavioral predisposition of human primates (Spinka, Newberry, & Bekoff, 2001), can place children at risk for a nip or bite. Such games are competitions in which one individual attempts to gain physical control over the other, and they can be aversive to dogs that either become tired of the game or become stimulated to defend themselves or "win."

As is true in all behavioral learning, it is never enough to tell children not to do something; in addition, parents must replace that action with an appropriate behavior. Professionals should encourage and coach parents to initiate positive interactions between their children and the family dog. Children (depending, of course, on their age) can be instructed to teach dogs a variety of tricks that keep both the dog and the child safe. Silvani and Eckhardt (2005) described a case in which a young boy who had previously been roughhousing with the dog learned to teach the dog to lie down when it heard the word "splat." The boy loved the humor in the cue and the dog loved the reinforcement, and the command resulted in an instant "time-out" that reduced arousal-based aggression. Children can be coached on a variety of engaging and safe games and tricks, including teaching dogs to find hidden objects (or people), learning new tricks such as "High Five" and "Sit Pretty," or learning games involving balls, such as fetch or soccer.

SUMMARY

The benefits of raising children with dogs are substantial, and denying children access to the many rewards of interspecies interactions would do them a disservice. However, emotional distress and physical injury may also accompany this multispecies interaction. Many practical efforts can be made to ameliorate the problems and increase the positive effects of dog ownership. These efforts include public education campaigns to teach parents to understand a small number of ethologically relevant signals, support for the efforts of breeders to select for docility in companion dogs, programs to condition dogs to respond without aggression to typical behaviors of children, and efforts to work with children to influence their behavior around dogs.

REFERENCES

Bates, E., (with Benigni, L, Bretherton, I., Camaioni, L., & Volterra, V). (1979). *The emergence of symbols: Cognition and communication in infancy*. New York: Academic Press (Elsevier).

Beckoff, M. (1995). Play signals as punctuation: The structure of social play in canids. *Behaviour, 132*(5/6), 419–429.

Bradley, J. (2005). *Dogs bite: But balloons and slippers are more dangerous*. Berkeley, CA: James and Kenneth Publishers.

Branson, N.J., & Rogers, L.J. (2006). Relationship between paw preference strength and noise phobia in *Canis familiaris*. *Journal of Comparative Psychology, 120*(3), 176–183.

Centers for Disease Control and Prevention. (2003, July 4). Nonfatal dog bite-related injuries treated in hospital emergency departments—United States, 2001. *Morbidity and Mortality Weekly Report, 52*(26), 605–610.

Darwin, C. (1998). *The expression of the emotions in man and animals.* (P. Ekman, Ed.). New York: Oxford University Press. (Original work published 1889)

de Waal, F. (1989). *Peacemaking among primates.* Cambridge, MA: Harvard University Press.

Donahue, T., & Wann, D.L. (2009). Perceptions of the appropriateness of sport fan physical and verbal aggression: Potential influences of team identification and fan dysfunction. *North American Journal of Psychology, 11*(3), 419–428.

Ekman, P. (2004). *Emotions revealed: Recognizing faces and feelings to improve communication and emotional life.* New York: Owl Books.

Gilchrist, J., Sacks, J.J., White, D., & Kresnow, M.J. (2008). Dog bites: Still a problem percentage. *Injury Prevention, 14(5),* 296–301.

Goddard, M., & Beilharz, R. (1985). A multivariate analysis of the genetics of fearfulness in potential guide dogs. *Behavioral Genetics, 15*(1), 69–80.

Goodall, J. (1971). *In the shadow of man.* Boston, MA: Houghton Mifflin.

Grandin, T. (2009). *Animals make us human: Creating the best life for animals.* Orlando, FL: Houghton Mifflin Harcourt Publishing.

Handelman, B. (2008). *Canine behavior: A photo illustrated handbook.* Wenatchee, WA: Woof and Word Press.

Hetts, S., & Estep, D. (2000). *Canine behavior program: Body postures and evaluating behavioral health.* Denton, TX: Animal Care Training.

London, K.B., & McConnell, P.B. (2008). *Play together, stay together: Happy and healthy play between people and dogs.* Black Earth, WI: McConnell Publishing,

McConnell, P.B. (2005). *The cautious canine: How to help dogs conquer their fears.* Black Earth, WI: McConnell Publishing.

McConnell, P.B. (2007). *For the love of a dog: Understanding emotion in you and your best friend.* New York: Ballantine.

Nicholls, H. (2009). My little zebra: The secrets of domestication. *New Scientist,* 2728.

Panskepp, J. (1998). *Affective neuroscience: The foundations of human and animal emotions.* New York: Oxford University Press.

Pelar, C. (2009). *Kids and dogs: A professional's guide to helping families.* Woodbridge, VA: Dream Dog Productions.

Reid, P. (1996). *Excel-erated learning: Explaining in plain English how dogs learn and how best to teach them.* Oakland, CA: James and Kenneth Publishers.

Rheingold, H.L. (1961). The effect of environmental stimulation upon social and exploratory behaviour in the human infant. In B.M. Foss (Ed.), *Determinants of infant behavior, 1,* 143–177. New York: Wiley.

Robson, K.S. (1967, May). The role of eye-to-eye contact in maternal–infant attachment. *Journal of Child Psychology & Psychiatry, 8*(1), 13–25.

Smith, D.W. (2006). *Decade of the wolf: Returning the wild to Yellowstone.* Guilford, CT: Lyons Press.

Silvani, P., & Eckhardt, L. (2005). *Raising puppies and kids together: A guide for parents.* Neptune City, NJ: T.F.H. Publications.

Spinka, M., Newberry, R.C., & Bekoff, M. (2001). Mammalian play: Training for the unexpected. *The Quarterly Review of Biology, 76,* 141–168.

Suomi, S. (1998). *Genetic and environmental factors influencing serotonergic functioning and the expression of impulsive aggression in rhesus monkeys.* Plenary lecture at the Italian Congress of Biological Psychiatry, Naples, Italy.

Ward, C., Bauer, E.B., & Smuts, B.B. (2008). Partner preferences and asymmetries in social play among domestic dog, *Canis lupus familiaris,* littermates. *Animal Behavior, 76,* 1187–1199.

Weiss, H.B., Friedman, D.I., & Coben, J.H. (1998). Incidence of dog bite injuries treated in emergency departments. *The Journal of the American Medical Association, 279*(1), 51–53.

Windle, R.J., Kershaw, Y.M., Shanks, N., Wood, S.A., Lightman, S.L, & Ingram, C.D. (2004, March 24). Oxytocin attenuates stress-induced c-*fos* mRNA expression in specific forebrain regions associated with modulation of hypothalamo–pituitary–adrenal activity. *Journal of Neuroscience, 24,* 2974–2982.

Zimen, E. (1983). A wolf pack sociogram. In F.H. Harrington & P.C. Paquet (Eds.), *Wolves of the world: Perspectives of behavior, ecology and conservation.* Park Ridge, NJ: Noyes Publications.

Animals and Therapeutic Intervention

Domesticated animals are already involved in many aspects of human life beyond being pets and sharing peoples' indoor living space. Guide dogs for people with severe visual impairments and assistance animals for people with disabilities or specific diseases are common today. School classrooms, especially those for younger children, sometimes have pets or mascots in the classroom, such as fish, hamsters, or guinea pigs, who provide teachers with a venue for teaching shared responsibility, among other lessons. The inclusion of animals in therapeutic interactions is perhaps less familiar, but it is gaining attention and becoming more common. Many of the ways in which animals are involved in therapy have been insufficiently studied, yet they lend themselves to scientific scrutiny, although there are some clear research design challenges.

Animals have been included in therapeutic interactions in both formal and informal contexts. Examples include therapeutic horseback riding to help children with cerebral palsy attain better truncal control, interactions with therapy dogs to improve social interaction among children with autism, and animals whose presence or interaction calms children prior to medical procedures. What is needed is not just scientifically obtained data on whether these approaches work or not—although certainly that is important to know—but information on how and why such interventions work or not, under what conditions they are effective, and for which individuals or sets of individuals they work. The chapters in this section delve into what is known about the inclusion of animals in schools and therapeutic settings and suggest how these issues might best be explored.

McCardle, McCune, Netting, Berger, and Maholmes discuss the therapeutic use of human–animal interaction (HAI), especially with children. They present a brief overview of the potential for clinical studies and the types of research that would be required to prove the efficacy of HAI, setting the stage for the chapters that follow in this section. Gee examines the role that pets have played and can play in schools and other educational environments. In the classroom pets seem to support the development of responsibility, independence, and empathy in children and also improve children's attention to their lessons. However, a number of obstacles restrict the use of pets in classrooms, including animal welfare issues, liability with regard to accidents, and allergies.

Prothmann and Fine provide an overview of the effects of animal-assisted intervention (AAI) in child psychiatric treatment and outpatient therapy. These authors, speaking from experience, their knowledge of others' research, and their own work, highlight both the basic effects of AAI on children's well-being and the challenges and criteria for the incorporation of animals in psychotherapy. They also discuss the impact of HAI on the interactive behavior of children with specific conditions, such as children with autism and adolescents with speech and/or hearing difficulties.

Horses are certainly not the first animals that come to mind when one thinks of pets or assistance animals. Yet they deserve to be included in any discussion of the potential for therapeutic interactions involving animals. Freund, Brown, and Buff, in their chapter, discuss available research findings and the types of studies that are currently being conducted. They outline the potential benefits of involving horses in therapeutic activities, including the potential benefit for children who may not carry a formal diagnosis but may simply benefit from this type of activity by building their self-confidence. They address the topics of hippotherapy and therapeutic horseback riding for children with developmental disabilities (e.g., improved postural control in children with cerebral palsy, improved social interaction abilities and self-esteem among children with Down syndrome and autism). They also make recommendations for both practice and research involving horses, explain the limitations of hippotherapy, and refer to the North American Riding for the Handicapped Association standards.

The last chapter in this section covers the value of interaction with pets and/or therapy animals for children with a specific diagnosis: autism spectrum disorder (ASD). Anecdotal evidence indicates that pets may greatly benefit some children with ASDs. This chapter reviews the scant HAI literature that relates to autism and points to research that is needed. Because ASDs present as such a variable condition, it is particularly difficult to evaluate the effects of HAI. Temple Grandin, speaking from both her knowledge as a scientist and her personal experiences as a person with an ASD, provides an inside view with insights as to what individuals with autism may be experiencing, why they may respond in particular ways, and how to plan for the safe and successful inclusion of animals in interactions with them. She focuses on differences in sensory sensitivities that may affect the use of HAI for children with autism.

Sal, the Canine Therapist

Connor, a high school student, generally handles stress well and prides himself in his ability to multitask and manage competing priorities. He always has a full plate of extracurricular activities and works at a part-time job after school to help out at home. However, on top of a particularly busy schedule, Connor had to suddenly cope with the illness and subsequent death of his father. During his father's illness, Connor's grades slipped, he missed work a lot to visit his father in the hospital, and he lost his job. When his father died, Connor felt lonely and depressed and started to withdraw from his family and friends. At the request of Connor's mother, his teacher referred him to the school social worker for grief counseling and support. The school social worker thought that Connor would be a good candidate for a new program which the school district was supporting in collaboration with the university mental health research center. The program involved animals as a therapeutic intervention for students who were dealing with stressful experiences such as loss. Connor was carefully matched with Sal, a golden retriever whose temperament and training seemed a good fit. It was typically hard for Connor to share his thoughts and feelings, but on the day that Sal was brought into a therapy session, he seemed to relax more. After a few sessions, Connor was feeling much more comfortable and began to express his feelings more openly. He later told the therapist that having Sal at these sessions made him relax and feel more like talking. He even thought that maybe he'd ask his mom about getting a dog.

CHAPTER 6

Therapeutic Human–Animal Interaction

An Overview

PEGGY McCARDLE, SANDRA McCUNE,
F. ELLEN NETTING, ANN BERGER, AND VALERIE MAHOLMES

Human–animal interaction (HAI) can be, and has been, used therapeutically with children and youth. Animals have been included in interventions, both formally and informally, in a variety of settings, as presented and discussed throughout this volume. Chapter 3 touched on the use of formal therapeutic interventions involving animals, which are generally termed animal-assisted therapy (AAT) or animal-assisted intervention (AAI). These interventions are often, but not always, conducted in mental health clinics or counseling settings; they also may occur in schools and communities such as residences and institutions for the elderly. In addition, animal-assisted activities (AAA) can contribute to typical, healthy development in children who are already developing typically, and they can occur in various settings, including schools, community centers, after-school programs, and boys and girls clubs. Both AAI and AAA can occur in medical settings; one use of AAI and AAA in such settings is for palliative care[1], to ease pain and suffering. In this chapter, the research presented offers an overview of the

---

[1]Palliative care, as defined by the World Health Organization (2010), is "an approach that improves the quality of life of patients and their families facing the problem associated with life-threatening illness, through the prevention and relief of suffering by means of early identification and impeccable assessment and treatment of pain and other problems, physical, psychosocial, and spiritual."

therapeutic uses of HAI with children and youth who are in abusive or potentially abusive or violent situations and in palliative care. Other chapters in this section explore the role that animals can play in classroom settings (Chapter 7), animal-assisted therapy and child psychiatric treatment (Chapter 8), and the use of horses in AAT and AAA (Chapter 9).

ANIMAL-ASSISTED THERAPY AND CHILD MALTREATMENT

In order for researchers to examine the potentially therapeutic role of HAI for maltreated children and to consider how best to develop interventions and study their effectiveness, we as researchers must first understand the complex nature of the relationship between children and animals. Researchers must take into account what is known about child development in general and about abusive contexts in particular. Animals may be a source of support for some children who have been exposed to domestic violence or who have been abused emotionally, physically, or sexually, and researchers must learn how and when animals fulfill this supportive role. In addition, various AAAs and AATs are being used as interventions to encourage responsible behavior in children who have engaged in antisocial behaviors. We will examine each of these tenets and then examine the use of animals in palliative care.

Understanding the complex nature of the relationship between children and animals is an essential goal of research on HAI. In 1987, researchers on an expert panel convened by the National Institutes of Health examined the role of pets in child development. They indicated that on the one hand, research suggests that exposure to pets should facilitate the establishment and maintenance of relationships with peers, especially in grade and high school. On the other hand, children who establish too intense a relationship with a pet may suffer by not developing sophisticated and meaningful relationships with other people. The panel called for more research to determine the long-term consequences of children's relationships with pets and to identify the conditions, situations, or characteristics of particular children whose specific relationships with their pets put them at risk for developing problems in subsequent social, emotional, and cognitive development (National Institutes of Health, 1987).

The complexity of such relationships is highlighted in two earlier chapters in this book. Chapter 1, by James Serpell, traces the history of HAI across time and cultures. In Chapter 5, Patricia McConnell explains how adults can learn, and teach children, to read the expressions of dogs in order to know when and how to safely interact with them.

Wynne, Dorey, and Udell (2010) presented information about the responsiveness of pet dogs to human cues, discuss factors that precipitate dog attacks on children, and analyze the importance of appropriate socialization of dogs to ensure that child–dog interactions are maximally beneficial with minimal risk. They call for experimental research on the nature of child–pet interactions. Such research is foundational to the successful design of interventions and HAI activities, especially those intended for use with vulnerable children, such as children who have been abused.

In addition, what is known about the contexts and interactions of maltreated children must be incorporated into the design and delivery of both formal interventions and less formal activities. A pet may be able to provide a buffer for a child who is in desperate need of support, but it would be naive to think that if the animal were placed in the same living situation as the abuser, the abuser would not triangulate and manipulate both the child and the animal. Furthermore, children who have been treated cruelly or have witnessed violence are more likely to treat animals cruelly. As Ascione, Friedrich, Heath, and Hayashi have pointed out, "Cruelty in one sphere—toward animals—is a red flag for cruelty toward others" (2003, p. 208). Children learn from their experiences. Arkow (2007) argued that animal maltreatment co-occurs with child maltreatment with such frequency that children who are exposed to abuse are likely to view abusive experiences as a familial norm. Thus, a great deal of caution must be exercised in implementing AAAs or AATs with children who are experiencing instability in the home environment.

It is also important to keep in mind that a child's immediate environment may not be the only context through which these understandings of abuse are perpetuated. Rather, children may internalize and respond to the behaviors that they observe in an increasingly violent society. Thus, activities that teach all children about how to care for and interact safely and compassionately with companion animals should be an important preliminary to any AAT or AAA. (Other chapters in this book offer information about how to teach children safe and caring ways to interact with animals.)

As previously noted, animals can serve as a source of support for some children who have been exposed to domestic violence or who have been abused emotionally, physically, or sexually. Children with deep-seated emotional problems may be difficult to treat, but typically they are not unresponsive to treatment. Frick and White (2008) noted that research on the unique developmental mechanisms which underlie antisocial behavior can provide clues about the types of interventions that may be most effective and serve as a basis for intervention development. There is hope for treatment, but interventions and activities must be built intentionally on the understandings about child development and risk factors.

Children who have been maltreated or who show cruelty toward animals may exhibit other conduct problems or antisocial behaviors (Arluke, Levin, Luke, & Ascione, 1999). Children who have engaged in antisocial behaviors may be good candidates for AAA or AAT interventions, to break the cycle and encourage responsible behavior. As noted, however, any such interventions must be undertaken with great care and preparation. Although AAAs offer an approach to violence prevention, most of them have not been rigorously evaluated (Arluke, 2007). Researchers and practitioners are working to design programs that build on the potential for at-risk children to benefit from interaction with animals, but they lack the resources to fully evaluate these promising interventions. Collaborations between people who are delivering services and those who have the time and expertise to conduct research on the effectiveness and mechanisms through which such interventions work are key. Such collaborations can move AAIs to a firm evidence base that transitions the field to evidence-based practice.

THEORY BUILDING AND CHILD-FOCUSED HUMAN–ANIMAL INTERACTION INTERVENTIONS

The following interconnected themes are based on sets of assumptions that lead to different empirical approaches:

- The complex nature of the relationship between children and animals can best be understood with regard to what is known about child development in general and what is known about abusive contexts in particular.

- Children who have been exposed to domestic violence or who have been abused may find support in interacting with animals.

- Responsible behavior in children who have engaged in antisocial behaviors may be encouraged through interventions involving animals.

These three approaches require cross-discipline dialogue and interdisciplinary and interprofessional collaboration.

In order to study the first theme, consider the following questions:

- How do children, animals, and abusers interact in a household?

- What meaning do animals have for abused children?

These questions are focused on meaning-making and understanding. We must increase understanding of child development, risk factors, and animal abuse and deepen understanding of the developmental mechanisms that underlie antisocial behavior. Research that seeks to understand is interpretive, and its primary methods may be highly qualitative (e.g., ethnographies, case studies, phenomenological studies, descriptive studies). Professionals who are skilled in rigorous interpretive research may want to collaborate with professionals who are skilled in child welfare and participants who have "lived" the experience.

Questions that could be asked in order to study the second theme might include the following:

- Are children who abuse animals more likely to engage in violent behavior as adults?

- Are children who are exposed to community violence more likely to abuse animals?

These questions focus on theory building and testing. Grounded theory research methods can lead to theory building, which in turn can lead to theory testing. Also, there are theories that have already been developed which warrant further testing. A major criterion for testing theories is that instrumentation be built on strong conceptual frameworks. This type of research must give attention to traditional issues of random assignment, control groups, valid and reliable data collection instruments, and standardized data analysis.

Questions that are pertinent to the third theme might include the following:

- Does the intervention of an animal companion reduce an at-risk child's antisocial behaviors?

- Can an at-risk child develop responsibility and increase his or her self-esteem by participating in an AAA program?

These questions focus on intervention and change. Such intervention studies require evaluation research in the form of evidence-based programming. The literature on evaluation research and outcome-based measurement can inform these types of activities, which must be evidenced based rather than anecdotal. Note that they need not be totally quantitative in their measurement criteria; indeed, these types of programs lend themselves to mixed methods research that collects both narrative (descriptive) and quantitative data. For example, outcome measurements can be combined with critical ethnographies, cooperative or collaborative inquiry, participatory action research, appreciative inquiry, and empowerment evaluation. However, for programs with initial efficacy data, experimental or quasi-experimental studies would be optimal.

ANIMAL-ASSISTED INTERVENTIONS AND PALLIATIVE CARE

Another area of HAI intervention is the medical setting, where it can serve as an aspect of palliative care for individuals with chronic or life-threatening illnesses. Great strides have been made in medicine in the last century. Nevertheless, many of the illnesses that people develop are chronic and/or life threatening. Such illnesses can, and usually do, have a huge impact on an individual's quality of life. The consequences of chronic and life-threatening illness are many, including depression, decreased socialization, agitation, impaired ability to move around, slowed rehabilitation progress, malnutrition, sleep disturbances, and more visits to doctors and hospitals. It is known that many individuals with chronic and/or life-threatening illnesses have multiple symptoms that have been undertreated (see Becker, Gates, & Newsom, 2004; Lorig, Ritter, & Gonzalez, 2003; Wagner, et al., 2001). Research has shown that a more holistic approach to dealing with patients with chronic illnesses offers promise, and practitioners have begun to extend their treatment approaches beyond traditional methods (Meier, 2010). In some cases, this has included AAIs.

Individuals who have chronic diseases have both physical symptoms and suffering that involves psychological and coping needs; lack of social support; grief issues related to loss of friends, family, personal belongings, and pets; fear of death; financial concerns; and spiritual or meaning-of-life concerns (Benkel, Helle, & Molander, 2009). To help relieve such suffering, the entire health care team needs to be involved, most notably those on the team who use nonpharmacologic approaches: social workers, spiritual care counselors, recreation therapists, art therapists, body work therapists (e.g., massage therapists, Reiki therapists), music therapists, animals, and others. Although AAIs are increasingly being introduced into health care settings, they are just beginning to emerge in discussions of complementary medical interventions that help individuals heal from their suffering and grow (Geisler, 2004; Meier, 2010). There is also interest in demonstrating the efficacy of AATs in health care environments.

Conducting HAI research in these settings is not easy because it requires capturing and quantifying the individual experience. The research presented here shows that the experience of suffering, healing, and feeling interconnected with an animal can be captured best by using a mixed-method design with both quantitative and qualitative measures. The researcher must define endpoints and clinical significance and must use an array of valid measures, along with face-to-face dialogue. It is important to understand that reality is individually constructed by people assigning meaning to their experiences, and there is no reality that is devoid of its context and separate from the one who experiences it. Objectivity seems nebulous at best under these conditions, which makes research with individuals in palliative care especially challenging. An intricate, well-integrated combination of qualitative and quantitative data may lead to a deeper understanding of the illness and the human response rather than a verification of truth or simply the prediction of an outcome. Therefore, some research or aspects of research studies must use inductive rather than (or in addition to) deductive approaches and include a naturalistic, holistic perspective to be able to fully understand how AAI may benefit individuals in health care settings.

In order to understand the health benefits of AAI for people in palliative care, researchers must understand the aspects of human suffering that they are experiencing, the special relationships or connections that people have with animals, and what is meant when discussing healing and growth for people who are coping with a chronic or life-threatening illness. From preliminary research, it is clear that various forms of HAI may provide clinical benefits (e.g., Allen, Shykoff, & Isso, 2001; Baun, Oetting, & Bergstrom, 1991; Benda, McGibbon, & Grant, 2003; Kaminski, Pellino, & Wish, 2002; Mallon, 1992; Martin & Farnum, 2002; Nimer & Lundahl, 2007; Orlandi et al., 2007; Snider, Korner-Bitensky, Kammann, Warner, & Saleh, 2007); now it is incumbent to further the research and understand how animals are helping to treat people's minds, bodies, and spirits to improve their health and quality of life.

SUMMARY AND CONCLUSION

In sum, three types of research with somewhat different purposes are needed to study the use of therapeutic HAI in vulnerable populations. The first type, meaning-making/understanding, seeks a deeper understanding of the relationships among children, their abusers, and the animals that may be abused in these situations, as well as a deeper understanding of individuals who have chronic or life-threatening illnesses. The second type, theory building and testing, calls for testing theoretical frameworks and causal relationships. The third type of research, intervention/change, investigates evidence-driven programs that are tied to outcome-based measurement, mechanisms of change, and the nature and extent of changes in people's quality of life. All three approaches require interdisciplinary collaborations between practitioners who have experience with children, animals, and their interactions, and researchers who have rigorous quantitative and qualitative skills and who can creatively design studies, given the challenges that are inherent in studying therapeutic HAI.

There are various ways to approach these types of research and methodologies. First, if one comes from a strengths perspective, then one might examine the literature on risk and resilience, psychopathology, pain, and suffering, in order to understand these complex areas of study and to design experimental clinical efficacy studies. Definitions of aberrant versus typical behavior, ways of dealing with pain and suffering, and perceptions of animals and human–animal interactions will vary by culture. Researchers may need to consider cultural differences in their research on effectiveness, to help understand why and for whom a certain type of intervention works, fails, or has a particular type of effect. Future research may need to focus on multiple units of analysis; for instance, when situations in which violence occurs are studied—at the clinical, community, and societal levels—researchers must be able to contextualize abuse and violence beyond the individual. With patients who are chronically ill or those in hospice settings, there may be differential responses for patient, family, and clinician. Again, these situations call for collaborations between diverse disciplines and professionals that span the micro–macro continuum. Connecting researchers of child health and development with child welfare practitioners who deal with abusive situations on a daily basis, or pain specialists and palliative care clinicians, would likely reveal much about the interactions between children and pets. Finally, in a move to join the growing trend toward university–community partnerships (community engagement), connecting practitioners with faculty and student researchers to design evidence-based programs that are built on strong conceptual frameworks with defined outcomes is a way to study and create interventions simultaneously.

REFERENCES

Allen, K., Shykoff, B., & Isso, J. (2001). Pet ownership, but not ace inhibitor therapy, blunts home blood pressure responses to mental stress. *Hypertension, 38,* 815–820.

Arkow, P. (2007). Animal maltreatment in the ecology of abused children: Compelling research, and responses for prevention, assessment, and intervention. *Protecting Children, 22,* 66–79.

Arluke, A. (2007). *Animal assisted activities for at-risk and incarcerated children and young adults: An introductory ethnography of five programs.* Paper presented at the National Technology Assessment Workshop on Animal-Assisted Programs for Youth at Risk, Baltimore.

Arluke, A., Levin, J., Luke, C., & Ascione, F.R. (1999). The relationship of animal abuse to violence and other forms of antisocial behavior. *Journal of Interpersonal Violence, 14,* 963–975.

Ascione, F.R., Friedrich, W.N., Heath, J., & Hayashi, K. (2003). Cruelty to animals in normative, sexually abused, and outpatient psychiatric samples of 6- to 12-year-old children: Relations to maltreatment and exposure to domestic violence. *Anthrozoos, 16*(3), 194–212.

Baun, M., Oetting, K., & Bergstrom, N. (1991). Health benefits of companion animals in relation to the physiologic indices of relaxation. *Holistic Nursing Practice, 15,* 16–23.

Becker, G., Gates, R.J., & Newsom, E. (2004). Self-care among chronically ill African Americans: Culture, health disparities, and health insurance status. *American Journal of Public Health, 94,* 2066–2073.

Benda, W., McGibbon, N., & Grant, K. (2003). Improvements in muscle symmetry in children with cerebral palsy after equine-assisted therapy. *Journal of Alternative and Complementary Medicine, 9,* 817–825.

Benkel, I., Helle, W., & Molander, U. (2009). Managing grief and relationship roles influence which forms of social support the bereaved needs. *American Journal of Hospice and Palliative Medicine, 26,* 241–245.

Frick, P.J., & White, S.F. (2008). Research review: The importance of callous unemotional traits for developmental models of aggressive and antisocial behavior. *Journal of Child Psychology and Psychiatry, 49*(4), 359–375.

Geisler, A.M. (2004). Companion animals in palliative care: Stories from the bedside. *American Journal of Hospice and Palliative Medicine, 21,* 285–288.

Lorig, K.R., Ritter, P., & Gonzalez, V.M. (2003). Hispanic chronic disease self-management: A randomized community-based outcome trial. *Nursing Research, 52*(6), 361–369.

Kaminski, M., Pellino, T., & Wish, J. (2002). Play and pets: The physical and emotional impact of child-life and pet therapy on hospitalized children. *Children's Health Care, 31,* 321–335.

Mallon, G. (1992). Utilization of animals as therapeutic adjuncts with children and youth: A review of the literature. *Child and Youth Care Forum, 21,* 53–67.

Martin, F., & Farnum, F. (2002). Animal assisted therapy for children with pervasive developmental disorders. *Western Journal of Nursing Research, 24*(6), 657–670.

National Institutes of Health. (1987). *The health benefits of pets.* Retrieved September 30, 2009, from http://consensus.nih.gov/1987/1987Health BenefitsPetsta003html.htm

Nimer, J., & Lundahl, B. (2007). Animal-assisted therapy: A meta-analysis. *Anthrozoos, 20,* 225–238.

Orlandi, M., Trangeled, K., Mambrini, A. Tagliani, M., Ferrarini, A., Zanetti, L., et al. (2007). Pet therapy effects on oncological day treatment patients undergoing chemotherapy treatment. *Anticancer Research, 27,* 4301–4303.

Snider, L., Korner-Bitensky, N., Kammann, C., Warner, S., & Saleh, M. (2007). Horseback riding as therapy for children with cerebral palsy: Is there evidence of its effectiveness? *Physical and Occupational Therapy in Pediatrics, 27,* 5–23.

Wagner, E.H., Austin, B.T., Davis, C., Hindmarsh, M., Schaefer, J., & Bonomi, A. (2001). Improving chronic illness care: Translating evidence into action. *Health Affairs, 20*(6), 64–78.

Wynne, C., Dorey, N., & Udell, M. (2010). The other side of the bond: Domestic dogs' human-like behaviors. In P. McCardle, S. McCune, J. Griffin, & V. Maholmes (Eds.), *How animals affect us: Examining the influence of human-animal interaction on child development and health.* Washington, DC: American Psychological Association.

World Health Organization. (2010). *WHO definition of palliative care.* Retrieved April 30, 2010, from http://www.who.int/cancer/palliative/definition/en

CHAPTER 7

Animals in the Classroom

NANCY R. GEE

> In contemporary Western society, nonhuman animals play an
> extraordinarily salient role in the lives of children.
>
> (Serpell, 1999, p. 87)

Serpell (1999) pointed out that nonhuman animals dominate the media (e.g., cartoons, television, film). It is obvious that children love zoos, aquariums, and natural history museums. Furthermore, a majority of parents believe that children benefit from interactions with animals. Parents believe that children learn responsibility by caring for the family pet and that the presence of an animal encourages caring attitudes among children; provides companionship, security, comfort, amusement, and an outlet for affection; promotes respect and compassion for animals and nature; and often teaches children about "the facts of life." From their interactions with animals, children probably learn things and acquire skills that they might not learn or acquire in other ways (Myers, 1996; Shepard, 1978).

The classroom is another environment where children have an opportunity to encounter animals. Although animals have long been involved in classroom and educational settings in varied ways, there exists little scientific research supporting this practice (Rud & Beck, 2003). This chapter begins with a discussion of the reported effects of animals in the classroom in terms of anecdotal evidence and correlational studies. We will focus on the existing controlled experimental investigations into the subject.

TRADITIONAL INVOLVEMENT
OF ANIMALS IN CLASSROOM CURRICULA

Animals are an integral part of educational experiences at virtually all levels of education; in many cases they have made the ultimate sacrifice for the purpose of human learning. For example, animals have been the objects of dissection exercises in biology courses in elementary, middle, and high school, as well as college. Earthworms (Moore, 2001), frogs (Fleischmann, 2003), and fetal pigs (e.g., Barr & Herzog, 2000), among other species, have been utilized to teach students about anatomy and physiology through hands-on surgical dissection. Animals have also been the subjects of behavioral experimentation in many psychology and animal behavior courses and programs (Belke, 2002). In the years following the development of the Skinner box (Skinner, 1938) the use of rats and pigeons in behavioral research and education became commonplace (e.g., Mazur, 2005; Thorpe & Wilke, 2005). More recently, Ackil and Ward (1982) advanced an argument for using chickens in introductory psychology laboratory courses in place of rats.

Whereas the use of rats, pigeons, and chickens in laboratory courses was stimulated by research based on the Skinner box, elementary school teachers who began bringing animals into their classrooms for targeted learning did so without waiting for a formal scientific foundation to justify the practice. Appealing animals such as butterflies, rabbits, and birds are commonly found in elementary school classrooms as class pets or mascots (Tomasek & Matthews, 2008). Classroom teachers hope that their presence will help to advance the curriculum, encourage student involvement with lessons, enhance children's understanding of responsibility through their care and maintenance, and teach them the humane treatment of animals. Generally speaking, there has been little scientific assessment of whether classroom pets achieve the purposes for which they are intended. Such an approach is akin to the advent of using guide dogs for the blind. No scientific research with regard to the dogs' effectiveness was conducted prior to the implementation of the guide dog system, but there is an obvious utility to the practice. Similarly, the practical impact of bringing animals into the classroom is demonstrated by the wide variety of classroom demonstrations or activities that involve them. For example, Siamese fighting fish have demonstrated the territorial behavior of animals defending their living spaces (Abate, 2005). Earthworms and houseflies have been used to demonstrate classical conditioning (Abramson, Onstott, Edwards, & Bowe, 1996). Endreny (2006) used crayfish (sometimes called *crawdads*) to teach students about habitats, adaptations, and methods of scientific inquiry. Tomasek and Matthews (2008) presented a number of educational activities that are centered on reptiles and amphibians, and Adams (2006) described an activity involving the isopods commonly known as *pill bugs* or *roly-polies*. Hull (2003) reported an activity in which students observed zoo animals in order to learn the skills necessary to select, operationalize, observe, and record animal behavior accurately.

A recent development is the use of animals to educate people on topics that ultimately are likely to benefit the animals in the program or other animals. For example, Kogan and Kellaway (2004) developed a college course in which the students learned the basic tenets of classical and operant conditioning in the classroom and then applied their knowledge by training dogs at the local humane society. This activity provided the humane society with additional resources and presumably helped to make the dogs more adoptable. Nicoll, Trifone, and Samuels (2008) described the efficacy of an in-class humane education program on young students' attitudes toward animals. Dandoy and Scanlon (1999) used a skit with a dog to teach children about rabies prevention. Coleman, Hall, and Hay (2008) evaluated a pet ownership education program for school children in Australia.

All of those classroom demonstrations, activities, and educational programs share the common theme of using an animal as a way of focusing students' attention on specific learning objectives. Clearly, those educators and others before them saw the advantages of involving animals in their classrooms, even prior to the formal investigation of their effects. However, science has begun to seek evidence on the hows, whys, and extent of the advantages that classroom animals might provide. We now turn our attention to reviewing the work that has been done to investigate the impact of animals in the classroom.

Reported Effects of Animal Presence in Classroom Settings

Early observational work was reported by Margadant-van Arcken (1984, 1989) who brought a different pet each day to kindergarten classrooms (Cairn Terriers, cats, a guinea pig, a rabbit, white mice, earthworms, grasshoppers, a miniature goat, cockerels, and chicks). She made observational recordings on the kindergarten visits and conducted open interviews with children ages 6 to 12 years. This information allowed her to describe a structured pattern for the initial interactions between children and novel animals. In the pattern, the child is initially fearful of the animal, progresses to trust, and ultimately reaches what Margadant-van Arcken calls a fusion of horizons in which the two share one reality.

Nielsen and Delude (1989) reported the results of a study involving children in child care (ages 2 to 4 years) and in kindergarten (ages

5 to 6 years). The children were videotaped while they were allowed to freely interact, on separate days, with either real animals (tarantula, rabbit, cockatiel, or golden retriever) or toy animals (dog, bird). The researchers found that the children were largely indifferent to the toy animals, but the live animals were extremely effective at generating interest from the children. Further, the children preferred the dog as an object of affiliation over the other animals in the study.

Law and Scott (1995) discussed the use of pet care programs as educational interventions for students with pervasive developmental delays or autism. Typically, such programs involve the care and handling of domestic animals within the confines of the classroom. The authors presented the case that these programs reduce or eliminate the children's worry and fear associated with the animals involved and increase their confidence and comfort in handling those animals. The authors also argued that the animals serve as a vehicle for receptive and expressive language development and help the children improve decision making, problem-solving skills, and social interactions with adults and peers.

More than 25% of Indiana teachers surveyed by Rud and Beck (2003) indicated that their classrooms contained a variety of animals, mostly small vertebrates. The teachers reported using the animals to provide an enjoyable activity and a hands-on educational experience for the students. Rud and Beck (2000) also described their investigation into how human–animal interactions shape and potentially improve children's learning in the classroom. They reported that children are intensely interested in animals; there is growing evidence that interactions with animals have important implications for child development, especially in the areas of social growth and communication; and the interactions between the children and the animals tended to calm the children and made them more open to engaging in cognitive and social activities. As others, Rud and Beck pointed out the "scant research literature in the area" (p. 314).

INVESTIGATIVE CATEGORIES

The existing studies exploring the effects of animals in classrooms can be separated according to the six topics or educational goals for children that they examine or address:

- Developing empathy and caring attitudes toward animals
- Improving physical abilities and motor skills
- Practicing communication and reading

- Experiencing calm and emotional well-being

- Coping with loss/grief

- Improving cognitive task performance and motivation to learn

The following sections present the available research investigating each of these topics/educational goals.

Developing Empathy and Caring Attitudes Toward Animals

In the 1980s, some researchers examined children's attitudes and perceptions of pets. In a preliminary survey of children in kindergarten through sixth grade, Salomon (1981) found that although the majority of the children who were surveyed already owned pets (53%–94% across the various grade levels), almost all the children desired a pet (97%–98%). Salomon also questioned the children's parents and found that they associated owning a pet with an increased sense of respect for animals in their children.

Children's perceptions of pets have been noted to shift between the ages of 3 and 7 years (Kidd & Kidd, 1980). The younger group of children did not appear to notice that pets feel pain, and they demonstrated an egocentric approach to the animals, relishing in the cuddly tactile qualities of the pets' soft, furry coats. By contrast, the 7-year-olds frequently demonstrated awareness that pets had feelings. They showed empathy and concern about the pets' fear of pain and about the actual pain that the pet might endure during visits to the veterinarian. The 7-year-olds also spoke in terms of mutual rather than unilateral affection, although they were aware that pets and humans demonstrate affection differently.

Melson and Fogel (1989) presented a theoretical model accounting for developmental gender differences in nurturance behaviors. They argued that children develop knowledge about nurturance from a variety of sources, including animals, and that this may be particularly true for developing boys. The period between preschool and the early elementary years is a time when boys begin to resist involvement in nurturing human infants (Berman, 1980), but it is a time when they may become more interested in nurturing pets.

In a discussion of the importance of empathy and prosocial behavior development in children, Thompson and Gullone (2003) noted one particular method used to build empathy that involves direct contact with animals. Their rationale is that a child who develops a bond with an animal will feel more empathy toward other human beings. They pointed out that the reverse case, in which childhood cruelty toward animals is associated with the propagation of violent behaviors in adulthood, has been noted and discussed at length.

Poresky and Hendrix (1990) found that it is the degree to which people bond with an animal, not the mere presence of the animal, that influences empathy. A number of studies have indicated that there is a positive relationship between companion-animal bonding and empathy in children (Melson, 1991; Poresky, 1996; Vizek Vidović, Vlahovic Stetic, & Bratko, 1999). Daly and Morton (2003) initially found no difference in empathy scores for pet owners compared with nonowners of pets. (They did find that among people who owned pets, owners of dogs had higher empathy scores than owners of other animals and children tended to prefer dogs to cats, horses, fish, birds, and reptiles as pets.) However, in a follow-up survey (Daly & Morton, 2006) of 155 elementary school students, they found that children who preferred or owned both dogs *and* cats were more empathic than those who preferred or owned only one species or the other. In addition, children who were more attached to their pets were more empathic than children who were less attached. Those later determinations are consistent with the findings of Poresky and Hendrix that it is the bonding experience that leads to the empathy.

Empathy can be viewed as a learned behavior (Richardson & Norman, 2000), and thus it is reasonable to assume that its development can be facilitated. Soutar-Freeman (2003) developed a program, as yet untested, aimed at teaching empathy, compassion, and respect for life by having participants care for an animal. Ascione (1992) assessed a yearlong human-education program for first-, second-, fourth-, and fifth-grade children and reported that the program did enhance the children's animal-related attitudes and that animal-oriented empathy did generalize to human-directed empathy.

Although those studies are promising, more experimental research aimed at scientifically examining the efficacy of these types of programs is necessary. Hergovich, Monshi, Semmler, and Zieglmayer (2002) examined the effects of the presence of a dog in a Viennese first-grade classroom on a wide variety of social and cognitive variables. The children in this study were mostly immigrants and a variety of assessment instruments were used. Two classrooms were involved in the study, but only one classroom received visits from a dog, in this case the teacher's dog. The results showed that the children improved on all variables (field independence, social competence, empathy with animals, and social–emotional atmosphere), which seems to indicate that a dog can be an important factor in the social and cognitive development of children. Still, caution must be used in interpreting the results because the presence of the dog could not be randomly assigned to classrooms. It is possible that the teacher who owned the dog was motivated to obtain the best possible outcome in the study, even though the teachers were not informed of the details of the experiment at the time of data collection.

Another investigation into the efficacy of animal involvement in educational curricula was conducted by Zasloff, Hart, and Weiss (2003), who conducted a longitudinal study to examine the efficacy of the Teaching Love and Compassion (TLC) program. TLC is a humane education program for inner-city seventh graders in Los Angeles. An experimental group of children participated in discussion groups focusing on conflict management and interpersonal issues and were taught proper care and obedience training of shelter dogs. Their scores on a test of the information they were taught were compared with those of a control group of children who did not participate in the TLC program. Pretest–posttest analysis showed that the experimental group increased their knowledge of pet care and the needs of the animals more, and retained it longer, than the control group. In addition, follow-up testing revealed that the experimental group continued to show a decrease in fear of dogs. However, although the experimental group children were significantly less likely to approve of responding to violence with violence than were the control group children on the posttest, this difference was no longer significant in results from the follow-up test.

Improving Physical Abilities and Motor Skills

An intrinsically different aspect of the benefits of classroom pets is their impact on children's motor skills. Physical activity and childhood seem to go hand in hand, and preschool children (3- to 5-year-olds) tend to be more physically active than are children in older age groups (Pate, McIver, Dowda, Brown, & Addy, 2008). People of all ages need exercise as part of a healthy lifestyle, but movement and activity in children are essential to the typical development of many cognitive functions, such as sensation and perception, language, and some intellectual abilities in young children (Olds, Kranowitz, Porter, & Carter, 1994). The ability to move about one's environment affects children not only physically but emotionally, intellectually, and socially (Poest, Williams, Witt, & Atwood, 1990).

Gee, Harris, and Johnson (2007) observed that when children and dogs interact there is almost inevitably a motor component to their interactions. They recorded speed and accuracy of performance for preschool children executing a series of motor-skill tasks, such as crawling through a tunnel, running through dog agility weave poles, walking a balance beam, and throwing a ball, both when a trained therapy dog was present and when it was absent. Their results showed that the children executed the tasks faster but without sacrificing accuracy when the dog was present. In fact, in some cases the presence of the dog was also associated with improved accuracy of performance. They concluded that the dog served as an effective motivator for preschool children and point to other possible educational applications for the use of dogs with preschool children.

In a follow-up study, Gee, Sherlock, Bennett, and Harris (2009) examined preschoolers' adherence to instructions while they executed similar motor-skills tasks in the presence of a real dog, a stuffed dog (manipulated by a human), and a human co-performer. The researchers separated the motor-skills tasks into three general types:

- Modeling tasks, in which the children were asked to emulate the behavior of a model

- Tandem tasks, in which the children were asked to do the tasks at the same time as a human co-performer

- Competition tasks, in which the children were asked to do the tasks faster than a competitor

The results indicated that the children were more likely to adhere to task instructions in the presence of the dog than in the presence of the other two co-performers in modeling tasks, but this was not the case in the tandem or competition tasks. It appears that when the children watched the dog perform the task first, and then were asked to perform the same task, they more readily adhered to task instructions than they did under other conditions. The authors concluded that the presence of the dog likely serves as a highly salient stimulus that allows the children to restrict their attention and focus it on the execution of the task itself, reducing the need for instructional prompts.

Other more observation-based reports also have indicated a positive connection between preschool children and dogs. Gee (2008) presented an informal case study detailing how a therapy dog helped motivate a preschool child with physical challenges to perform his routine physical therapy. Williams, Carter, Kibbe, and Dennison (2009) described a pilot study to evaluate the Animal Trackers program, which was designed to increase structured physical activity and the practice of gross motor skills in preschool children. They indicated that the program increased structured physical activity time, and they presented anecdotal evidence that provides encouragement for this program, including children's and teachers' opinions of the program.

There are a number of programs aimed at increasing physical activity through dog walking (e.g., Cutt, Giles-Corti, & Knuiman, 2007; Thorpe et al., 2006). The efficacy of these programs, combined with the degree to which many children and young people seem to be drawn to animals, may make this a fertile ground for future program development and investigation in school settings. Given current budgetary conditions that reduce extracurricular activities, such as athletic programs, perhaps educators should consider potentially less expensive activities to encourage students to engage in physical activity through dog walking, or even through other movement-oriented dog sports.

Communication and Reading

There exists a body of evidence that indicates that the presence of an animal increases communication, but little of this work has taken place in a classroom setting. For example, Boris Levinson (1969) was the first to describe the "social lubricant" function of the presence of a dog in the therapeutic environment. Corson and Corson (1980) presented the example of a 19-year-old male suffering from schizophrenia who increased his mean number of words per answer from 3.4 to 21.1 following visits from a dog. Adams (1997) reported a case study of a 72-year-old female who had suffered multiple strokes that resulted in speech and language difficulties. Animal-assisted therapy increased her ability to produce one-word answers, object identification answers, and other verbalizations. Fick (1993) indicated that the presence of a dog increases verbal interactions in discussion groups of nursing home residents. In a study of peer interaction, a child was shown to be 10 times more likely to interact with a peer who had a disability if the peer was accompanied by a dog (Katcher, 1997). Serpell (2000) estimated that more than 70% of children of all ages tend to talk to and confide in animals.

Limond, Bradshaw, and Cormack (1997) examined the behavior of children who had learning disabilities in a repeated-measures design in which eight children with Down syndrome interacted for 7 minutes with a real dog and for 7 minutes with an imitation dog. They found differences across the two conditions for visual attention and verbal and nonverbal initiation and response behaviors. The findings suggested that the presence of the real dog increased and sustained focus for positive and cooperative interactions with the dog and the adult participant, relative to the imitation dog.

In a study by Kotrschal and Ortbauer (2003) at an elementary school in Vienna, children were observed during a control period (1 month) in the absence of a dog and during an experimental period (approximately 1 month) when a dog was present in the classroom. They found that the presence of the dog was associated with a decrease in aggressiveness and hyperactivity (more noticeable in boys than girls) and an increase in social cohesiveness and attention paid to the teacher. The findings must be interpreted with caution because it is possible that maturation of the children may be able to explain some of the results, as all of the experimental observations took place after the control observations. Nevertheless, this study is certainly provocative and indicates a need for further investigation.

In a seminal study conducted by Friedmann, Katcher, Thomas, Lynch, and Messent (1983), the effect of the presence of a friendly animal on children's blood pressure and heart rate was examined while the children were resting and while they were verbalizing by reading aloud. The researchers found that the presence of the dog reduced blood pressure in both conditions, and they concluded that the presence of the dog modified the children's perceptions of the experimental situation by creating a friendlier and less threatening environment. Friedmann, Thomas, and Eddy (2000) found that the presence of a calm, attentive dog appears to reduce anxiety relative to the presence of an adult or supportive friend when children are asked to read aloud. Melson (1988) reported that preschool children who owned pets engaged in more frequent "reading" behavior (being read to) than did preschool children without pets.

As a result of these positive indications of the impact of animals on children's communication and reading skills, a variety of programs have been developed that involve reading to dogs as a way of helping children learn to read. Jalongo, Astorino, and Bomboy (2004) reviewed one such program by Intermountain Therapy Animals called the "READ: Reading Education Assistance Dogs" program. This program started in Salt Lake City in 1999 and showed impressive results. All of the students who participated in the program for 13 months gained at least two grade levels and some gained four grade levels. A recent Internet search produced many similar programs throughout the country that are designed to help children learn to read by having them read to animals (primarily dogs). Here are some typical examples:

- BARK: Beach Animals Reading with Kids (http://bark.web.officelive .com/default.aspx)

- Reading with Rover (http://www.readingwithrover.org)

- Paws for Reading (http://www.supportdogs.org/Programs/ PAWS-For-Reading)

- Tail Waggin' Tutors Program through Therapy Dogs International (http://www.tdi-dog.org/OurPrograms.aspx?Page=Children+ Reading+to+Dogs)

- Puppy Dog Tales Reading Program sponsored by the San Francisco SPCA (http://www.sfspca.org/programs-services/animal-assisted-therapy/puppy-dog-tales-reading-program)

- Aurora Public Library's Wagging Tales program (http://www.auroragov.org/AuroraGov/Departments/LibraryAndCulturalSer vices/LibraryServices/ProgramsAndEvents/index.htm)

The popularity of these programs may be yet another indication that teachers' intuition is one step ahead of the science, but we must consider the possibility that science will reveal that the programs are not as effective as animal lovers would like to think. Controlled experimental examinations of the effects are needed; however, doing this type of research is very challenging. At a very basic level, it is impossible for the children to be blind to the presence of the dog. In addition, the therapy animals are typically owned and handled by well-meaning and self-sacrificing volunteers, all of whom would likely enjoy seeing a positive result from an experimental examination of their programs, and their preference might affect the experiment. That said, although a well-designed, scientifically rigorous investigation is possible, at some point, it must be considered whether such a study is necessary. The children reportedly enjoy the programs and are learning to read; that is enough to validate their implementation. Ultimately, however, if a scientific investigation were to reveal a substantial effect size, it might provide the evidence that is needed to move the programs into standardized reading curricula.

Calming Influence and Emotional Well-Being

Previous research has indicated that the presence of a dog can moderate stress by reducing observable signs of anxiety such as heart rate and blood pressure (Katcher, Friedmann, Beck, & Lynch, 1983). Weigel and Straumfjord (1970) reported that the presence of a dog in a marathon group-treatment setting for college students with emotional problems provided a catalytic function, as had been reported earlier by Levinson (1962, 1969). Blue (1986) described six aspects of the child–pet relationship, including love, attachment, and comfort, as well as benefits to both psychological and physical health. As mentioned earlier, the presence of a calm, attentive dog apparently reduces anxiety relative to the presence of an adult or supportive friend when children are asked to read aloud (Friedmann et al., 2000). Elementary school girls in Slavonia with a pet dog or cat had a lower posttraumatic stress response to the war in Croatia than did girls with other pets or girls without pets (Arambasic, Kerestes, Kuterovac-Jagodic, & Vizek

Vidović, 2000). Both boys and girls with a dog or cat expressed their emotions, sought social support, and used problem solving more than did other children.

Anderson and Olson (2006) examined how a dog's presence in a classroom of children with emotional disturbance affected the children's emotional stability and their ability to learn. They observed the children, interviewed children and parents, and recorded behavioral data. The presence of the dog appeared to contribute to the children's emotional stability, as evidenced by prevention and de-escalation of episodes of emotional crisis. The presence of the dog also appeared to improve the children's attitudes toward school and helped them learn lessons in responsibility, respect, and empathy. These results must be interpreted with caution due to a maturation confound: All students had more "crisis behaviors" in the 2 months prior to the dog entering the classroom than in the next 2 months when the dog was in the classroom, perhaps partially due to their own maturation. Nevertheless, Anderson and Olson's descriptions of the six children in the study are informative.

A study by Esteves and Stokes (2008) examined the impact of the presence of a dog on the social interactions of three children (ages 5–9) with developmental disabilities and their teacher at an elementary school. They implemented a baseline period during which social interactions were assessed in the presence of a toy dog and other play materials. The experimental change involved the additional presence of the real dog. The authors reported that all of the participants increased their positively initiated behaviors (both verbal and nonverbal) and decreased their negatively initiated behaviors. Esteves and Stokes also reported that these improved social interactions did generalize to the classroom after the completion of the experimental sessions. They argued that children with developmental disabilities do benefit from the use of skilled dogs as teaching assistants, but because the sample size was so small, caution must be exercised about generalizing the results. Clearly, the results of this study are intriguing and further research is needed.

In a twist on the concept of a dog's calming presence, Somervill, Swanson, Robertson, Arnett, and MacLin (2009) found that when children who were diagnosed with attention-deficit/hyperactivity disorder (ADHD) spent time with a therapy dog, they were more likely to experience an excitatory than a calming response to the dog. They found a significant increase in blood pressure for this group of students, which is contrary to the more commonly found decrease in blood pressure and cardiovascular responses found in other groups (Friedmann, Katcher, Thomas, & Lynch, 1980; Friedmann & Thomas, 1995; Friedmann, Thomas, Stein, & Kleiger, 2003) in the presence of a dog. Still, stimulants are a common treatment for children diagnosed with ADHD and are recommended by the American Academy of Pediatrics (2001), so the stimulating presence of the dog may in fact be beneficial to such children.

Coping with Loss/Grief

Crase and Crase (1976) argued that contemporary society avoids directly addressing issues that are related to aging and dying and allows most children to learn about death through vicarious violent death experiences in the media. By the age of 9, most children understand that death is inevitable and irreversible, and the authors made the case that open communication with children about death is of the utmost importance to help them avoid confusion and fear. One way to achieve such communication is by using the unfortunate but inevitable circumstance of the death of an animal—a pet or school mascot that is part of the lives of preschool or elementary school children. These situations can be used in a positive way by allowing the children to work through the process of grief for a pet. Through this experience, children can understand why there should be no wanton taking of life and no disregard for pain.

As previously mentioned, Blue (1986) examined the child–pet relationship and presented six aspects of that relationship. One of the aspects was the opportunity for children to learn about life, death, and grief. Kaufman and Kaufman (2006) present a literature review and a case analysis of childhood pet bereavement in which they argued that childhood grief and mourning may have immediate and long-term consequences, including depression, anxiety, social withdrawal, behavioral disturbances, and school underachievement. They emphasized the need for parents to avoid trivializing the death of pets, to appreciate the role that pets play in children's lives, and to assist children in multiple approaches toward expressing their feelings, including verbal, written, or artistic venues. The authors also pointed out that in this way a child may actually teach the entire family about coping with bereavement.

Cognitive Task Performance and Motivation to Learn

Allen, Blascovich, Tomaka, and Kelsey (1991) studied a group of adult female dog owners ages 27 to 55 years. They measured four physiological responses (conductance, systolic and diastolic blood pressure, and pulse rate, all of which typically elevate in response to stress) to the presence of a dog in the room while the subjects performed mental arithmetic and other tasks. The authors of the study found that when the women performed the mental arithmetic task in the presence of the dog, their physiological responses to three of the four measures were significantly reduced compared with their responses when they were asked to perform the same task in the presence of a close female friend. Although this study was not aimed specifically at examining the impact of the dog's presence on the accuracy of the cognitive task (mental arithmetic), it suggests that the presence of a dog may provide a calming influence that could have a beneficial effect during the execution of a challenging cognitive task.

To explore the effect of a dog's presence on children's ability to follow instructions, Gee, Crist, and Carr (2010) asked preschool children to participate in a very simple object recognition task in the presence of a coparticipant: either a real dog, a stuffed dog, or a human. They told the children that the coparticipant was going on a trip to visit his grandmother and showed the children 10 different three-dimensional objects that the coparticipant was planning to take on the trip. Next, the children engaged in a distracter task that involved a matching game and was unrelated to the current memory task. Then the experimenter told the child that the objects belonging to the coparticipant were inadvertently mixed up with another set of objects and asked the child to assist the coparticipant in picking out his own belongings. The children's performance on the memory task was at ceiling, as expected given the simplicity of the task, but the analysis of the children's ability to follow instructions was revealing. Gee and colleagues examined two different types of instructional prompts: task-specific (e.g., please pick one) and general prompts (e.g., please face this direction). They found that the children required fewer prompts of either type in the real-dog condition relative to the human condition and that the stuffed-dog condition required an intermediate number of prompts. They suggested that the presence of the real dog helps children to restrict their attention to the demands of the task. Further, they suggested that the children were more motivated to help the real dog, who might indeed need help sorting out his belongings, than the stuffed dog or the human, who was an adult college student and whom the children might believe did not really need their help.

Gee, Church, and Altobelli (2010) asked preschool children to participate in a match-to-sample object categorization task in which they showed the children a picture of an object (e.g., a poodle) and asked them to select another object that it "goes with." The children were shown pictures of three alternative choices: a taxonomic choice (e.g., a different dog), a thematic choice (e.g., a dog bone), or an irrelevant choice (e.g., a pair of scissors). As expected, the pattern of the data revealed that the younger children made more taxonomic choices (probably because those choices are based on simple surface-feature similarities between the two objects), and the older children made more thematic choices that involve a deeper level of comparison. The more interesting result was the number of irrelevant choices, or errors, that were made by the children. Overall, the children made fewer errors in the real-dog condition than in the stuffed-dog or the human condition. Gee and colleagues again considered this finding supportive of the notion that the presence of the dog allows preschool children to restrict, or focus, their attention on the demands of the task, which results in their making fewer errors on the task. They also considered the possibility that the dog provides an additional source of motivation for the children to perform well on the task.

A completely different approach to examining motivation in learning related to animals comes from Chen, Chou, Deng, and Chan (2007), who used a digital animal to help motivate Chinese children to learn by taking care of "animal companions." Their preliminary data with a fifth-grade class indicates that this digital classroom environment has a positive impact on academic performance and facilitates teamwork and interpersonal interaction and communication. The authors attributed these preliminary results to the ability of their digital environment to simulate the human attachment to pet keeping, and they suggested that animal companion research could focus on the trainability of animals with different competency levels to foster goal-setting and deeper engagement.

CONSIDERATIONS FOR FUTURE INVESTIGATIVE STUDIES

More than twenty-five years ago, Beck and Katcher (1984) made the argument that bringing pets into an institutional setting is no more effective than any other novel stimulus. They suggested that when people are evaluating pet-visitation programs, they tend to suspend critical judgment and use inappropriate statistical analyses, if they use statistics at all. Ultimately, they recommended that veterinarians consider pet therapy programs to be of recreational value and nothing more. Research on this topic has come a long way since 1984, but those sorts of criticisms must be borne in mind, lest they resurface in the future.

In general, people who are involved in research on human–animal interaction enjoy the company of animals and may have a personal bias in hoping to see positive outcomes of their research investigations. Researchers must maintain their scientific objectivity and the products of those investigations must be subjected to rigorous scientific scrutiny by peer reviewers. Reviewers have a responsibility to adhere to the highest standards of scientific inquiry to ensure that the findings and conclusions will stand the test of time and scrutiny of future researchers.

Imposing high scientific standards on research in this area will ultimately be beneficial not only because it will provide legitimacy to the practice of involving animals in educational settings, but because it will clearly delineate the circumstances under which the use of animals is most and least effective. In addition, a foundation of research can help establish clear guidelines for educators to consider regarding the care and involvement of the animals in their interactions with the classroom students to meet specific pedagogical goals. That said, a number of constraints are still involved in assessing the efficacy of certain types of animal-assisted interventions in the classroom.

Barker, Best, Fredrickson, and Hunter (2000) discussed the existence of the few controlled studies aimed at examining the impact of animal-assisted therapy and animal-assisted activities in educational settings while considering the constraints that hinder such research. They used a case study as their comparison point, and in so doing, they discussed the obstacles that they encountered that were likely to be an issue for future research. For example, they needed two 6-week blocks of consecutive school days to compare their intervention with their control condition. They found it very difficult to implement this schedule within the academic calendar, due to the number of sporadic days during which the children were not at school for various reasons, including school holidays. Other constraints were related to the animal handlers, the teachers, and external influences (e.g., an external review during the intervention noted that the school had animals on its premises without prior approval from a higher authority). Even though many of the issues that they raise will not apply to all investigations, and they do not claim to have described all possible constraints on research in this subject area, they do make a number of valuable suggestions. Following are some of their suggestions, which are really reminders about good scientific investigative techniques:

- Carefully consider the research design and the implications related to the design choice.

- Anticipate and address potential confounds and threats to internal validity in longer studies.

- Seek larger sample sizes (largely because they improve power and the efficacy of randomization).

- Use dependent measures that are sensitive to the effects under consideration.

- Train key personnel in proper data collection and coding.

Unfortunately, Barker and colleagues (2000) also made some less helpful recommendations, such as involving only teachers who volunteer in order to avoid complaints related to their workload. A potential bias will be built into the study if it includes only classrooms with the most motivated teachers. In addition, they suggested training the teachers about what to expect from anxious or excited dogs. This is the wrong approach; anxious or excited dogs should not be in these classrooms in the first place, as they are indeed more likely to have an accident or cause an injury. Only well-trained dogs, preferably certified with an appropriate organization and desensitized to the pressures of class-room environments, should be involved in this sort of research. Finally, Barker and colleagues suggested asking the teachers to have appropriate cleaning supplies on hand, a task that is not the teachers' responsibility. All certifying therapy dog organizations make it clear in their policies that the handler is responsible for having available appropriate cleaning supplies and using those supplies when necessary. It makes sense for research team members to support and assist the dog handlers when necessary, but this task should never fall to the other participants or volunteers in the project (e.g., teachers, aides, students).

OBSTACLES TO THE USE OF PETS IN A CLASSROOM SETTING

In addition to the concerns already listed that specifically affect research investigations into the use of pets in classrooms, several other concerns arise whenever pets are brought into an educational setting.

Safety and Liability Issues

Parents often express concern about safety issues when they are informed that an animal may be brought into the classroom. Because children and especially dogs tend to interact in a movement-oriented manner, there is an increased possibility of an accidental injury due to an inadvertent collision or trip. In addition, there exists the possibility of a dog bite. According to the American Academy of Otolaryngology (2009), young children are especially vulnerable to severe dog bites in the head and neck areas. Jalongo (2006, 2008) reported a variety of sobering statistics regarding the incidence of dog bites, especially among young children. Further, she indicated that dog bites most frequently occur with familiar dogs.

The good news is that, as Jalongo (2008) pointed out, such incidents are largely preventable. She made a very strong argument for the role of education in preventing such incidents and provides research-based, developmentally appropriate strategies and a variety of free resources that can be used to help children learn to safely interact with dogs. According to her suggestions, bringing a dog into a classroom can aid in dog safety education and actually reduce the incidence of dog bites outside of the classroom. (See also Chapter 4, which gives information on dog-bite frequency and safety suggestions for avoiding such occurrences.)

Along the same lines, adhering to the basic dog safety recommendations provided by organizations such as Therapy Dogs International or the Delta Society will greatly reduce the likelihood of an injury occurring in the classroom, assuming that the dog involved is a well-trained and well-handled certified therapy dog. Because the possibility of an injury will always exist, however, liability insurance coverage is a must.

Health Concerns

Some children or teachers may have allergies to the animals that might be brought into the classroom. It is essential to clarify whether this is the case prior to bringing any animal into a classroom and to obtain instructions from parents regarding how their child should be allowed to interact with the animal. It is important to bathe or groom the animal prior to the visit, thus removing a large portion of the dander that is most frequently the source of an allergic reaction. According to Jalongo and colleagues (2004), using an airy, well-ventilated area will also alleviate this particular concern.

Another common worry is that the animal might carry a zoonotic disease—that is, an infectious disease transmitted from animals to humans. (For a listing of common zoonoses and their sources and treatment, see Chapter 4.) According to Brodie, Biley, and Shewring (2002), the potential does exist, but the danger is minimal if responsible safety practices are observed. Their study focused primarily on health-care settings where more rigorous standards apply, but their basic recommendations for responsible safety practices when working with dogs are worth noting. Children and adults should wash their hands before and after interacting with the dog, the dog should sit on a disposable pad, the dog should be appropriately groomed, and the dog should have received appropriate routine veterinary health care, including vaccinations. Marty Becker (2009), a veterinary consultant to the *Good Morning America* television show, makes the argument that it is best not to allow dogs to lick people in the mouths simply because dogs investigate the world by putting things into their mouths that may carry harmful germs, and by licking a human's mouth they could inadvertently pass those germs on to the human. Therapy dogs are commonly trained not to lick.

Sanitation is also a common concern. Dogs, the most common animal visitors to classrooms, are typically housetrained (whereas some other pet visitors may not be), but even the best-trained dog may become sick and vomit, urinate, or defecate unexpectedly in the classroom (Jalongo et al., 2004). Preparation for this possibility is essential. Having the appropriate cleaning supplies available is important in avoiding such incidents, as is providing proper exercise for the dog before it enters the classroom setting.

Personal and Cultural Concerns

The possibility of a child fearing or feeling a general distaste for the animal in question must be taken into consideration. Jalongo and colleagues (2004) recommended not forcing the issue. If a child is afraid of dogs, for instance, then the teacher should allow that child to keep a distance from a dog in the classroom and simply watch his or her peers interact with it. In many cases, this approach results in the child quickly overcoming his or her fear. Cultural sensitivity is also essential. For example, in some cultures (e.g., those of the Middle East) dogs are considered to be unclean, and it is important to approach the situation in a culturally responsible manner.

ANIMAL WELL-BEING AND TREATMENT

Guidelines have been established for the care and treatment of animals in research settings. For example, the Committee on Animal Research and Experimentation published *Guidelines for the Use of Animals in School Science Behavior Projects* (1981) as a companion to the existing *Principles for the Care and Use of Animals* from the American Psychological Association (n.d.). However, there are no comparable guidelines for the use of classroom pets or mascots or for the situation in which teachers bring their own animals to class or invite others to do so. Obviously, animal-assisted therapy certifying programs such as Therapy Dogs International and the Delta Society have their own guidelines for such visits, but there is no overarching, commonly accepted set of guidelines that would formally address the wider variety of pedagogical applications of animal use. Andrew and Robottom (2001) discussed this issue within the confines of the educational system in Australia. They pointed out that a dilemma exists with regard to the ethical tensions between the objectivist, purely scientific approach to the use of animals in the science curriculum and in the classroom and the varying subjective ethical perspectives inherent in the societies in which the teaching occurs. They recommended that teachers recognize the existence of these disparate views and encourage the incorporation of ethical thinking in the classroom.

Although there has been much debate about the use of animals in educational activities involving dissection or other invasive techniques, that controversy falls outside the range of this chapter. Herzog (1990) presents a classroom activity that is designed to stimulate discussion of animal rights and animal research for teachers who wish to explore that area with their students.

SELECTED RESOURCES FOR INCORPORATING ANIMALS INTO CLASSROOMS

There are several resources available for information on adding animals to the classroom experience. A few of these resources are listed here:

- Roy (2004) has given valuable information in an article titled "Responsible Use of Live Animals in the Classroom."

- The Delta Society's (2005) book, *Animals in the Classroom,* represents a collection of information on many different issues that are related to the involvement of animals in the classroom. The book's contents range from opinion pieces and untested activities to refereed journal articles reprinted from other sources and descriptions of state and federal laws, so one must be discriminating in digesting this material. This book may be found at http://prostores2.carrierzone .com/servlet/deltasocietycom/Detail?no=98.

- Anderson's (2007) article aimed at helping people incorporate a dog into a classroom setting is available online at http://escholarship .bc.edu/education/tecplus/vol4/iss1/art4.

CONCLUSION

Clearly, there are many ways in which animals have been shown to be beneficial in educational settings. On one level, they have been educational "tools" to help students accomplish a specific learning objective—for example, in dissections and in demonstrations of animal behaviors. On another level, the presence of animals in classrooms has been shown to be effective in six general areas, ranging from the development of empathy and other emotion-related factors to the enhancement of cognitive and motor skills, communication and reading skills, and motivation to learn.

Efforts have been made to analyze the nature of these effects and to determine the specific circumstances under which the use of classroom animals is particularly effective or ineffective. Although much of this research is preliminary in nature, the continuation and expansion of these studies should be encouraged and supported, as they will serve to legitimize the involvement of animals in educational settings.

Even more important to the legitimization of animal use in the classroom will be the use of specially trained dogs for specific purposes in environments to which they have been desensitized. Household pets, no matter how well behaved they are at home or how well intentioned their owners are in volunteering them for service, are at a distinct disadvantage in becoming effective classroom adjuncts. Even trained therapy dogs may be unsuccessful if they have not been acclimated to the potential overstimulation of a classroom of noisy, active children. The best results, both in terms of the immediate classroom situation and the long-term validation of classroom animals, will depend on using well-trained, seasoned, qualified animals.

In today's hectic, technologically driven world, interaction with animals can be an especially meaningful experience in a child's world. Including animals in classrooms may be the ideal way to accomplish such interaction.

REFERENCES

Abate, M.E. (2005). Using a popular pet fish species to study territorial behavior. *Journal of Biological Education, 39*(2), 81–86.

Abramson, C.I., Onstott, T., Edwards, S., & Bowe, K. (1996). Classical-conditioning demonstrations for elementary and advanced classes. *Teaching of Psychology, 23*(1), 26–30.

Ackil, J.E., & Ward, E.F. (1982). Chickens in the classroom: Introductory laboratory courses in experimental psychology. *Teaching of Psychology, 9*(2), 107–108.

Adams, B. (2006). Inquiring about isopods. *Science and Children, 43*(7), 57.

Adams, D.L. (1997). Animal-assisted enhancement of speech therapy: A case study. *Anthrozoos, 10*(1), 53–57.

Allen, K.M., Blascovich, J., Tomaka, J., & Kelsey, R.M. (1991). Presence of human friends and pet dogs as moderators of autonomic responses to stress in women. *Journal of Personality and Social Psychology, 61*(4), 582–589.

American Academy of Otolaryngology. (2009, March 2). Dog bites a particular threat to young children, especially as temperatures rise. *ScienceDaily*. Retrieved September 27, 2009, from http://www.sciencedaily.com/releases/2009/03/090301094244.htm

American Academy of Pediatrics. (2001). Clinical practice guideline: Treatment of the school-aged child with attention-deficit/hyperactivity disorder. *Pediatrics, 108*, 1033–1044.

American Psychological Association Principles for the Care and Use of Animals Retrieved August 17, 2010, from http://www.apa.org/science/leadership/care/guidelines.aspx

American Psychological Association. (n.d.) *Principles for the Care and Use of Animals.* Retrieved August 17, 2010, from http://www.apa.org/science/leadership/care/guidelines.aspx

Anderson, K.L. (2007). Who let the dog in? How to incorporate a dog into a self-contained classroom. *TEACHING Exceptional Children Plus, 4*(1) Article 4. Retrieved October 15, 2009, from http://escholarship.bc.edu/education/tecplus/vol4/iss1/art4

Anderson, K.L., & Olson, M.R. (2006). The value of a dog in a classroom of children with severe emotional disorders. *Anthrozoos, 19*(1), 35–49.

Andrew, J., & Robottom, I. (2001). Sciences and ethics: Some issues for education. *Science Education, 85*(6), 769–780.

Arambasic, L., Kerestes, G., Kuterovac-Jagodic, G., & Vizek Vidović, V. (2000).
The role of pet ownership as a possible buffer variable in traumatic experi-
ences. *Studia Psychologica, 42,* 135–146.
Ascione, F.R. (1992). Enhancing children's attitudes about the humane treatment
of animals: Generalization to human-directed empathy. *Anthrozoös, 5,* 176–191.
Barker, S.B., Best, A.M., Fredrickson, M., & Hunter, G. (2000). Constraints in
assessing the impact of animals in education. *Anthrozoös, 13*(2), 74–79.
Barr, G., & Herzog, H. (2000). Fetal pig: The high school dissection experience.
Society & Animals, 8(1), 53–69.
Beck, A.M., & Katcher, A.H. (1984). A new look at pet-facilitated therapy.
Journal of the American Veterinary Association, 184(4), 414–421.
Becker, M. (2009, October). *The power of love: The science and soul behind the
affection-connection we call The Bond.* Paper presented at the joint meeting of
the International Society for Anthrozoology and the first annual Human-
Animal Interaction Conference in Kansas City, MO.
Becker, M. (2009, October) *The power of love: The science and soul behind the
affection-connection we call The Bond.* Paper presented at the joint meeting
of the International Society for Anthrozoology and the first annual Human-
Animal Interaction Conference in Kansas City, MO.
Belke, T.W. (2002). Context matters: My education at the Harvard pigeon lab.
Journal of Experimental Analysis of Behavior, 77(3), 373–374.
Berman, P. (1980). Are women more responsive than men to the young? A review
of developmental and situational variables. *Psychological Bulletin, 88,* 668–695.
Blue, G.F. (1986). The value of pets in children's lives. *Childhood Education,
63*(2), 84–90.
Brodie, S.J., Biley, F.C., & Shewring, M. (2002). An exploration of the potential
risks associated with using pet therapy in health care settings. *Journal of
Clinical Nursing, 11*(4), 444–456.
Chen, Z.H., Chou, C.Y., Deng, Y.C., & Chan, T.W. (2007). Active open learning
models as animal companions: Motivating children to learn through interacting with My-Pet and Our-Pet. *International Journal of Artificial Intelligence
in Education, 17,* 145–164.
Coleman, G.J., Hall, M.J., & Hay, M. (2008). An evaluation of a pet ownership
education program for school children. *Anthrozoös, 21*(3), 271–284.
Committee on Animal Research and Experimentation. (1981). Guidelines for
the use of animals in school science behavior projects. *American Psychologist,
36,* 686.
Corson, S.A., & Corson, E.O. (1980). Pet animals as nonverbal communication
mediators in psychotherapy in institutional settings. In S.A. Corson & E.O.
Corson (Eds.), *Ethology and Nonverbal Communication in Mental Health*
(pp. 83–110). Oxford, United Kingdom: Pergamon Press.
Crase, D.R., & Crase, D. (1976). Helping children understand death. *Young
Children, 32*(1), 21–25.
Cutt, H., Giles-Corti, B., & Knuiman, M. (2007). Encouraging physical activity
through dog walking: Why don't some owners walk with their dogs?
Preventive Medicine, 46(2), 120–126.
Daly, B., & Morton, L.L. (2003). Children with pets do not show higher empa-
thy: A challenge to current views. *Anthrozoös, 16,* 113–127.
Daly, B., & Morton, L.L. (2006). An investigation of human–animal interactions
and empathy as related to pet preference, ownership, attachment, and atti-
tudes in children. *Anthrozoös, 19*(2), 113–127.
Dandoy, S., & Scanlon, F. (1999). Teaching kids about rabies. *American Journal of
Public Health, 89*(3), 413–414.
Delta Society. (2005). *Animals in the classroom.* Bellevue, WA: Author.
Endreny, A. (2006). Crazy about crayfish: Using crayfish to teach habitats,
adaptations, and inquiry. *Science and Children, 43*(7), 32–35.

Esteves, S.W., & Stokes, T. (2008). Social effects of a dog's presence on children with disabilities. *Anthrozoös, 21*(1), 5–15.

Fick, K.M. (1993). The influence of an animal on social interactions of nursing home residents in group settings. *The American Journal of Occupational Therapy, 47*, 529–534.

Fleischmann, K.R. (2003). Frog and cyberfrog are friends: Dissection simulation and animal advocacy. *Society & Animals, 11*(2), 123–143.

Friedmann, E., Katcher, A.H., Thomas, S.A., & Lynch, J.J. (1980). Animal companions and one-year survival of patients after discharge from a coronary care unit. *Public Health Reports, 95*(4), 307–312.

Friedmann, E., Katcher, A.H., Thomas, S.A., Lynch, J.J., & Messent, P.R. (1983). Social interaction and blood pressure: Influence of animal companions. *The Journal of Nervous and Mental Disease, 171*(8), 461–465.

Friedmann, E., & Thomas, S.A. (1995). Pet ownership, social support, and one-year survival after acute myocardial infarction in the cardiac arrhythmia suppression trial (CAST). *The American Journal of Cardiology, 76*, 1213–1217.

Friedmann, E., Thomas, S.A., & Eddy, T.J. (2000). Companion animals and human health: Physical and cardiovascular influences. In A.L. Podbersceck, E.S. Paul, & J.A. Serpell (Eds.), *Companion animals and us: Exploring the relationship between people and pets* (pp. 125–142). New York: Cambridge University Press.

Friedmann, E., Thomas, S.A., Stein, P.K., & Kleiger, R.E. (2003). Relation between pet ownership and heart rate variability in patients with healed myocardial infarcts. *The American Journal of Cardiology, 91*, 718–721.

Gee, N.R. (2008). Describing that which cannot be measured, catalogued, or classified. *Reflections*, 23–26.

Gee, N.R., Church, M.T., & Altobelli, C.L. (2010). Preschoolers make fewer errors on an object categorization task in the presence of a dog. Manuscript submitted for publication.

Gee, N.R., Crist, E.N., & Carr, D.N. (2010). Preschool children require fewer instructional prompts to perform a memory task in the presence of a dog. Manuscript submitted for publication.

Gee, N.R., Harris, S.L., & Johnson, K.L. (2007). The role of therapy dogs in speed and accuracy to complete motor skills tasks for preschool children. *Anthrozoös, 20*(4), 375–386.

Gee, N.R., Sherlock, T.R., Bennett, E.A., & Harris, S.L. (2009). Preschoolers' adherence to instructions as a function of presence of a dog and motor skills task. *Anthrozoös, 22*, 267–276.

Hergovich, A., Monshi, B., Semmler, G., & Zieglmayer, V. (2002). The effects of the presence of a dog in the classroom. *Anthrozoos, 15*(1), 37–50.

Herzog, H.A. (1990). Discussing animal rights and animal research in the classroom. *Teaching of Psychology, 17*(2), 90–94.

Hull, D.B. (2003). Observing animal behavior at the zoo: A learning laboratory. *Teaching of Psychology, 30*(2), 117–119.

Jalongo, M.R. (2006). On behalf of children. *Early Childhood Education Journal, 33*(5), 289–292.

Jalongo, M.R. (2008). Beyond a pets theme: Teaching young children to interact safely with dogs. *Early Childhood Education Journal, 36*, 39–45.

Jalongo, M.R., Astorino, T., & Bomboy, N. (2004). The influence of therapy dogs on young children's learning and well-being in classrooms and hospitals. *Early Childhood Education Journal, 32*, 9–16.

Katcher, A.H. (1997). New roles for companion animals mean new roles for veterinarians. *The Newsmagazine of Veterinary Medicine, 29*(6), 12–16.

Katcher, A.H., Friedmann, E., Beck, A.M, & Lynch, J.J. (1983). Looking, talking, and blood pressure: The physiological consequence of interaction with the

140 Gee

living environment. In A.H. Katcher & A.M. Beck (Eds.), *New perspectives on our lives with companion animals* (pp. 351–359). Philadelphia: University of Pennsylvania Press.

Kaufman, K.R., & Kaufman, N.D. (2006). And then the dog died. *Death Studies, 30,* 61–76.

Kidd, A.H., & Kidd, R.M. (1980). Personality characteristics and preferences in pet ownership. *Psychological Reports, 46,* 939–949.

Kogan, L.R., & Kellaway, J.A. (2004). Applied animal behavior course: A service-learning collaboration with the humane society. *Teaching of Psychology, 31*(3), 202–204.

Kotrschal, K., & Ortbauer, B. (2003). Behavioral effects of the presence of a dog in the classroom. *Anthrozoös, 16*(2), 147–159.

Law, S., & Scott, S. (1995). Tips for practitioners. Pet care: A vehicle for learning. *Focus on Autistic Behavior, 10*(2), 17–18.

Levinson, B.M. (1962). The dog as a "co-therapist." *Mental Hygiene, 46,* 59–65.

Levinson, B.M. (1969). *Pet oriented child psychotherapy.* Springfield, IL: Charles C Thomas.

Limond, J.A., Bradshaw, J.W.S., & Cormack, K.F.M. (1997). Behavior of children with learning disabilities interacting with a therapy dog. *Anthrozoos, 10,* 84–89.

Margadant-van Arcken, M. (1984). There's a real dog in the classroom: The relationship between young children and animals. *Children's Environments Quarterly, 1*(3), 13–16.

Margadant-van Arcken, M. (1989). Environmental education, children and animals. *Anthrozoös, 3*(1), 14–19.

Mazur, J.E. (2005). Effects of reinforcer probability, delay, and response requirements on the choices of rats and pigeons: Possible species differences. *Journal of Experimental Analysis of Behavior, 83*(3), 263–279.

Melson, G.F. (1988). Availability of and involvement with pets by children: Determinants and correlates. *Anthrozoos, 2*(1), 45–52.

Melson, G.F. (1991). Studying children's attachment to their pets: A conceptual and methodological review. *Anthrozoös, 4,* 91–99.

Melson, G.F., & Fogel, A. (1989). Children's ideas about animal young and their care: A reassessment of gender differences in the development of nurturance. *Anthrozoös, 2,* 265–273.

Moore, R. (2001). Dissection: Where and when is it appropriate in the teaching laboratory? *Journal of Applied Animal Welfare Science, 4,* 139–141.

Myers, O.E. (1996). Child–animal interaction: Nonverbal dimensions. *Society and Animals, 4*(1), 19–35.

Nicoll, K., Trifone, C., & Samuels, W.E. (2008). An in-class, humane education program can improve young students' attitudes toward animals. *Society and Animals, 16,* 45–60.

Nielsen, J.A., & Delude, L.A. (1989). Behavior of young children in the presence of different kinds of animals. *Anthrozoös, 3*(2), 119–129.

Olds, A.R., Kranowitz, C.S., Porter, R., & Carter, M. (1994). Building in opportunities for gross motor development. *Exchange, 97,* 31–50.

Pate, R.R., McIver, K., Dowda, M., Brown, W.H., & Addy, C. (2008). Directly observed physical activity levels in preschool children. *Journal of School Health, 78*(8), 438–444.

Poest, C.A., Williams, J.R., Witt, D.D., & Atwood, M.E. (1990). Challenge me to move: Large muscle development in young children. *Young Children, 45*(9), 4–10.

Poresky, R.H. (1996). Companion animals and other factors affecting young children's development. *Anthrozoös, 9,* 159–168.

Poresky, R.H., & Hendrix, C. (1990). Differential effects of pet presence and pet-bonding on young children. *Psychological Reports, 67,* 51–54.

Richardson, R.C., & Norman, K.I. (2000). Intrinsic goodness: Facilitating character development. *Kappa Delta Pi Record, 36*(4), 168–172.

Roy, K. (2004). Responsible use of live animals in the classroom. *Science Scope,*
    27(9), 10–11.
Rud, Jr., A.G., & Beck, A.M. (2000). Kids and critters in class together. *Phi Delta*
    Kappan, 82(4), 313–315.
Rud, Jr., A.G., & Beck, A.M. (2003). Companion animals in Indiana elementary
    schools. *Anthrozoös, 16*(3), 241–251.
Salomon, A. (1981, June). Animals and children, the role of the pet. *Canada's*
    Mental Health, 9–13.
Serpell, J.A. (1999). Guest editor's introduction: Animals in children's lives.
    Society and Animals, 7(2), 87–94.
Serpell, J.A. (2000). Creatures of the unconscious: Companion animals as medi-
    ators. In A.L. Podberscek, E.S. Paul, & J.A. Serpell (Eds.), *Companion animals*
    and us: Exploring the relationship between people and pets (pp. 108–124). New
    York: Cambridge University Press.
Shepard, P. (1978). *Thinking animals.* New York: Viking Press.
Skinner, B.F. (1938). *The behavior of organisms: An experimental analysis.* New
    York: D. Appleton-Century Co.
Somervill, J.W., Swanson, A.M., Robertson, R.L., Arnett, M.A., & MacLin, O.H.
    (2009). Handling a dog by children with attention-deficit/hyperactivity dis-
    order: Calming or exciting? *North American Journal of Psychology, 11*(1),
    111–120.
Soutar-Freeman, B.M. (2003). Animal-assisted therapy program for children
    identified with behavioral problems. *Dissertation Abstracts International:*
    Section B: The Sciences and Engineering, 63(11-B), 5503.
Thompson, K.L., & Gullone, E. (2003). Promotion of empathy and prosocial
    behavior in children through humane education. *Australian Psychologist,*
    36(3), 175–182.
Thorpe, C.M., & Wilke, D.M. (2005). Spatial associative memory: A possible
    species difference in rats and pigeons. *Behavioral Processes, 70*(3), 301–306.
Thorpe, Jr., R.J., Simonsick, E., Brach, J.S., Ayonayon, H., Satterfield, S., Harris,
    T.B., et al. (2006). Dog ownership, walking behavior, and maintained mobil-
    ity in late life. *Journal of the American Geriatrics Society, 54*(9), 1419–1424.
Tomasek, T., & Matthews, C.E. (2008). Using reptiles and amphibian activities
    in the classroom. *Sciences Activities, 44*(4), 123–127.
Vizek Vidović, V., Vlahovic Stetic, V., & Bratko, D. (1999). Pet ownership, type
    of pet, and socio-emotional development of school children. *Anthrozoös, 12,*
    211–217.
Weigel, R.G., & Straumfjord, A.A. (1970). The dog as a therapeutic adjunct in
    group treatment. *Voices, 6*(2), 108–110.
Williams, C.L., Carter, B.J., Kibbe, D.L., & Dennison, D. (2009). Increasing phys-
    ical activity in preschool: A pilot study to evaluate animal trackers. *Journal*
    of Nutrition Education and Behavior, 41, 47–52.
Zasloff, R.L., Hart, L.A., & Weiss, J.M. (2003). Dog training as a violence pre-
    vention tool for at-risk adolescents. *Anthrozoös, 16*(4), 352–359.

CHAPTER 8

Animal-Assisted Interventions in Child Psychiatry

ANKE PROTHMANN AND AUBREY H. FINE

In the fields of nursing, medicine, and psychotherapy, animal-assisted therapy (AAT) has received growing acceptance as a means of support for people who are sick or challenged. It is believed that animals can play an important role in a multitude of therapeutic settings. Animals are comparatively often involved as cotherapists in psychotherapy with children and adolescents in the Anglo-Saxon sphere, and they have been the subject of increasing attention worldwide since the 1990s. Nevertheless, although there are many positive anecdotal examples, there is limited empirical support and research validating the overall effectiveness of AAT (Fine, 2002, 2003; Serpell, 1983). Fine suggested that this lack of documentation and thorough investigation leaves a large void in demonstrating the efficacy of animal-assisted therapy (AAT) (Fine, 2006).

Recent studies (Heimlich, 2001; Mansfeld, 2002; Odendaal, 2000) have shown that contact with animals causes complex physiological, psychological, and social effects in people, responses that might be valuable for psychiatry and psychotherapy. (See Table 8.1.)

Children and adolescents have a pronounced and natural interest in animals, which is why AATs are implemented relatively often for the treatment of psychological disorders. The next section provides an overview of the main scientific findings that relate to the use of AAT to treat particular mental disorders.

Table 8.1. Physiological, psychological, and social responses of people to contact with animals

Physiological Responses

Cardiovascular system	Normalizing and stabilizing of the circulation
Musculoskeletal system	Muscular relaxation, lessening of spasticity, and improvement in body equilibrium
Nervous system	Secretion of endorphines, changes in pain perception, and neuroendocrinal influences
Health behavior	Motoric activation, increase in motion, muscular training, activation of the digestive tract, motivation to healthier eating habits, better personal hygiene, reducing overweight, reducing alcohol and nicotine consumption, help for regulating a daily schedule
Practical living assistance	Compensation for limited functioning of senses, guiding and accompanying people with disabilities (e.g., blind, deaf, limited mobility)

Psychological Responses

Mental state	Experiencing acceptance, sympathy, recognition, consolation, encouragement, endearment, bodily closeness, and enthusiasm
Self-perception, self-esteem, and self-confidence	Esteem and admiration, experience of self-efficacy, feeling of usefulness, responsibility, accomplishment, and competence
Control over oneself and one's environment	Experience of control through the care, provision, guidance and upbringing of a house pet, self-control, sensitization of one's own needs and capabilities, active dealing with coping skills, competence, confidence
Surety and reduction of fear	Acceptance, nonjudgmental, constant affection, uncritical admiration, nonthreatening and strain-free possibility of interaction
Stress	Change in the perception and evaluation of stress situations; composure, consolation, reassurance, diversion from sources of fear, upgrading of small pleasures
Social systems	Requirement for contact, relationship, security, closeness, and common interests
Reflection, projection, and relief	Quiet listening, affective relief and emotional openness, recall aid, identification and projection vehicle
Mood	Mutuality, trust, grounding, devotion, reframing of stress situations, furthering active coping skills, activity, responsibility, dependency, consolation, encouragement, pleasure, spontaneity, and fun; antidepressive and antisuicidal effect

Social Responses

Isolation	Direct through the closeness to the animal, removal of loneliness; indirect by catalyzing interactions with other people, facilitation of social contact through an icebreaker function
Nearness, intimacy, and bodily contact	Substitute for lack of intimate social relationships (e.g., for singles)
Conflict behavior, family bonding, shaping of relationships	Subject of discussion, stronger intrafamily communication, strengthening the feeling of togetherness
Social attribution	Sympathy bonus, facilitating open and relaxed interactions

Source: Nestmann, (1994).

ANIMAL-ASSISTED INTERVENTIONS
IN CHILDREN WITH PSYCHOSES

Psychoses are comparatively infrequent and appear typically during late childhood and early adulthood. They are accompanied by serious disruptions in thinking, perception, motivation, and affect. Drugs are indispensable in treating psychoses, but they are less effective for socially relevant symptoms such as listlessness, anhedonia, or lack of empathy. Many patients lose their interest in social interaction. The main therapeutic goal, therefore, is to rebuild interest in social contacts, an effort for which animals, as social catalysts, are exceptionally well suited. One challenge associated with animal use is the concern that the patients could develop strong fears of animals.

A randomized study (Beck, Seraydarian, & Hunter, 1986) showed that for patients with acute and chronic psychotic disorders, the hospital atmosphere was less frightening and alarming when animals (in this case, a cage with finches) were present. When animals were present in the therapy room, the patients took part in group therapies significantly more often, and displayed social animosity significantly less often, than did a comparison group without animals. The "finch group" was more popular among patients, and members of this group were more involved. Another study observed as early as the 1970s that young patients with schizophrenia demonstrated an increase in their communicative abilities, as well as an improved daily routine, when they had opportunities to interact with animals (Corson & Corson, 1980).

In a controlled study of 230 acute care patients with severe psychiatric disorders, researchers investigated whether AAT led to a greater reduction in anxiety than did conventional relaxation methods (Barker & Dawson, 1998). A statistically significant decrease in anxiety was found among patients with psychoses, affective disorders, and certain other disturbances. In the group receiving conventional relaxation therapy, only patients with affective disorders demonstrated a similar level of improvement. Animal-assisted interventions (AAIs) seem to be highly attractive for patients with acute or chronic psychoses.

Therapists seem to make more progress when they use animals than when they use other therapy methods with patients who have serious communication and interaction deficits. Such patients rarely benefit from group therapies otherwise (Holcomb & Meacham, 1989). Animals appear able to change the quality of life of those patients by alleviating negative symptoms of psychoses (Nathans-Barel, Feldman, Berger, Modai, & Silver, 2005). After only 5 weeks of group therapy with a dog, the patients described a significant improvement in their ability to feel pleasure and desires. This phenomenon continued to grow up to the 10th therapy session. Patients were recreationally more active and were more motivated. Their anticipation of approaching therapy sessions also led to improved personal hygiene and more intensive communication with the clinic staff. The presence of the dog was perceived as pleasant, stabilizing, and fear reducing. The communication between patient and dog was simple and was not influenced by problematic communication phenomena such as expressed emotions or double-bind messages (a human-specific paradoxon, or discrepancy between verbally and nonverbally transmitted information). The dog presented no verbal–cognitive demands but provoked thought through its natural behavior, which often led to an interaction between the dog handler and the patients.

It is apparent that animals provide a unique contribution to the therapeutic outcome of treatment. Melson and Fine hypothesized that animals may "slip under the radar of human defense mechanisms" (2006, p. 5). The presence of animals in the therapeutic setting, either directly or indirectly (e.g., as a story character), may help open a dialogue or an interaction that may have therapeutic benefits. Animals can also help put the patient more at ease.

Pomp (1998) pointed out that the animal's presence encourages clients to readjust their boundaries of social comfort. Most clients appear more willing to open up and become more actively engaged in therapy as a consequence of being surrounded by animals. Other researchers report that the presence of the animals enables patients to begin feeling more comfortable and safer, thus leading to a stronger therapeutic alliance (Prothmann, Bienert, & Ettrich 2006; Forner 2007).

Researchers such as Bowers and MacDonald (2001) stressed that a skilled therapist needs to be in charge of the therapy to interpret the interactions in order to achieve the most effective therapeutic gain. Fine (2006) contended that it may not necessarily be the fact of using animals in therapy that leads to the breakthrough; rather, he argues that what is important is understanding *how* an animal may lead to a positive result. That perception is critical in the view of both authors. AAT should be incorporated into treatment only by well-trained clinicians who know how to incorporate therapy animals and work alongside them.

ANIMAL-ASSISTED INTERVENTIONS IN CHILDREN WITH MOOD DISORDERS (DEPRESSION)

Up to this point, there have been no studies demonstrating the effectiveness of AAT in childhood depression. Like adults, children may suffer from depressive moods characterized by sadness, fatigue, lack of concentration, cognitive deficits, and thoughts of suicide. They may feel lonely, have few friendships, and live in complicated, stressful family situations. Treatment involves training the patients to learn both cognitive and social skills, in order to create a gateway to pleasant and positively reinforced surroundings such as friendships.

People with depression interact less with others than do people without depression. Although they desire conviviality, they find it difficult to initiate communication. Animals such as dogs and cats can help directly, because they naturally seek contact with people without having particular expectations. For example, Fine (2006) reported that trained therapy animals can act as a social lubricant and a catalyst for children with depression who are in therapy. The animals can effectively ease the stress of the initial phase of therapy and act as a link in the conversation between therapist and client. Fine went on to explain that a calm animal may also act as a signal of a safe environment.

In a case study, Fine and Eisen (2008) discussed how a therapy dog affected the overall treatment of a 14-year-old girl who was referred for psychotherapy due to depression and suicidal ideations. They reported that the client initially utilized the presence of the animal to reduce her anxiety and tension. During the course of treatment, the client walked with, groomed, and interacted with the therapy dog. She stated that the dog assisted her in self-revelation in therapy and that taking care of the animal helped her realize that she was capable and a worthwhile person.

With cat owners, the individual's current mood influenced the interaction with his or her pet (Rieger & Turner, 1999). The more depressed a participant felt, the less interaction he or she had with the cat. The cat owners' desire for interaction (e.g., with their spouses or partners, who were, however, not continuously available) led to increased inhibition, a behavior typical for people with depression, who seek contact with others but often fear social rejection. Concerning a pet (e.g., a cat), the situation clearly is different: Pets are always present at home, need not be addressed before starting an interaction, and are not influenced by the present mood of the owner in their interactive behavior.

A survey of 150 people concerning critical life events yielded no difference between people who owned cats and people without cats at the time of the critical occurrence (Bergler, 2003). Both groups of people were equally intensively affected by the critical event. However, it is interesting to observe how they mastered that critical phase of their lives. Bergler observed that the cat owners' involvement with their cats strongly increased during the stressful time, so that the cat became a substantial source of consolation, reassurance, diversion, amusement, physical closeness, intimacy, and understanding. The animal was more important for their well-being than it had been before the critical event occurred. The perception of positive feelings in the cat owners' relationships with their animals contributed considerably to a higher quality of life. The cat owners more readily developed an active mastery of coping mechanisms and a positive attitude, whereas people without cats were more likely to develop a resigned, depressive disposition. Furthermore, the social network of the cat owners was larger and more versatile than that of the people without cats. Cat owners tend to overcome critical life events more actively than people without cats. Cats mediate social contacts and can, in critical phases of life, break the vicious cycle of resignation and depression. Their meaning for the individual increases strongly in a crisis.

Clinical observations show that children with depression react differently during AAIs than do those without affective disorders (Prothmann, 2007). They show little initiative, especially at the beginning of a therapy session, and only marginally offer ideas or show an inclination to engage. The children seem to talk little and take a longer time to react to the dog's invitation to play. Only later do they develop their own creative input. It is interesting to observe that the dogs do not abandon the children, but remain close, looking for physical contact. As soon as the child initiates an activity, the dog reacts promptly and willingly. Hence, the children in this situation experience no criticism or rebuff due to their reluctance; rather, they are immediately rewarded with attention and appreciation when they show initiative. Thus, the dog reinforces the desired behavior in an ideal manner.

This pattern was evident in one case that Fine and Eisen (2008) reported of a teenage girl. Over the course of treatment, the client made it known that it was the animals that fostered her openness and involvement; the therapy animals seemed, to her, to promote a warmer and friendlier environment.

Fine (2006) suggested that therapists need to give more attention to the elements that enhance the therapeutic environment. Obviously, living beings such as animals and plants could be utilized to complement the work environment, making it more appealing and comfortable. In their study on anxiety and discomfort before and during dental surgery, Beck and Katcher (1983) reported that patients who viewed an aquarium in the dentist's office appeared to be more comfortable and less anxious than did patients in a control group who did not view an aquarium. Lockwood (1983) hypothesized that such an outcome may occur because people perceive most situations with animals to be safer and perhaps more benign.

Beck and colleagues (1986) initiated a study in Haverford, Pennsylvania, to test whether animals would alter the therapeutic environment and make it less threatening to patients with various mental illnesses. Results suggested that the experimental group had a better attendance rate and participated more frequently than did the control group. In addition, outcomes from the Brief Psychiatric Rating Scale identified a reduction in hostility scores among clients in the experimental group.

ANIMAL-ASSISTED INTERVENTIONS IN CHILDREN WITH EMOTIONAL DISORDERS (ANXIETY DISORDERS, PHOBIAS, POSTTRAUMATIC STRESS DISORDER)

Childhood fears are widespread and represent typical phases of development. The content of fears changes with age. Infants and toddlers, for example, often show fear of the dark and animals. As a rule, children learn to cope with these fears or integrate them into their lives, but the fears become a problem when they interfere with a child's capability potential. Many adults help children cope with fears intuitively; in problematic situations (e.g., a confrontation with an unfamiliar dog), the adults act to prevent fears from developing or being aggravated. They touch the child reassuringly, try to calm the child by speaking with a comforting voice, explain the dog's behavior, and remain in the situation until the fears decrease significantly. Such behavior is called *reverse conditioning*. Inappropriate behavior in parents, such as talking with an agitated voice or rapidly leaving the situation, can intensify the child's fears.

For 6%–8% of children, temporarily emerging developmental fears manifest themselves in clinical syndromes. Emotional disorders, such as anxiety and phobias, represent the most common disorders during childhood (Davison & Neale, 1996). Everyone, even children, can suffer from specific phobias, but generalized fear and panic disorders appear more commonly in adolescents. The goal of phobia treatment is to expose the child step by step to the situation that causes the fear. With support, the child learns relaxation methods and acquires competencies in other areas (e.g., cognitive reframing, self-regulation, self-managing of fear-inducing situations). In addition to directly training the child, therapists may use group modeling. Children who notice that other children are free of fear in a dreaded situation are more likely to observe and emulate their behavior.

How significant can animals be in a behavioral therapeutic directed-treatment approach to emotional disorders? Evaluation studies show that nondirective AAT can have a highly significant influence on the experience of general fear. Observations of interactions emphasize that children with socially motivated fear disorders (e.g., school anxiety, social phobias) are especially likely to seek out the dog and pat it intensively (Prothmann et al., 2005; Prothmann, Bienert, & Ettrich, 2006). Agreeable physical contact, such as patting one's body, results in relaxation by releasing large amounts of the neurohormone oxytocin. It simultaneously blocks the secretion of stress-associated hormones (DeVries, Glasper, & Detillion, 2003; Pickering, 2003). Odendaal (2000) observed that during patients' interactions with a dog, their levels of beta-endorphin, oxytocin, prolactin, and dopamine increased significantly and the level of cortisol (associated with stress) sank significantly. These changes occurred not only in humans but also in the animals. Children with anxiety disorders (with the exception of animal phobia) can learn from such interactions: Through the use of intensive patting, they can calm themselves and thus become able to tolerate an unknown, fear-provoking situation better and longer. Therefore, animals, as agreeable and positively perceived stimuli, can be successfully incorporated into classical conditioning situations with therapeutic value (Virues-Ortega & Buela-Casal, 2006).

Fine and Eisen (2008) described how a gentle golden retriever became an integral component in the treatment of a child with selective mutism. The dog was initially utilized to help initiate conversation, but it was evident that petting the dog had palliative effects. When the dog was present, the child was able to initiate a dialogue with the therapist. The dog participated throughout the child's 5 months of therapy as she practiced communicating and opening up with her teacher and her peers.

Various researchers have suggested that a therapist who conducts therapy with an animal present may appear to be less threatening, and consequently the client may be more willing to reveal him- or herself (Beck et al., 1986; Kruger, Trachtenberg, & Serpell, 2004; Peacock, 1986). Vormbrock and Grossberg (1988) suggested that animals appear to have a calming effect on humans: Their study linked tactile contact with a dog with experimentally induced lower blood pressures. Fine (2006) suggested that a gentle animal may help a client view the therapist in a more endearing manner. Peacock (1986) reported that when she conducted interviews with children in the presence of her dog, the children appeared more relaxed and seemed more cooperative; she concluded that the dog served to reduce the initial tension and assisted in developing an atmosphere of warmth. Numerous studies have elicited similar findings.

On one hand, animals reduce fears, which leads to a pleasurable state of emotion (relaxation); on the other hand, they catalyze social interactions (skills training). Children with pets have been observed to be more popular with classmates (Guttmann, Predovic, & Zemanek, 1983), which can be useful in building friendly relationships. Dogs cause children to go outdoors and, through various sports activities such as fly-ball or junior dog-handling work, facilitate contact with children of similar ages and interests. In addition, animals provide a sympathy bonus, because people with animals are more positively perceived than those without.

Intense feelings of fear and the desire to avoid frightening stimuli also play a central role in posttraumatic stress disorder (PTSD). The treatment of PTSD involves coping with the crisis directly by working through the traumatic experiences. Therefore, a fear-free atmosphere is indispensable, which is why animals are so helpful in such therapy settings. Animals reduce fears, promote companionship and communication, and offer physical closeness. Particularly for people who have been sexually abused, animals can play an important role; patients can experience nearness and affection without danger of retraumatizing. Petting an animal causes the release of relaxing hormones. Llamas and alpacas in particular can be applied in the therapy of patients who have experienced physical or sexual violence. These animals approach people cautiously, so the patients can slowly relearn how to allow and endure physical closeness.

Barker (1999) ascertained that, for some children with abuse experiences, their pet was their most important source of support. She noted that adults who had been abused in childhood suffered less severe consequences of that abuse if they had had a strong bond to a pet as a child. Reichert (1994) reported that, in an animal-assisted group therapy program for 9- to 13-year-old children who had experienced trauma, the dog helped the children to master the transition from passive endurance to active coping. Children often tell their experiences to the dog before they present them to the group. The animal is perceived to be absolutely trustworthy, and what the patients tell it remains a secret. The chance that their experiences could be passed on and cause further consequences is not a consideration with a dog.

Another important use of therapy dogs is to treat people who have survived bomb and terror attacks, an idea that was used after World War I with veterans who had experienced trauma. Wasserman (2004) observed that the patients found it easier to relax and, concurrently, to think clearly when a dog was present. Some patients were able only to report their experiences by telling them to the dog, an action that had, however, the same relieving effect as telling their experiences to another person. There exist to-date no comparable scientific data for children and adolescents. According to Altschuler (1999), these effects should be systematically investigated. Patients with PTSD who, after an appropriate recommendation, acquire a pet, could be compared with those who did not desire a pet, in order to match the results on a long-term basis.

Despite the pleasant effects of animal contact, some children react in panic to the sight of an animal and avoid every approach to it, as previously mentioned. Parents play an important role as a model in overcoming animal, and especially dog, phobias. As is known from primate experiments, fear behavior can be learned. This makes sense from an evolutionary perspective: If the stimulus or situation can be life threatening, then learning through direct experience is not optimal (e.g., infant apes must not first gather experience with dangerous snakes in order to learn to avoid them later; Davison & Neale, 1996). Usually, infants and toddlers do not fear animals. Between the ages of 2 and 3, when children become more mobile and physically active, they may begin to develop fears of animals. If parents react and inadvertently affirm the children's fears during this phase, serious challenges can develop out of children's natural fears. Parents of children with a manifest dog phobia themselves often react, in the presence of the child, with extreme fear to the approach of a dog. Thus, children can develop massive fear disorders without having had a personal negative experience with dogs. As a result of his or her fear, the child will avoid contacts with dogs and have no chance to gain experience with their proper handling. Happily, fears can be "unlearned." Children can observe how other children interact fearlessly with an animal and attempt to emulate their behavior. Using this premise, an 8-week group therapy treatment program has been developed that leads to a significant reduction of dog phobia (Zimmermann, 2003).

ANIMAL-ASSISTED THERAPY IN CHILDREN WITH AUTISM

Autism is a pervasive developmental disorder that is characterized by distinctive deficits in social interaction and communication, accompanied by stereotyped, repetitive behaviors. People with autism display impaired perception and processing of emotional and communicative signals (Dalton et al., 2005; Pelphrey et al., 2002); pronounced differences in joint attention skills (Carpenter, Pennington, & Rogers, 2002); and limitations in certain social thought processes, such as theory of mind (Rutter, 2005). Many children with autistism spectrum disorders (ASDs) also have difficulty recognizing central coherences (Frith, 1989) and exhibit impairments in certain executive functions (Volkmar & Pauls, 2003).

Autism is not considered curable and is difficult to treat. Treatment focuses on improving quality of life and, at the same time, is open to alternative, individually conceived, empirically tested therapy approaches (Freeman, 1997). Therapy programs that treat ASDs target the training of social skills. One important aspect in many treatment programs for children with ASDs is the production of multisensory stimulation within a controlled environment in which the children can experience reproducible relationships between their own behavior and its consequences; a strengthening of motivation to social interaction, particularly through natural support; and a furthering of self-initiated social interactions (Hetzroni & Tannous, 2004). Animals are well suited to the therapy of autism-specific symptoms, for several reasons:

- Newborn children already prefer moving to static visual stimuli, and 4-month-old infants can recognize biological movement patterns, presumably due to an intrinsic capability of the visual system.

- Even before they begin speaking, children can differentiate between animate and inanimate objects. Often before they learn the names of objects, children identify animals (e.g., bow-wow) as an independent category of language development.

- Animals are highly attractive stimuli for children, who feel drawn in by and attracted to the behavior of living creatures. The fascinating ingredient for children is presumably the variability of animal behavior. Whereas the activity possibilities of a toy car, for example, are limited, animals can move independently and more flexibly act and react, thus offering stronger sensory stimuli than inanimate objects.

- Animals are "intentional actors" (Tomasello, 1999; Tomasello, Carpenter, Call, Behne, & Moll, 2005). Their behavior follows certain aims and inspires children to better understand animal and, later, human intentions.

- Children and adults are thought to have an intrinsic need for contact with animals (Wilson, 1984). In the presence of animals, children seem to have a sense of well-being, safety, and security that leads to a measurable reduction in stress and produces an atmosphere conducive to learning (Kotrschal & Ortbauer, 2003).

- Pets provide multisensory stimuli: auditory, visual, tactile, and olfactory. They do not overtax children in verbal, communicative (i.e., cognitive) ways; at the same time, animals stimulate in many children the need to communicate verbally and nonverbally. Dogs particularly stimulate children to play with them, to pat them, and to speak to them.

Dogs react directly to the behavior of children and thus function as a natural reinforcer. Particularly for children with developmental and communication disorders, therapy methods that initiate and encourage interactive behavior are indispensable. Because dogs, due to their long coexistence with humans, understand better than primates human mimic and gesture, they are considered to be the strongest social catalysts (Agnetta, Hare, & Tomasello, 2000; Gácsi, Miklósi, Varga, Topál, & Csányi, 2006; McKinley & Sambrook, 2000; Miklósi, Polgárdi, Topál, & Csányi, 1998). In fact, some AAT studies have shown a higher reactivity and an increased enjoyment of social interaction by children with impaired communication and autism (Levinson, 1962; Martin & Farnum, 2002; Prothmann, Ettrich, & Prothmann, 2009; Redefer & Goodman, 1989). Children with ASDs showed behaviors when they were interacting with animals that they rarely showed with humans: Not only did they readily seem to recognize the feelings and needs of the animal, but they also had no aggressive impulses while handling it (McNicholas & Collis, 1995).

Similar findings have been reported by Fine and Eisen (2008) in their work with children who have ASDs. In one case with a 12-year-old child, qualitative reports identified a reduction in the child's aggressive behaviors toward others and an increase in her prosocial skills as a result of her interactions with a therapy dog. Although she showed initial reluctance to interact with the dog, the child became extremely attached to the therapy animal, especially when she was told that she was the dog's primary instructor. Over the course of her treatment, she always responded gently and kindly toward the dog. She spent time outside the program drawing and writing about her experiences. These findings are similar to findings noted by McNicholas and Collis (1995).

PROBLEMATIC NATURE OF MEASURING THERAPY EFFECTS

Although the number of empirical studies on the efficacy of AAT has risen greatly since the early 1990s, there is still a lack of well-designed and controlled studies in the field of child and adolescent psychotherapy (Draper, Gerber, & Layng, 1990; Martin & Farnum, 2002). The evaluation of psychotherapeutic methods involves certain challenges. First, research methods to investigate treatment efficiency, which are widely applied in the field of human medicine, do not sufficiently meet the requirements of psychotherapy, where the relationship between the patient and the therapist is one of the most important therapeutic factors. Nonspecific factors, such as the nature of the therapeutic relationship and the therapist's sincerity and authenticity, which decide the success of psychotherapy, are difficult to standardize and summarize in a manual (Chatoor & Krupnick, 2001; Grawe, Donati, & Bernauer, 1994; Orlinsky, Grawe, & Parks, 1994; Schmidtchen, 2002).

Second, therapy methods, which are effective when they are tested under experimental conditions, can be regarded as truly effective only if they can be sensibly integrated into clinical routines and can demonstrate their effectiveness under those circumstances. Therapeutic methods that have been classified as successful under experimental conditions are often considerably less effective in a clinical situation. Taking into consideration the problematic nature of measuring efficacy, future evaluations of therapies should be conducted primarily under genuine hospital conditions (Remschmidt & Mattejat, 2003).

In efficacy research in the fields of medicine and psychology, there are two important approaches to measuring modifications: direct and indirect measurement. Direct measurement of modifications assesses change that has been subjectively experienced and self-reported by the person who is the subject of the intervention. In contrast, when researchers measure the modification indirectly, they assess the parameter changes through external observers at two or more times (Schulte, 1993).

Generally, long-term effects (influences of variables over a longer period of time) and short-term effects (the influence of a single factor on a person in the current situation) are easily distinguishable. When researchers measure long-term effects, persisting changes in a person that might be caused by AAIs are of greatest interest. Therefore, personality variables and their alterations need to be considered. Relevant studies investigate the effects of pet keeping on certain groups (e.g., children, older adults, people with disabilities) and pre-suppose long-term, constant, and preferably daily contact with an animal. Studies in institutions such as hospitals, where the patients spend only a short time, are fundamentally different. The time for interaction with a visiting pet in a clinic is considerably less than with pets at home. However, the way in which visiting or therapy animals may influence the patient's experience of the hospital situation and their cooperation in the therapeutic process could be key. The most valuable research methods—including subjective ones—are able to reflect possible short-term modifications of the experience and the patient's perception both of his or her own personality and of the situation. Such methods offer the opportunity to examine the efficacy of short-term contact with animals in the framework of an animal-visiting program or the integration of animals as a complementary therapy in a clinical setting. Information about the patient's motivation and mood seem to be particularly useful. These parameters can give insight into how a person experiences a particular situation (e.g., therapy), so that changes can be attributed primarily to different environmental factors (Hobi, 1985).

Of the existing studies concerning children and adolescents, relatively few use random samples. The investigations are limited to a selected group of patients or are not conducted in a clinical setting. Therefore, little can be stated about the influence of animals on children with psychiatric disorders. The question of whether and how AAT affects children and adolescents with different disorders in a psychiatric clinic remains unanswered. Questionnaires, interviews, and well-established, standardized instruments must be used to measure these effects (Parshall, 2003).

In one study, we investigated the short-term influence of AAT on the state of mind of children and adolescents in inpatient psychiatric treatment (Prothmann et al., 2006). We investigated the extent to which the clinical diagnosis influences the efficacy of AAT and whether certain disorders respond particularly well or not at all to AAT. Sixty-one children and adolescents participated, during their inpatient stays, in a maximum of five separately conducted and video-recorded therapeutic sessions with a certified therapy dog. Thirty-nine children were assigned to a comparison group and did not receive AAT. Current well-being of the patients was measured with the Basler Befindlichkeits-Skala (BBS), a well-established and standardized self-rating method for patients with severe psychiatric disorders that is designed to measure changes in state of mind over time (Brickenkamp, 2002; Hobi, 1985). It is especially suitable for the evaluation of the progress of psychotherapy and can be used to determine the state of mind in four dimensions: vitality, intraemotional balance, social extroversion, and alertness. An increase in total score between at least two measurement events represents an improvement in state of mind. The dog therapy was conducted as a nondirective play therapy for 30 minutes once a week. Each participating patient assessed his or her current mood 5 minutes before the start and again after the end of the therapy session. The same measurement procedure was followed with the patients who did not have dog therapy.

The results showed a significant increase in all scores after contact with the therapy dog, but no increase in the control group. Correlations between the initial BBS scores and the extent to which they changed revealed a significant negative correlation between the initial BBS score and the difference between pre- and posttest scores. In other words, the lower the initial BBS score, the larger the difference was between the measurements before and after therapy. In addition to tests of significance, the effect size is another important dimension used to evaluate the efficacy of a therapy method (Rosenthal, 1994; Schulte, 1993). The effect size, according to Cohen (as cited by Rosenthal, p. 236), is standardized difference between two means and is commonly represented by d. It is calculated by the formula

$$d = \frac{\text{Mean value}_{\text{group 1}} - \text{Mean value}_{\text{group 2}}}{\text{standard deviation}_{\text{pooled}}}$$

This formula produced an effect size of 0.38, which corresponds very well with the overall effect size of 0.39 calculated in a meta-analysis by Nimer and Lundahl (2007) for patients with different psychiatric disorders.

After having ascertained the general efficacy of animal contact on the state of mind of children and adolescents with various psychiatric disorders, it is important to determine whether some participants experienced either no effects or a deterioration in their state of mind. Such an outcome would be interesting in two respects. On the one hand, negative differences in the state of mind would indicate that the participants had not reacted in a socially desirable way. On the other hand, in the context of all therapeutic interventions, it is necessary to find people for whom the intervention does not have the desired effect. From this information, it would be possible to elicit indications or contraindications for treatment.

In our study (Prothmann et al., 2006), patients were categorized into the following six groups on the basis of their diagnoses according to the ICD-10: 1) eating disorders, 2) emotional disorders, 3) depressive disorders, 4) personality disorders, 5) conduct disorders, and 6) psychoses. (See Figure 8.1.)

In an analysis of variance, no differences between the diagnosis groups could be found ($F = 0.611$; $p = 0.692$). Seven of the sixty-one

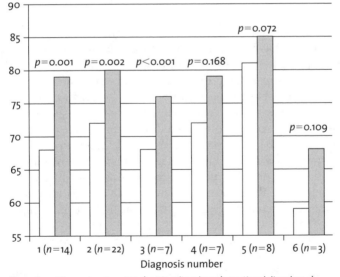

Figure 8.1.   Diagnosis categories: 1) eating disorders, 2) emotional disorders, 3) depressive disorders, 4) personality disorders, 5) conduct disorders, and 6) psychoses. (*Key: n*, number in subsample; *p*, probability.) (Originally published in Prothmann, Bienert, and Ettrich [2006]. Reprinted with permission, International Society of Anthrozoology.)

patients (11.5 %) experienced a deterioration in their current mood, but the deteriorations were not related to any specific diagnosis group. Those patients spontaneously attributed the worsening of their state of mind to subjective problems with the therapy settings (e.g., simultaneous video recording) and not to the dog itself.

The presence of a dog had a highly significant influence on the children's state of mind. To a large extent, the dog's presence appeared to increase the alertness and attention of the children, cause more trust and desire for social contact and conviviality, promote the perception of healthiness, and stabilize the children in such a manner that they felt better balanced. The effects were stronger for children or adolescents who felt worse before having contact with the dog. The lowest initial scores, indicating patients with the worst well-being, were produced by patients who were being treated for psychoses. Those patients in particular seemed to benefit from the presence of a dog and demonstrated the highest increase in well-being in each measured dimension, possibly due to the strong relationship with reality that is created by an animal. No diagnosis group remained unaffected by the influence of the dog. However, further analysis showed that not all patients benefited from dog therapy: Some suffered from a deterioration in their state of mind. Again, no patients with psychoses were among those individuals. This outcome confirms the results of studies in the field of adult psychiatry that were previously mentioned.

In sum, children and adolescents with different psychological disorders undergoing inpatient treatment experience the presence of a dog as very pleasant. They feel encouraged to communicate with other people who are present and to associate with others, and they feel more attentive, better able to concentrate, less easily distracted, and more balanced. Situation-dependent anxiety and fear decrease, allowing the patients to feel secure and cared for in the clinical environment. Animals seem to be able to cause a profound change in the atmosphere of a therapy session. The children feel transported into a warm and empathetic atmosphere, which facilitates the establishment of a reliable relationship with the therapist. Such criteria, across all psychotherapeutic schools, are regarded as the basis of a strong relationship between the patient and the therapist and the foundation that encourages the patient to strive for change. Because such positive results have been observed, and because of the potentially dramatic impact of including animals in therapeutic settings for children and adults, it is important for researchers to continue to study these interactions, using rigorous, well-designed studies.

REFERENCES

Agnetta, B., Hare, B., & Tomasello, M. (2000). Cues to food location that domestic dogs (Canis familiaris) of different ages do and do not use. Animal Cognition, 3, 107–112.

Altschuler, E.L. (1999). Pet-facilitated therapy for posttraumatic stress disorder. Annals of Clinical Psychiatry, 11, 29–30.

Barker, S.B., & Dawson, K.S. (1998). The effects of animal-assisted therapy on anxiety ratings of hospitalized psychiatric patients. Psychiatric Services, 49, 797–801.

Beck, A.M., & Katcher, A.H. (1983). Between pets and people: The importance of animal companionship. New York: G.P. Putnam's Sons.

Beck, A.M., Seraydarian, L., & Hunter, G.F. (1986). Use of animals in the rehabilitation of psychiatric inpatients. Psychological Reports, 58, 63–66.

Bergler, R. (2003). Katzen und Krisen. In R. Bergler (Ed.), Gesund durch Heimtiere: Beiträge zur Prävention und Therapie gesundheitlicher und seelischer Risikofaktoren. Köln, Deutschland: Deutscher Instituts-Verlag.

Bowers, M.J., & MacDonald, P. (2001). The effectiveness of equine-facilitated psychotherapy with at-risk adolescents. Journal of Psychology and Behavioral Sciences, 15, 62–76.

Brickenkamp, R. (2002). Handbuch psychologischer und pädagogischer Tests 2. Göttingen, Germany; Hogrefe.

Carpenter, M., Pennington, B.F. & Rogers, S.J. (2002). Interrelations among social-cognitive skills in young children with autism. Journal of Autism and Developmental Disorders, 32, 91–106.

Chatoor, I., & Krupnick, J. (2001). The role of non-specific factors in treatment outcome of psychotherapy studies. European Child and Adolescent Psychiatry, 10, I/19–I/25.

Corson, S.A., & Corson, E.O.L. (1980). Pet animals as nonverbal communication mediators in psychotherapy in institutional settings. In S.A. Corson & E.O.L. Corson (Eds.), Ethology and nonverbal communication in mental health (pp. 83–110). Oxford, United Kingdom: Pergamon Press.

Dalton, K.M., Nacewicz, B.M., Johnstone, T., Schaefer, H.S., Gernsbacher, M.A., Goldsmith, H.H., et al. (2005). Gaze fixation and the neural circuitry of face processing in autism. Nature Neuroscience, 8, 519–526.

Davison, G.C., & Neale, J.M. (1996). Abnormal psychology. New York: John Wiley & Sons, Inc.

DeVries, A.C., Glasper, E.R., & Detillion, C.E. (2003). Social modulation of stress responses. Physiology & Behavior, 79, 399–407.

Draper, R.J., Gerber, G.J., & Layng, E.M. (1990). Defining the role of pet animals in psychotherapy. Psychiatric Journal of the University of Ottawa, 15, 169–172.

Fine, A.H. (2002). Animal assisted therapy. In M. Hersen & W. Sledge (Eds.), Encyclopedia of Psychotherapy (pp. 49–55). New York: Elsevier Science.

Fine, A.H. (2003, November). Animal assisted therapy and clinical practice. Presented at the Psycho-Legal Associates CEU meeting, Seattle, WA.

Fine, A.H. (2006). Animals and therapists: incorporating animals in outpatient psychotherapy. In A.H. Fine (Ed.), Handbook on animal-assisted therapy (pp. 167–206). New York: Academic Press.

Fine, A.H., & Eisen, C. (2008). Afternoons with puppy. West Lafayette, IN: Purdue University Press.

Forner, F. (2007). Der Einfluss tiergestützter Therapie mit Therapiebegleithund auf die Befindlichkeit von Kindern und Jugendlichen sowie auf die therapeutische Beziehung in der Einzelpsychotherapie. Unpublished diploma thesis, University of Leipzig, Department of Psychology.

Freeman, B.J. (1997). Guidelines for evaluating intervention programs for children with autism. *Journal of Autism and Developmental Disorders, 27*, 641–651.

Frith, U. (1989). *Autism: Explaining the enigma.* London: Blackwell.

Gácsi, M., Miklósi, A., Varga, O., Topál, J., & Csányi, V. (2004). Are readers of our face readers of our minds? Dogs (*Canis familiaris*) show situation-dependent recognition of human's attention. *Animal Cognition, 7*(3), 144–153.

Grawe, K., Donati, R., & Bernauer, F. (1994). *Psychotherapie im Wandel—von der Konfession zur Profession.* Göttingen, The Netherlands: Hogrefe Verlag.

Guttmann, G., Predovic, M., & Zemanek, M. (1983). Einfluss der Heimtierhaltung auf die nonverbale Kommunikation und die soziale Kompetenz bei Kindern. In *Die Mensch-Tier-Beziehung: Dokumentation des Internationalen Symposiums Anlass des 80. Geburtstages von Nobelpreistrager Prof. DDr. Könrad Lorenz, 27* und 28 October; 62–66. Wien: IEMT.

Heimlich, K. (2001). Animal-assisted therapy and the severely disabled child: A quantitative study. *Journal of Rehabilitation, 67*, 48–54.

Hetzroni, O.E., & Tannous, J. (2004). Effects of a computer-based intervention program on the communicative functions of children with autism. *Journal of Autism and Developmental Disorders, 34*, 95–113.

Hobi, V. (1985). *Basler Befindlichkeits-Skala. Ein Self-Rating zur Verlaufsmessung der Befindlichkeit.* Weinheim: Beltz Verlag.

Holcomb, R., & Meacham, M. (1989). Effectiveness of an animal-assisted therapy program in an inpatient psychiatric unit. *Anthrozoös, 2*, 259–264.

Kotrschal, K., & Ortbauer, B. (2003). Behavioral effects of the presence of a dog in a classroom. *Anthrozoös, 16*, 147–159.

Kruger, K., Trachtenberg, S., & Serpell, J.A. (2004). *Can animals help humans heal? Animal-assisted interventions in adolescent mental health.* Philadelphia: University of Pennsylvania School of Veterinary Medicine. Retrieved January 29, 2009, from http://research.vet.upenn.edu/Portals/36/media/CIAS_AAI_white_paper.pdf

Levinson, B.M. (1962). The dog as a "co-therapist." *Mental Hygiene, 46*, 59–65.

Lockwood, R. (1983). The influence of animals on social perception. In A.H. Katcher & A.M. Beck (Eds.), *New perspectives on our lives with companion animals* (pp. 351–362). Philadelphia: University of Pennsylvania Press.

Mansfeld, K. (2002). *Meta-analysis of animal-assisted therapy: A literature review.* Doctoral thesis, University of Vienna, School of Humanities and Social Sciences, Institute of Psychology.

Martin, F., & Farnum, J. (2002). Animal-assisted therapy for children with pervasive developmental disorders. *Western Journal of Nursing Research, 24*, 657–670.

McKinley, J., & Sambrook, T.D. (2000). Use of experimenter-given cues by domestic dogs (*Canis familiaris*) and horses (*Equus caballus*). *Animal Cognition, 3*, 13–22.

McNicholas, J., & Collis, G.M. (1995, September 6–9). *Relationships between young people with autism and their pets.* Paper presented at the 7th International Conference on Human–Animal Interactions, Geneva, Switzerland.

Melson, G., & Fine, A.H. (2006). Animals in the lives of children. In A.H. Fine (Ed.), *Handbook on animal-assisted therapy* (pp. 207–226). New York: Academic Press.

Miklósi, A., Polgárdi, J., Topál, J., & Csányi, V. (1998). Use of experimenter-given cues in dogs. *Animal Cognition, 1*, 113–121.

Nathans-Barel, I., Feldman, P., Berger, B., Modai, I., & Silver, H. (2005). Animal-assisted therapy ameliorates anhedonia in schizophrenia patients. A controlled pilot study. *Psychotherapy and Psychosomatics, 74*, 31–35.

Nestmann, F. (1994). Tiere helfen heilen. *Wissenschaftliche Zeitschrift der Technischen Universität Dresden, 43*, 64–74.

Nimer, J., & Lundahl, B. (2007). Animal-assisted therapy: A meta-analysis. *Anthrozoös, 20*, 225–238.

Odendaal, J.S.J. (2000). Animal-assisted therapy: Magic or medicine? *Journal of Psychosomatic Research, 49,* 275–280.

Orlinsky, D.E., Grawe, K., & Parks, B. (1994). Process and outcome in psychotherapy. In A.E. Bergin & S.L. Garfield (Eds.), *Handbook of Psychotherapy and Behavior Change* (pp. 270–376). New York: Wiley.

Parshall, D.P. (2003). Research and reflection: Animal-assisted therapy in mental health settings. *Counseling and Values, 48,* 47–56.

Peacock, C.A. (1986). *The role of the therapist's pet in initial psychotherapy sessions with adolescents: An exploratory study.* Unpublished doctoral dissertation, Boston College. Retrieved January 29, 2009, from http://escholarship .bc.edu/dissertations/AAI8522289

Pelphrey, K.A., Sasson, N.J., Reznick, S.J., Paul, G., Goldman, B.D., & Piven, J. (2002). Visual scanning of faces in autism. *Journal of Autism and Developmental Disorders, 32,* 249–259.

Pickering, T.G. (2003). Men are from Mars, Women are from Venus: Stress, pets, and oxytocin. *Journal of Clinical Hypertension, 5,* 86–88.

Pomp, K. (1998). Attachment functions of animal-facilitated child psychotherapy. Unpublished manuscript. Karl Menninger School of Psychiatry and Mental Health Sciences, Topeka, KS.

Prothmann, A. (2007). *Tiergestützte Kinderpsychotherapie.* Frankfurt/Main, Deutschland: Peter Lang GmbH, Europäischer Verlag der Wissenschaften.

Prothmann, A., Albrecht, K., Dietrich, S., Hornfeck, U., Stieber, S. & Ettrich, C. (2005). Analysis of child-dog play behavior in child psychiatry. *Anthrozoös, 18* (1), 43–58.

Prothmann, A., Bienert, M., & Ettrich, C. (2006). Dogs in child psychiatry: Effects on children's state of mind. *Anthrozoös, 19*(3), 265–277.

Prothmann, A., Ettrich, C., & Prothmann, S. (2009). Preference and responsiveness to people, dogs and objects in children with autism. *Anthrozoös, 22*(2), 161–171.

Redefer, L.A., & Goodman, J.F. (1989). Brief report: Pet-facilitated therapy with autistic children. *Journal of Autism and Developmental Disorders, 19,* 461–467.

Reichert, E. (1994). Play and animal-assisted therapy: A group-treatment model for sexually abused girls aged 9–13. *Family Therapy, 21,* 55–62.

Remschmidt, H., & Mattejat, F. (2003). Evaluation of therapy in psychological disorders in childhood and adolescence. *Deutsches Ärzteblatt, 100,* C840–C846.

Rieger, G., & Turner, D.C. (1999). How depressive moods affect the behavior of singly living persons towards their cats. *Anthrozoös, 12,* 224–233.

Rosenthal, R. (1994). Parametric measures of effect size. In H. Cooper & L.V. Hedges (Eds.), *The handbook of research synthesis* (pp. 231–244). New York: Russell Sage Foundation.

Rutter, M. (2005). Autism research: Lessons from the past and prospects for the future. *Journal of Autism and Developmental Disorders, 35,* 241–257.

Schmidtchen, S. (2002). Neue Forschungsergebnisse zu Prozessen und Effekten der klientenzentrierten Kinderspieltherapie. In C. Boeck-Singelmann, B. Ehlers, T. Hensel, S. Jürgens-Jahnert, & C. Monden-Engelhardt (Eds.), *Personenzentrierte Psychotherapie mit Kindern und Jugendlichen, Band 1* (pp. 153–194). Göttingen, The Netherlands: Hogrefe.

Schulte, D. (1993). How treatment success could be assessed. *Zeitschrift für Klinische Psychologie, 22,* 374–393.

Serpell, J.A. (1983, Spring). Pet psychotherapy. *People–Animal–Environment,* 7–8.

Tomasello, M. (1999). *The cultural origins of human cognition.* Cambridge, MA: Harvard University Press.

Tomasello, M., Carpenter, M., Call, J., Behne, T., & Moll, H. (2005). Understanding and sharing intentions: The origins of cultural cognition. *Behavioral and Brain Sciences, 28,* 675–691.

Virues-Ortega, J., & Buela-Casal, G. (2006). Psychophysiological effects of human-animal interaction: Theoretical issues and long-term interaction effects. *Journal of Nervous and Mental Disease, 194*, 52–57.

Volkmar, F.R., & Pauls, D. (2003). Autism. *The Lancet, 362*, 1133–1141.

Vormbrock, J., & Grossberg, J. (1988). Cardiovascular effects of human–pet dog interactions. *Journal of Behavioral Medicine, 11*, 509–517.

Wasserman, A. (2004). Terror attack victims: The rehabilitation process of post traumatic patients with the aid of a therapy dog. Paper presented at the International Association of Human–Animal Interaction Organizations Conference, Glasgow, Scotland.

Wilson, E.O.L. (1984). *Biophilia*. Cambridge, MA: Harvard University Press.

Zimmermann, F. (2003). Behandlungskonzept für hundephobische Kinder. In E. Olbrich & C. Otterstedt (Eds.), *Menschen brauchen Tiere. Grundlagen und Praxis der tiergestützten Pädagogik und Therapie*. Stuttgart, Deutschland: Franckh-Kosmos.

Saint Tonto

We could never afford a horse when I was a kid, but I played horses and constantly thought of horses, horses, horses. When I had my own little girl, I looked forward to playing horses with her. But when she was 18 months old, she went into heart failure and suddenly her father and I were faced with the unthinkable. She needed a heart transplant. At age 2, she was put on the transplant list, and after agonizing months of waiting, she had her new heart. She recovered well, but would always be on strong medications to keep her body from rejecting her new heart.

My daughter continued to grow but had several learning and behavior problems. She was very immature and continued to fail in school. The medicine she had to take made her "moon-faced" and increased the hair on her body. Other kids laughed at her. She often came home in tears and it broke my heart. One day when she was 8 years old, I noticed that she was playing "horses" by herself. I asked her if she wanted to learn to ride and her face lit up. That was it . . . I didn't care what it cost, she was going to learn to ride a horse. I went to a local riding center where she started to learn how to take care of a horse and how to ride. She loved it and it was something fun we could do together. But we both started to want more.

One day, I took a chance and answered an ad about a 13-year-old paint pony. I knew nothing, but when I saw him, I thought he was "cute" and the price was low. I bought him for my daughter for Christmas that year. His name was Tonto. When he arrived at his new home, he was nasty; he even tried to bite my daughter first thing. He was shaggy and bedraggled and kind of skinny. But my daughter didn't care. As we continued to care for him, he started to fill out, his coat started to shine, and he started to nuzzle and nicker when my daughter came around. He never tried to bite again. When she was at the barn, no one laughed at her. She still didn't have a lot of friends, but she always had Tonto there for her. He didn't judge her and I think she was learning that she really could be loved for who she was. She was also learning to really ride and jump her pony in lessons. For fun, my daughter would go for long trail rides in the summer and spend hours just grooming him. She said, "You know Mom, there just is nothing that smells so good as a pony in the summer!" A true horse lover! And Tonto always took care of her in extraordinary ways. Some of the trainers at the horse center started to call him Saint Tonto.

It turned out Tonto was a good jumper and mover. My daughter wanted to go to horse shows. We started attending local shows from mini-stirrup, short-stirrup, and finally pony hunter. She started to collect ribbons, and more ribbons, and more ribbons and even a year-end trophy. One day she told me, "You know, I can't do many things very good, but Tonto and I can sure jump. He's my best friend, you know." God, how I love that pony . . . what he gave my daughter was invaluable . . . a loving friend, a sense of responsibility to something outside of herself, a sense of pride and accomplishment. He really eased the pain she would experience from being rejected at school; knowing she could jump a pony somehow helped her cope with ongoing medical procedures. As time went by, my daughter began to mature, make some friends, and have more success at school. Today she's 17 years old and doesn't ride Tonto any more. We still own him but he is helping another little girl learn to ride and do lead line. In my mind, he is truly Saint Tonto . . . he healed my daughter's heart in ways that medicine never could.

CHAPTER 9

Equine-Assisted Activities and Therapy for Individuals with Physical and Developmental Disabilities

An Overview of Research Findings and the Types of Research Currently Being Conducted

LISA S. FREUND, OCTAVIA J. BROWN, AND PRESTON R. BUFF

Sierra was a very special horse I owned. She taught me, at age 40+ years, how to ride and care for a horse, a dream I have had since I was a small girl. Sierra loved people; she would follow me around the pasture when I was filling water troughs or looking for lost halters. She nickered when she saw me arrive at the barn and stared after me when I left for home. Eventually I became the owner of another horse, a beautiful show horse. When it was clear that Sierra really wasn't cut out for the kind of show competition I seemed to crave, I knew she belonged where she'd get more attention from people, including lots of pats and hugs, and where her kindness would be appreciated. She became a stellar therapy horse, helping adults with multiple sclerosis and children with cerebral palsy. Now and then I hear from the physical therapist and horse handler to whom I donated Sierra and they always tell me how she has inspired such effort and motivation in her riders with disabilities. I'm told Sierra has helped her riders increase their balance, posture, and muscle coordination, but most of all, I hear how the riders rarely skip a session because "they and Sierra would miss each other too much."

L. Freund

What is it about Sierra that helps the physical therapist achieve such results? Why are her riders with disabilities so motivated? Is it something unique about Sierra or the physical therapist, or is it simply because a horse is involved? Is it primarily the physical activity of riding Sierra that achieves results, or is it her apparent emotional bond with the riders? Are the client results real or just hoped for?

Sierra is part of an equine-assisted activities and therapy (EAA/T) program employing the technique of *hippotherapy*. Hippotherapy is a somewhat unorthodox mode of physical, occupational, or speech and language therapy for individuals who have physical and/or speech-related limitations. Its incredibly loyal, dedicated, and enthused therapists and clients are convinced of its value. There is another type of equine therapy involving similarly inspired therapists and clients that emphasizes the social and emotional aspects of the activity, rather than working on physical or speech-related problems. That type of equine-centered therapy may or may not involve actual horseback riding. It has been used by clinician therapists as a means of increasing communication skills, increasing behavior control, decreasing depression symptoms, and exploring emotions with their clients. In this chapter, we will discuss various forms of EAA/T, including hippotherapy and equine-facilitated psychotherapy. The chapter will review the scientific attempts that have been made to answer questions about EAA/T and will offer suggestions for future research that may help better understand this unique mode of animal–human interaction.

HISTORY AND DESCRIPTION OF HIPPOTHERAPY

Working with horses as partners to meet therapeutic goals became popular in several European countries after World War II. Programs were developed to help soldiers with injuries or amputated limbs increase their postural control. Children who had survived polio were placed on horseback as a way to strengthen their residual muscles and improve their balance. The success of these therapeutic horseback riding programs eventually led to the establishment of organizations in the United States such as the North American Riding for the Handicapped Association, now known as NARHA, in the 1960s. Over the years, NARHA and the American Hippotherapy Association have developed certification and licensing programs for instructors and therapists in order to improve EAA/T as a professional, allied health field. NARHA and many similar, affiliated organizations have helped foster the growth of EAA/T in the United States.

Horses have been the focus as therapeutic agents for improving physical disabilities because the movement of the horse's back when walking simulates a human walk. When an individual sits on the back of a walking horse, the horse's stride moves the rider's pelvis similarly to the way that the pelvis is moved when a person walks typically on the ground. Furthermore, movement of the horse's back requires the rider to continuously adjust his or her posture, balance, coordination, and flexion (Lessick, Shinaver, Post, Rivera, & Lemon, 2004). For this reason, a number of physical and occupational therapists and other professionals who work with individuals with physical disabilities have incorporated horseback riding into their clients' therapeutic regimens. In the most common approach, hippotherapy, the client sits on the horse passively while working with a physical therapist. A horse handler and two side-walkers (usually trained volunteers, one on each side of the horse) help the rider remain safely on the horse. The physical therapist engages the rider in various physical coordination exercises ranging from maintaining balance while the horse walks to more challenging activities such as turning one's head from side to side, extending arms, or turning one's torso while the horse continues walking with a steady gait (NARHA, 2009). The side-walkers and the therapist focus completely on the rider and horse and give frequent positive reinforcement to the rider. Sessions are often very enjoyable events, with much smiling and eagerness apparent on the faces of riders and side-walkers alike. The sheer joy of movement experienced by the rider can be quite compelling.

The hippotherapy approach has been used with children and adults who have cerebral palsy, multiple sclerosis, various developmental disorders, primary or secondary scoliosis, diplegia, and paraplegia (Pauw, 2000). Similar activities are used by occupational therapists who concentrate more on fine motor control and activities that can generalize to daily life. Speech and language pathologists use the movement of the horse to stimulate erect posture and free movement of the pelvis, which in turn leads to improved ability to take deep breaths and produce louder sounds for improved phonation (Macauley & Gutierrez, 2004).

Articles, books, and Internet blogs resound with enthusiastic anecdotes from clinicians, clients, and their families about the benefits of EAA/T as an intervention for physical and speech-related disability. The numerous EAA/T centers that are established in the United States and Canada—800 are affiliated officially with NARHA alone (NARHA, 2009)—also attest to the popularity of this approach. The scientific literature documenting the benefits of EAA/T, however, is unfortunately sparse. This is a concern, because parents want to know whether hippotherapy is truly a useful therapy for their children with disabilities, insurance companies want to know whether there are real benefits that outweigh the costs, and any individual with a physical disability who is considering hippotherapy needs solid grounds on which to decide whether to invest his or her time, efforts, and money.

HIPPOTHERAPY RESEARCH: REVIEW AND CRITIQUE

A review of published studies through the mid-1990s identified 11 studies related to EAA/T (MacKinnon, Noh, Laliberte, Lariviere, & Allan, 1995). Most of the studies assessed hippotherapy, but some addressed equine-facilitated socioemotional interventions. The review concluded that only limited effects on gross motor function and self-esteem were documented by outcome studies. The authors identified several limitations of the studies, including poor scientific rigor, small samples, and heterogeneous populations. Nonstandardized observational techniques prevailed, and the use of standardized, quantifiable measures was limited.

Children with Cerebral Palsy

Children and adolescents with cerebral palsy compose the most studied group engaged in hippotherapy. Cerebral palsy is a neurological disorder that is present at birth or acquired in very early childhood and that permanently affects body movement and muscle coordination. In one study, Cherng, Liao, Leung, and Hwang (2004) assessed 14 children ages 3–11 years with spastic cerebral palsy who participated once a week for 16 weeks in traditional therapy and once a week for 16 weeks in hippotherapy. (Half the children had traditional therapy followed by therapeutic riding, and the other half had hippotherapy followed by traditional therapy.) The greatest improvement in gross motor function was seen after the hippotherapy segment, but only among children with hemi- or diplegia cerebral palsy, not among those with quadriplegia. That finding was supported by a subsequent study of children with diplegia cerebral palsy, who participated in a 12-week hippotherapy program and showed significant improvements in posture, head/trunk stability, and efficiency of movement when reaching for a target (Shurtleff, Standeven, & Engsberg, 2009).

In another study, Benda, McGibbon, and Grant (2003) evaluated 15 children with spastic cerebral palsy who were randomly assigned to one of two groups. The children in one group participated for 8 minutes in hippotherapy, and the children in the other group sat astride a stationary barrel for the same amount of time. A surface electromyography measure (EMG), which measures muscle activity of the trunk and upper legs, was used to assess symmetry of muscle activation. The children who received the brief hippotherapy session showed significantly greater improvement in muscle activity symmetry than those who sat on the barrel. The inclusion of biomechanical outcome measures such as EMG in hippotherapy research is especially warranted in order to establish comprehensive, evidence-based conclusions regarding the benefits of the therapy.

Biomechanical measures also may help refine how hippotherapy is used with different populations. For example, using a heart rate monitor, Dirienzo, Dirienzo, and Baceski (2007) found that individuals with cerebral palsy who are nonambulatory have significantly higher heart rates than do ambulatory riders with cerebral palsy following hippotherapy sessions. Although more research is needed regarding the effects of hippotherapy activity on heart rates, Dirienzo and colleagues suggest that heart-rate monitoring be conducted routinely with the individuals who have cerebral palsy during riding sessions.

Given that hippotherapy has been used by allied health professionals since at least the 1960s in North America, it is surprising that so very few scientifically valid studies of its efficacy have been published. Pauw (2000) reviewed research published through 1998 that involved hippotherapy for individuals with a variety of physical disabilities. The review included only the eight studies that provided statistical evaluation of results. Although the few studies that meet standards for scientific rigor clearly show that patients with cerebral palsy had improvements in balance, posture, and muscle coordination from engaging in hippotherapy, the studies taken as a whole are somewhat mixed in outcome. This mixed outcome is attributed to the very small sample sizes available (no study included more than 15 subjects per group, and most studies had fewer than 10 subjects per group), lack of adequate comparison groups, and inconsistent use of long-term outcomes. Furthermore, although the studies measured the same variables of balance and posture, they used different instruments and scales.

Recent reviews of hippotherapy studies continue to echo earlier reviews citing criticisms of small sample sizes, heterogeneity of the participants, lack of control groups, and nonstandardized outcome measures (Snider, Korner-Bitensky, Kammann, Warner, & Saleh, 2007; Sterba, 2007). Snider and colleagues and Sterba each looked specifically at studies published through 2004 that evaluated the effectiveness of hippotherapy for individuals with cerebral palsy. Those studies reported evidence that hippotherapy improves gross motor function, joint stability, postural stabilization, and muscle symmetry in the torso compared with typical physical therapy interventions or no intervention. However, the studies generally did not use rigorous, scientific designs and lacked standardized measures. In addition, no experimental hippotherapy research in the most recent reviews assessed long-term changes in other activities as a result of the hippotherapy.

Only one study in the reviews by Snider and colleagues (2007) and Sterba (2007) met the criteria for a *randomized clinical trial*. A randomized clinical trial is a research design in which the participants are randomly assigned to one of two or three groups: the target intervention (e.g., hippotherapy), a comparison intervention (often traditional therapy), or a waiting list (clients receive no intervention and are placed on a waiting list for therapy). This type of research allows the scientist to better control many factors that could bias or seriously compromise the results of a study. Without more such trials, the EAA/T field as a whole cannot establish full credibility within traditional medical and clinical fields, nor can it fully support claims of therapeutic efficacy.

Criticisms about the quality of scientific rigor in published research assessing the effectiveness of hippotherapy continue to be valid, but a review of studies published since 2005 is encouraging. Six studies of the physical effects of hippotherapy published since the reviews by Snider and coworkers (2007) and Sterba (2007) were identified through the electronic publication databases PubMed, Scopus, and PsychInfo. (See Table 9.1.) Most of the studies included groups of more than 15 subjects, used a pre/post design with quantitative measures, and included statistical analyses. One study used interviews of parents and children who participated in hippotherapy (qualitative analysis) and one study was a fully randomized clinical trial. Standardized observational measures were used, as well as biomechanical measures such as EMG, an electronic carpet for measuring spatial and temporal gait parameters, and video motion capture. Results of these recent evaluations of hippotherapy were somewhat mixed. One study found no effect of hippotherapy (although the results were gathered after a single treatment session with only 9 subjects). Another study found only a small improvement for gait speed and distance (although the subject population was not well defined). The remaining studies report significant effects for improved postural stability, ability to reach for a target, adductor asymmetry, and overall increased balance and mobility. These latter studies included at least 12 weeks of weekly hippotherapy sessions that were at least 30 minutes long. Two of the studies also reported that improvements were maintained at a follow-up 7–12 weeks later.

Children with Language and Communication Difficulties

There are preliminary indications that hippotherapy can increase verbal communication as well as offering physical benefits, suggesting that the therapy's effects on language constitute another avenue for

Table 9.1. Summary of published hippotherapy studies from 2005 through 2009

Author	Clients	Number of Clients (N), Age Range	Design	Duration	Measures	Results
Debuse, Gibb, & Chandler (2009)	Cerebral palsy	N = 17 4–63 years	Qualitative	Varied	Self- and parent-report: muscle tone, trunk control, walking, self-esteem, confidence	All measures reported as improved
McGee & Reese (2009)	Cerebral palsy	N = 9 7–18 years	Pre/post	1 session	Gait with auto walkway	No significant difference between pre- and post-intervention
McGibbon, Duncan, Benda, & Silkwood-Sherer (2009)	Cerebral palsy	N = 47 initially N = 6 at follow-up 4–6 years	Pre/post randomized control with follow-up	10 minutes hippotherapy or 10 minutes barrel sitting; follow-up = 12 weeks baseline, 12 weeks hippotherapy 1 time/week, 12 weeks follow-up	Pre/post: adductor muscle by EMG Follow-up: gross motor and self-perception	Pre/post: improved adductor asymmetry Follow-up: improvement over baseline
Schwesig et al. (2009)	Motor dysfunction	N = 22 5–13 years	Pre/post with follow-up	8 weeks, 1 time/week; 7 week follow-up	Gait and posture with interactive balance system	Small effect on gait speed and distance and no effect on posture control
Silkwood-Sherer & Warmbier (2007)	Multiple sclerosis	N = 15 29–63 years	Pre/post with comparison: N = 9 (treatment group), N = 6 (no treatment)	14 weeks, 1 time/week	Balance, mobility	Post: effect of treatment on balance and mobility Follow-up: effect of treatment on balance

Key: EMG, electromyelogram.

research. Macauley and Gutierrez (2004) evaluated the effects of hippotherapy on three children who were diagnosed with language learning disabilities. The children's parents and the children themselves reported greater improvement in speech and language abilities after hippotherapy compared with improvements they observed after traditional speech and language therapy.

Although more recent studies of the effects of hippotherapy tend to use improved designs and standardized and biomechanical measures, further randomized controlled clinical trials are still needed, comparisons with other physical therapy techniques, and better reporting of client compliance with hippotherapy treatment. At this point, it simply is not know whether reported improvements are the result of the actual hippotherapy or the clients' increased motivation to consistently engage in hippotherapy compared with other types of therapy.

EQUINE-FACILITATED PSYCHOTHERAPY

Investigations of the psychotherapeutic or socioemotional benefits of hippotherapy for individuals with mobility impairment suggest that it can indeed bring improvements in self-esteem and self-confidence (McGibbon, Benda, Duncan, & Silkwood-Sherer, 2009; Sole, 2007). The psychological benefits of equine-facilitated psychotherapy (EFP) have been investigated in other populations as well, including children and adults with autism, emotional disturbance, intellectual disabilities, brain injuries, learning disabilities, attention-deficit/hyperactivity disorder, emotional disorder, depression, and anxiety. EFP activities can include horse handling, grooming, longeing (asking the horse on a long lead line to walk, trot, and canter in a large circle around the horse handler), driving, riding, or vaulting (gymnastic moves from the back of a horse) (NARHA, 2009). An EFP session can involve unmounted activities as simple as putting a halter on a horse, entering a round pen with an untethered horse, or trying to herd a group of horses to a particular area of an arena. In this latter exercise, for example, many clients try directive actions such as shouting, raising their hands, or even running at the horses to get them to move to where they want them to go. It can take quite some time for the client to realize that just standing quietly in the desired area will arouse the horses' curiosity and they will usually come slowly to the client of their own accord. This experience can be used by the therapist to identify with the client how he or she can use less aggressive or inappropriate approaches when he or she desires something from others.

EFP falls within the class of experiential psychotherapy and involves equines, a licensed mental health professional, and a horse handler. The therapeutic aspect uses the client's experiences during the activity to work on identified behavioral, socioemotional, or communication goals. Practitioners of this approach are equally enthusiastic and committed to the benefits of EFP as those who engage in traditional hippotherapy. EFP has been formalized by such groups as the Equine Facilitated Mental Health Association (EFMHA), which was established in 1996 as a professional section of NARHA. The EFMHA provides guidelines, training, and a code of ethics for EFP professionals, as does a similar organization, the Equine Assisted Growth and Learning Association (EAGALA), established in 1999.

The instinctual behavioral programming of the horse is the reason that this animal is particularly well suited for psychotherapeutic and personal development work. Horses are prey animals, not predators, and their survival has been based on their extreme sensitivity to the environment. As a herd animal, the horse can detect fear in a distant herd member and act on that feeling without hesitation. This ability appears to have become transferrable to humans over the past 5,000 years or so that people and horses have interacted (Vilà et al., 2001). There are countless reports of horses "reading" people's feelings and intentions. Horses are extremely adept at discerning people's moods and responding to human behaviors immediately, even when people try to hide their feelings, and as a result, encounters with horses may allow clients to learn about relationships through nonverbal communication. Furthermore, the physical size and power of horses demands respect and requires the humans around them to increase their focus and attention. Perhaps most important, the horse is not judgmental. Horses do not have expectations or prejudices. The horse responds immediately to the rider's or handler's behavior without criticism. Thus, the equine-facilitated psychotherapeutic or well-being activity involves three to four partners (including the handler and the sidewalkers): the therapist or facilitator (who may or may not also be the horse handler), the horse, and the client.

Equine-Facilitated Psychotherapy with Individuals with Autism

EFP work with children, adolescents, and adults with autism spectrum disorders (ASDs) has been reported anecdotally as particularly effective and rewarding. The population of people with ASDs is a good example of a group demonstrating the benefits of EFP. ASDs form is a group of disorders with similar features ranging from mild to severe. The primary symptoms of autism include problems with verbal and nonverbal communication, difficulty holding a conversation, difficulty understanding how others think and feel, engaging in repetitive behaviors, showing hypersensitivity to sensory input, and obsessively following routines or schedules (National Institute of Child Health and Human Development, 2008). There is no known cure for ASDs at this time. The behavioral and communication difficulties of individuals with ASDs can be especially challenging for therapists, parents, and teachers.

An EFP session with a child with an ASD can address several areas of potential benefit. For example, learning to groom the horse requires following a routine (to which both the child and horse can readily adapt) and requires the child to focus on the activity, to inhibit abrupt behaviors, and to modulate his or her vocal productions and the intensity of his or her actions. The tactile senses are stimulated. The horse's coat is smooth, the mane and tail are rougher, and the nose is especially soft. Discovery of these sensations not only can help the child accept sensory inputs, but often helps establish nonverbal communication with the horse (e.g., increased eye contact) and even verbal communication with the therapist and other staff. The rhythmic motion of riding a horse causes the child to focus on the movement, which is slow and relaxing. This calming effect of riding appears to facilitate further social interaction and emotional expression. Often, the child will make interaction overtures toward the horse first (e.g., making eye contact with the horse or stroking the horse) and then with other people. Learning to groom, tack (put on a saddle and bridle), and ride a horse are skills that can increase the child's self-confidence, and the enjoyment of such learning may well generalize to learning in other settings, such as at home or school. Perhaps most important, the child is engaged in an activity about which he or she seems motivated to communicate with others.

Equine-Facilitated Psychotherapy Research Review and Critique

As exciting as EFP sounds as a tool for working with individuals who have developmental disabilities or emotional problems, the scientific investigation of the efficacy of EFP is in its infancy. Most of the published literature regarding equine-facilitated therapeutic programs is based on nonexperimental case studies, focus groups, and theoretical literature (Vidrine, Owen-Smith, & Faulkner, 2002). Table 9.2 lists studies using EFP or other equine-assisted wellness activities published from 1990 through 2009. These studies were identified through the PubMed, Scopus, and PsychInfo electronic databases. Several of the reports are dissertation abstracts, suggesting that there is increasing interest in academic settings in the EFP approach.

Table 9.2. Studies of the effect of equine-facilitated psychotherapy and other equine-assisted activities on behavior and emotional functioning, 2000–2009

Authors	Clients	Number of Clients (N), Age Range	Design	Duration	Measures	Results
Bass, Duchowny, & Llabre (2009)	Children with autism spectrum disorders (ASDs)	N = 19, treatment group N = 15, comparison group 4–10 years	Pre/post with comparison group	12 weeks, 1 time/week	Social responsiveness scale sensory profile	Treatment group showed greater sensory seeking, sensitivity, social motivation; less inattention, distractibility
Bizub, Joy, & Davidson (2003)	Adults with psychiatric disability (schizophrenia spectrum)	N = 5 26–46 years	Qualitative	10 weeks, 1 time/week	Semistructured interviews	Reported increase in self-efficacy and self-esteem
Burgon (2003)	Adults with mental health issues	N = 6 > 21 years	Qualitative	24 weeks, 1 time/week	Semistructured interviews	Increased confidence, self-concept, social stimulation
Cawley, Cawley, & Retter (1994)	Adolescents with special education needs	N = 29 Adolescents	Pre/post	Unknown	Self-concept	Increased for younger adolescents only
Farias-Tomaszewski, Jenkins, & Keller (2001)	Adults with physical impairments	N = 22 > 21 years	Pre/post	12 weeks, 1 time/week	Physical self-efficacy, behavior confidence	Increased on both measures
Gray[a] (2008)	Children with autism	Unknown	Pre/post	6 sessions	Social Communication Questionnaire, CBCL, Piers-Harris Self Concept Scale	Decrease in abnormal behaviors
Häkanson, Möller, Lindström, & Mattsson (2009)	Clients with severe back pain	N = 24 13–53 years	Qualitative	12 weeks, 1–2 times/ week but varied	Pain reduction, psychological well-being	Increased self-image; enhanced mood, sense of competence; reduced pain

(continued)

Table 9.2. *(continued)*

Authors	Clients	Number of Clients (N), Age Range	Design	Duration	Measures	Results
Hemenway[a] (2007)	Female, adolescent horseback riders without disabilities	N = 10	Qualitative	Varied	Semistructured interviews	Improved mood, reduced depressed feelings
Honda & Yamazaki (2006)	Adults without disabilities	N = 22 > 21 years	Pre/post	2 days, 2 times/day	Mood, state anxiety, fatigue, vigor	Mood enhanced, anxiety reduced, fatigue reduced, vigor increased
Iannone[a] (2003)	Adolescents with emotional disturbance	N = 19 treatment group N = 8 wait-list controls 13–17 years	Pre/post	1 time/week	Self-esteem; community involvement, locus of control, psychiatric symptoms, behavior conduct	Sign increases in self-esteem; increased community involvement
Kaiser, Smith, Heleski, & Spence (2006)	Children at risk, children in special education	N = 17 (at risk) N = 14 (with special education needs) 8–18 years	Pre/post	At risk: 8 weeks, 1 time/week; those with special education needs: 4 weeks, 2 times/week	Children's Inventory of Anger; State-Trait Anxiety Inventory for Children; Self-Perception Profile for Children; State-Trait-Cheerfulness Inventory; Connor's Self Report; Connor's Parent Report	At risk: no effect; those with special education needs: anger decreased, boys; decreased attention problems, girls; parents of boys rated fewer problem behaviors
Klontz, Bivens, Leinart, & Klontz (2007)	Adults in equine-assisted psychotherapy program	N = 31 23–70 years	Pre/post	4.5 days, 28 hours of EAP	Brief Symptom Inventory; Personal Orientation Inventory	Reduced psychological distress, increased psychological well-being
Koch[a] (2008)	Women horse owners	N = 8	Qualitative	Varied time as horse owners	Observation, interviews, journal entries	Increased trust and positive bonding experience; risk taking had negative impact on well-being

Meinersmann, Bradberry, & Roberts (2008)[a]	Adult women who experienced abuse	N = 5 27–49 years	Qualitative	Varied	Semistructured interview	Increased power, self-efficacy
Russell-Martin[a] (2007)	Adult couples	N = 10 couples (treatment) N = 10 couples (control) 21–45 years	Pre/post with control	6 weeks, 1 time/week	Dyadic Adjustment Scale (DAS)	Positive effect on DAS
Scialli[a] (2003)	Parents of children, varying disabilities (learning disability, intellectual disabilities, orthopedic, autism)	N = 64 children ages 4–19 years	Pre/post	Varied	Horseback Riding Survey (subscales include: Self-Care, Cognitive/School Learning, Physical-Motor, Psychological/Emotional, Social Communication, Interaction)	Improved self-esteem, self-confidence, self-image
Sole[a] (2007)	Cerebral palsy	N = 12 children 9–12 years; N = 12 adolescents 13–17 years	Pre/post	8 weeks, 1 time/week	Self-efficacy	No significant improvement
Weber[a] (2005)	Children with unspecified disabilities	Unknown	Pre/post with comparison group; qualitative	Varied	Rosenberg Self-Esteem Scale; focus groups	No effect, but qualitative analysis of focus groups indicated parents saw positive impact
Yorke, Adams, & Coady (2003)	Adults recovering from trauma	N = 6 > 21 years	Qualitative	Varied	Semistructured interviews, videotapes of horse–rider interaction	Positive impact on recovery

[a]Dissertation abstract.

Some of the nonexperimental reports of EFP outcomes have used well-structured, qualitative approaches to evaluate the experiences of individuals in EFP through semistructured interviews, surveys, journal entries, and even videotapes of horse–rider interactions (e.g., Weber, 2005; Yorke, Adams, & Coady, 2008). A variety of populations have been investigated with these approaches. For example, Scialli (2003) interviewed 64 parents of children ages 4–19 years with varying disabilities. All the children were involved in an EFP program. Parents reported via a survey that in addition to improving physically, their children improved in self-esteem and self-confidence. Both Bizub, Joy, and Davidson (2003) and Burgon (2003) conducted semistructured interviews with a small number of adults with long-standing psychiatric disabilities who participated in weekly therapeutic riding sessions. Clients from both studies identified increased confidence and self-esteem as a result of their therapeutic equine experiences. In a qualitative study of females who had experienced abuse, themes of increased sense of power (self-efficacy) and self-confidence were identified after a series of EFP sessions (Meinersmann, Bradberry, & Roberts, 2008).

The nonexperimental studies just cited have been useful in consistently identifying parent- or self-reported positive effects of EFP, but they do not help to evaluate the effectiveness of EFP as a viable psychotherapeutic tool. Experimental EFP outcome studies have primarily used the preintervention–postintervention assessment design, which has the potential to provide more solid evidence. In one such study, psychosocial and socioemotional functioning of adolescents was assessed before and after an 8-session EFP program involving a group of adolescents at risk for failure in school and another group of adolescents in special education programs (Kaiser, Smith, Heleski, & Spence, 2006). Positive results were seen for the male adolescents who were enrolled in special education programs only. The subjects' anger was significantly decreased after the riding program, and the boys' mothers saw significant improvements in their sons' behaviors at the end of the program. In another EFP program, self-reported improvement in self-concept from pre- to postintervention was observed in 29 adolescents who had special education needs (Cawley, Cawley, & Retter, 1994). The group as a whole showed no statistical improvement in scores, but evaluation of just the younger adolescents (13–15 years) revealed significant improvement in self-concept. Unfortunately, neither of these studies included a comparison or control group. Thus, it cannot be determined for certain whether the documented improvements are the result of the EFP intervention, time itself, or other factors that are unrelated to treatment.

The few existing experimental reports that have assessed children with developmental disabilities (e.g., autism) have reported benefits of

EFP. Using a preintervention–postintervention design, Bass, Duchowny, and Llabre (2009) compared 19 children with ASDs participating in EFP with 15 children with ASDs in a wait-list control group. This well-controlled study found that children with ASDs who were exposed to EFP exhibited increased sensory seeking and social motivation and showed significantly less inattention, distractibility, and sedentary behaviors. Gray (2008) also looked at children with ASDs, using standardized behavioral measures such as the Social Communication Questionnaire (Rutter, Bailey, & Lord, 2003) and the Child Behavior Checklist (Achenbach, 1991). After EFP, atypical social communication behaviors were significantly decreased, but repetitive behaviors (e.g., hand-flapping) did not decrease. The lack of improvement in behavior may be the result of only 6 weekly EFP sessions compared with the 12 weekly sessions that Bass and coworkers (2009) used in their study.

FUTURE DIRECTIONS FOR HIPPOTHERAPY AND EQUINE-FACILITATED PSYCHOTHERAPY RESEARCH

The major criticisms of the published experimental outcome studies of EFP are similar to criticisms of hippotherapy research. Most of the studies lack an appropriate comparison or control group, thus compromising confidence in their results. No identified study of EFP included a randomized clinical trial, and no study has compared the effects of different types of psychotherapy to EFP. Few if any long-term effects have been assessed. Sample sizes are generally small. These problems continue to hamper both hippotherapy and EFP in establishing credibility in traditional medical and allied health fields and with health insurers. After reviewing the available studies that evaluate either hippotherapy or EFP, it is our opinion that the time for pilot studies and nonrigorous research approaches is over. Clearly, the involvement of horses in EAA/T programs creates inherent difficulties for researchers. Such programs usually involve small numbers of clients, are spread across different areas, and involve different therapists—factors that hamper standardization of the therapeutic interaction. These challenges mean that future studies need to coordinate across therapy sites in order to obtain larger samples and institute more standardized intervention approaches.

The funds to support such research are limited and will remain so until more evidence-based studies are published. Clinician therapists and physical therapists considering EEA/T should be encouraged, however, by the fact that the National Institutes of Health has expressed an interest in human–animal interaction research (National

Institute of Child Health and Human Development, 2010) and foundations have been established specifically to support valid EAA/T research projects (e.g., the Horses & Humans Research Foundation, http://www.horsesandhumans.org). Research that is relevant to EAA/T is currently underway through these organizations and through academic programs that are focused on understanding and using human–animal interaction in therapeutic settings. Such research promises to push the field forward. Researchers may not be able yet to answer definitively the questions that we posed at the beginning of this chapter, but the next decade holds great promise for establishing the scientific basis and clinical effectiveness of EAA/T.

REFERENCES

Achenbach, T.M. (1991). *Integrative guide to the 1991 CBCL/4-18, YSR, and TRF profiles.* Burlington, VT: University of Vermont, Department of Psychology.

Bass, M.M., Duchowny, C.A., & Llabre, M.M. (2009). The effect of therapeutic horseback riding on social functioning in children with autism. *Journal of Autism Developmental Disorders, 39*(9), 1261–1267.

Benda, W., McGibbon, N.H., & Grant, K.L. (2003). Improvements in muscle symmetry in children with cerebral palsy after equine-assisted therapy (hippotherapy). *Journal of Alternative and Complementary Medicine, 9*(6), 817–825.

Bizub, A.L., Joy, A., & Davidson, L. (2003, Spring). "It's like being in another world": Demonstrating the benefits of therapeutic horseback riding for individuals with psychiatric disability. *Psychiatric Rehabilitation Journal, 26*(4), 377–384.

Burgon, H. (2003). Case studies of adults receiving horse-riding therapy. *Anthrozoos, 16*(3), 263–276.

Cawley, R., Cawley, D., & Retter, K. (1994). Therapeutic horseback riding and self-concept in adolescents with special educational needs. *Anthrozoos, 7*(2), 129–134.

Cherng, R.-J., Liao, H.-F., Leung, H.W.C., & Hwang, A.-W. (2004, April). The effectiveness of therapeutic horseback riding in children with spastic cerebral palsy. *Adapted Physical Activity Quarterly, 21*(2), 103–121.

Debuse, D., Gibb, C., & Chandler, C. (2009). Effects of hippotherapy on people with cerebral palsy from the users' perspective: A qualitative study. *Physiotherapy Theory and Practice, 25*(3), 174–192.

Dirienzo, L.N., Dirienzo, L.T., & Baceski, D.A. (2007). Heart rate response to therapeutic riding in children with cerebral palsy: An exploratory study. *Pediatric Physical Therapy, 19*(2), 160–165.

Farias-Tomaszewski, S., Jenkins, S.R., & Keller, J. (2001). An evaluation of therapeutic horseback riding programs for adults with physical impairments. *Therapeutic Recreation Journal, 35*(3), 250–257.

Gray, A.C. (2008). The effects of therapeutic horseback riding with autistic children. *Dissertation Abstracts International, 168*(11), 7663B. (UMI No. 3288822)

Häkanson, M., Möller, M., Lindström, I., & Mattsson, B. (2009). The horse as the healer: A study of riding in patients with back pain. *Journal of Bodywork and Movement Therapies, 13*(1), 43–52.

Hemenway, R. (2007). Effects of horseback riding on depression and self-esteem in adolescent girls. *Dissertation Abstracts International, 67*(7), 4133B. (UMI No. 3227367)

Honda, A., & Yamazaki, K. (2006). Effects of horseback riding and contact with horses on mood change and heart rate. *Japanese Journal of Health Psychology, 19*(1), 48–55.

Iannone, V.N. (2003). Evaluation of a vocational and therapeutic riding program for severely emotionally disturbed adolescents. *Dissertation Abstracts International, 64*(3), 1493B. (UMI No. 2084421)

Kaiser, L., Smith, K.A., Heleski, C.R., & Spence, L.J. (2006). Effects of a therapeutic riding program on at-risk and special education children. *Journal of the American Veterinary Medical Association, 228*(1), 46–52.

Klontz, B.T., Bivens, A., Leinart, D., & Klontz, T. (2007). The effectiveness of equine-assisted experiential therapy: Results of an open clinical trial. *Society and Animals, 15*(3), 257–267.

Koch, L.F. (2008). Equine therapy: What impact does owning or riding a horse have on the emotional well-being of women? *Dissertation Abstracts International, 69*(1), 406A. (UMI No. 3291950)

Lessick, M., Shinaver, R., Post, K.M., Rivera, J.E., & Lemon, B. (2004). Therapeutic horseback riding. Exploring this alternative therapy for women with disabilities. *AWHONN Lifelines/Association of Women's Health, Obstetric and Neonatal Nurses, 8*(1), 46–53.

Macauley, B.L., & Gutierrez, K.M. (2004, Summer). The effectiveness of hippotherapy for children with language-learning disabilities. *Communication Disorders Quarterly, 25*(4), 205–217.

MacKinnon, J.R., Noh, S., Laliberte, D., Lariviere, J., & Allan, D.E. (1995). Therapeutic horseback riding: A review of the literature. *Physical and Occupational Therapy in Pediatrics, 15*(1), 1–15.

McGee, M.C., & Reese, N.B. (2009). Immediate effects of a hippotherapy session on gait parameters in children with spastic cerebral palsy. *Pediatric Phyisical Therapy, 21*(2), 212–218.

McGibbon, N.H., Benda, W., Duncan, B.R., & Silkwood-Sherer, D. (2009). Immediate and long-term effects of hippotherapy on symmetry of adductor muscle activity and functional ability in children with spastic cerebral palsy. *Archives of Physical Medicine and Rehabilitation, 90*(6), 966–974.

Meinersmann, K.M., Bradberry, J., & Roberts, F.B. (2008). Equine-facilitated psychotherapy with adult female survivors of abuse. *Journal of Psychosocial Nursing and Mental Health Services, 46*(12), 36–42.

NARHA. (2009). *NARHA.* Retrieved February 16, 2010, from http://www.narha.org

National Institute of Child Health and Human Development. (2008). *Autism spectrum disorders (ASDs).* Retrieved February 16, 2010, from http://www.nichd.nih.gov/health/topics/asd.cfm

National Institute of Child Health and Human Development. (2010). *Human–animal interaction (HAI) research.* Retrieved February 16, 2010, from http://www.nichd.nih.gov/about/org/crmc/cdb/prog_hai/index.cfm

Pauw, J. (2000). Therapeutic horseback riding studies: Problems experienced by researchers. *Physiotherapy, 86*(10), 523–527.

Russell-Martin, L.A. (2007). Equine facilitated couples therapy and solution focused couples therapy: A comparison study. *Dissertation Abstracts International, 67*(9), 5421B. (UMI No. 3234094)

Rutter, M., Baily, A., & Lord, C. (2003). *Social Communication Questionnaire (SCQ).* Los Angeles: Western Psychological Services.

Schwesig, R., Neumann, S., Richter, D., Kauert, R., Becker, S., Esperer, H.D., et al. (2009). Impact of therapeutic riding on gait and posture regulation. *Sportverletz Sportschaden, 23*(2), 84–94.

Scialli, A.L. (2003). Parent perceptions of the effectiveness of therapeutic horseback riding for children with varying disabilities. *Dissertation Abstracts International, 63*(7), 2717A. (UMI No. 3059032)

Shurtleff, T.L., Standeven, J.W., & Engsberg, J.R. (2009). Changes in dynamic trunk/head stability and functional reach after hippotherapy. *Archives of Physical Medicine and Rehabilitation, 90*(7), 1185–1195.

Silkwood-Sherer, D., & Warmbier, H. (2007). Effects of hippotherapy on postural stability, in persons with multiple sclerosis: A pilot study. *Journal of Neurologic Physical Therapy, 31,* 77–84.

Snider, L., Korner-Bitensky, N., Kammann, C., Warner, S., & Saleh, M. (2007). Horseback riding as therapy for children with cerebral palsy: Is there evidence of its effectiveness? *Physical and Occupational Therapy in Pediatrics, 27*(2), 5–23.

Sole, D.P. (2007). Effects of equine-facilitated therapy on self-efficacy beliefs of cerebral palsied pre-adolescents and adolescents. *Dissertation Abstracts International, 67*(8), 4723B. (UMI No. 13228130)

Sterba, J.A. (2007). Does horseback riding therapy or therapist-directed hippotherapy rehabilitate children with cerebral palsy? *Developmental Medicine and Child Neurology, 49*(1), 68–73.

Vidrine, M., Owen-Smith, P., & Faulkner, P. (2002). Equine-facilitated group psychotherapy: Applications for therapeutic vaulting. *Issues in Mental Health Nursing, 23*(6), 587–603.

Vilà, C., Leonard, J.A., Gotherstrom, A., Marklund, S., Sandberg, K., Liden, K., et al. (2001). Widespread origins of domestic horse lineages. *Science, 291*(5503), 474–477.

Weber, P.C. (2005). The effect of therapeutic horseback riding on self-esteem of children with disabilities. *Dissertation Abstracts International, 66*(5), 1962A–1963A. (UMI No. 3176972)

Yorke, J., Adams, C., & Coady, N. (2008). Therapeutic value of equine–human bonding in recovery from trauma. *Anthrozoos, 21*(1), 17–30.

CHAPTER 10

The Roles That Animals Can Play with Individuals with Autism

TEMPLE GRANDIN

This chapter starts with a general introduction to autism and then goes on to discuss the role of animals for helping individuals with autism. I am a person with autism, and I will explain some of the problems that are faced by individuals with autism. This discussion will assist the reader in understanding the role that animals can play in assisting both children and adults on the autism spectrum. To work effectively with individuals with autism, it is necessary to understand how they perceive the world.

Autism is a highly variable disorder that ranges from very severe to mild. It is a spectrum of traits. A core neurological deficit in autism is difficulty relating to other people socially (Volkmar, Carter, Grossman, & Klin, 1997). In a severe case, an individual remains nonverbal and must live in a supervised living situation for the rest of his or her life, whereas in a mild case an individual might be a brilliant scientist or skilled computer programmer who lives independently. Another characteristic of autism and the milder variant, Asperger syndrome, is an obsessive interest in a favorite subject (e.g., trains, dinosaurs, sports stars). With the help of creative teachers and mentors, children on the milder end of the spectrum can become successful adults. I was one of those autistic kids. My science teacher got me interested in science by redirecting my obsessive interests. For example, when I got fixated on optical illusions after seeing them in a movie, he challenged me to make the illusions and to read scientific articles about them. Many brilliant scientists, musicians, and artists, including Einstein, Mozart, and Andy Warhol, would probably be labeled as either autistic or as having Asperger syndrome today (Grandin, 1996; Ledgin, 2002).

On the other end of the spectrum are children and adults with severe autism who cannot speak and whose sensory systems provide jumbled, scrambled information. First-person reports from individuals on the spectrum provide valuable insights into their sensory problems (Grandin, 2006; Mukhopadhyay, 2008; Williams, 1988). Tito Mukhopadhyay, a nonverbal man with autism, is able to type independently and describe how he perceives a fragmented world. Many people with severe autism are also *monochannel;* they are not able to hear and see at the same time (Mukhopadhyay, 2008; Williams, 1988). They either have to look at something or listen to it, but cannot do both at the same time. People who are monochannel will have a preferred sense and will usually learn best if the preferred sense is used.

SENSORY PROBLEMS IN AUTISM

Scientific research clearly shows that the sensory systems are abnormal and often hypersensitive in individuals with autism spectrum disorders (Davis, Bockbrader, Murphy, Hetrick, & O'Donnell, 2006; Leekam, Nieto, Libby, Wing, & Gould, 2007; Wiggens, Rubins, Bakemann, & Adamson, 2009). The sensory problems discussed in this section may also occur in other disorders such as head injury, dyslexia, and learning problems. In my own case, loud noises hurt my ears and feel like a dentist's drill hitting a nerve. The sound of the school bell was torture, and I often screamed when a sudden loud noise occurred. Problems with oversensitive senses can be extremely variable. One child may love the sound of running water and want to play in it, and another child may run away from it screaming because it hurts his or her ears. High-pitched, sudden sounds, such as smoke alarms, are often the sounds that are most likely to be painful to a person with autism.

Problems with auditory processing of speech sounds have been documented in scientific studies (Russo, Zecker, Trammer, Chen, & Kraus, 2009). It has also been noted that the autistic brain has problems filtering out distracting sounds (Teder-Sälejärvi, Pierce, Courchesne, & Hillyard, 2005). Although a person with autism may have a normal ability to hear faint sounds, there may be deficits in hearing auditory detail. When I was tested for auditory processing disorders in the early 1990s, my test results showed that my auditory acuity was normal but I had difficulty hearing and processing hard consonant sounds (Grandin, 1996). I often have difficulty determining whether somebody said "cat" or "pat." To figure this out, I have to go by the context of the speech.

In addition to having problems with auditory processing, some people with autism cannot tolerate fluorescent lights, and they are more likely to engage in repetitive behaviors in a room with fluorescent lights (Coleman, Frankel, Ritvoe, & Freeman, 1976). Individuals who cannot tolerate fluorescent lights often report that the room is flickering like a strobe light. They can see the 60-cycle flicker of standard fluorescent lamps. Many small compact fluorescents that screw into a lamp also flicker. It is best to use incandescent bulbs or electronic fluorescent lights that have a much higher cycle rate than 60 cycles.

Touch sensitivity is also a challenge for some individuals. For example, I cannot stand the feeling of itchy, scratchy wool against my skin. It is like rough sandpaper on raw exposed nerve endings. Other individuals who have more severe problems with touch sensitivity have reported that certain fabrics caused a burning sensation. An autistic child or adult who has a tantrum every time he or she goes into a large supermarket usually has severe sensory oversensitivity in more than one sense. These are individuals who cannot tolerate a noisy restaurant, large crowds, or loud movies. Problems with sensory oversensitivity are often worse when the person gets tired. A trip to the supermarket that may be uneventful in the morning may not be possible when the individual becomes fatigued in the afternoon.

Sensory Preferences

Some individuals on the autism spectrum, like me, learn visually presented information better, and others learn better through the auditory sense. Each person uses the sense that gives him or her the most accurate information. Reports from auditory thinkers indicate that vision often produces a jumble of patterns and hearing works better for them (Mukhopadhyay, 2008; Williams, 1988). Mukhopadhyay writes, "My dominant sensory channel is hearing. It dominates to such an extent that I dream in sounds." Visual thinkers like me much prefer written words and learn better when they can use vision. I have a terrible time remembering long strings of verbal directions.

Some individuals have such severe sensory problems that they probably do not receive accurate information through their malfunctioning visual and auditory systems. These individuals perceive the world by touch and smell because those senses provide more accurate information. A touch schedule may help such individuals schedule their lives. One innovative group home had good results and fewer tantrums when a touch schedule was used with nonverbal clients. Some nonverbal people cannot learn to use a picture schedule. One client was given a spoon to hold 5 minutes before dinnertime so that he would know that dinner was coming soon. A washcloth was given to him shortly before shower time. This system enabled him to be mentally ready for the next event, and it prevented the panic that is caused by sudden surprises.

For my kind of mind, all thoughts are in pictures. When I think about the sounds that hurt my ears, such as a horn on a ferryboat, I see a picture of the boat before I hear its awful horn. When I think of a sound word such as "bang bang," I immediately see visual images in my imagination of the places and the objects that make banging sounds that hurt my ears. My mind works like the Google search engine for images. The first image that flashed into my imagination was some stuntmen staging a western gunfight in Arizona. Research done with brain scans shows that people with autism process nonvisual information such as written words in the visual cortex (Gaffney et al., 2007; Kana, Keller, Cherkassky, Minshew, & Just, 2006), although nonautistic people use the language parts of the brain.

Attention Shifting Is Slow

Scientific research has also shown that people on the autism spectrum shift attention much more slowly than do people without autism and that the brains of individuals with severe autism process information extremely slowly compared with those of people without autism (Teder-Sälejärvi et al., 2005). They have difficulty shifting their attention away from a stimulus after it has locked in their attention (Landry & Bryson, 2004). It takes a much longer time to shift back and forth between two different stimuli. This delay can vary from half a second for a person on the higher end of the spectrum to up to 5 minutes for more severe cases. Teachers must be careful to avoid the problem of *clipping*. Clipping occurs when an individual fails to hear the first part of a sentence because his or her attention has not shifted. To avoid this problem, get the individual's attention first before giving him or her directions. For instance, you might say, "Tommy, I need to talk to you." This sentence will shift the child's attention and then he will hear the next sentence with the instructions in its entirety.

One use of this technique in a human–animal interaction setting would be giving the client in a riding class a riding helmet to hold 5 minutes before class begins. Holding the helmet will enable the client to get his or her attention shifted to "It's time for riding." The next step would be to let him touch the horse 5 minutes before it is time to mount and ride.

Fractured Perception

Reports from individuals on the spectrum with severe sensory processing problems can give the reader a glimpse into the world of malfunctioning sensory systems. Mukhopadhyay writes that he has difficulty perceiving both the shape of an object and its color at the same time. For example, when he sees a door, he has to perceive its color first and then its shape (Mukhopadhyay, 2008). New things are often frightening to individuals on the spectrum. To prevent this fear, teachers and therapists should present each new thing slowly and give the person time to perceive it. They must remember that the autistic brain processes information slowly. A report from one individual with both autism and severe visual processing problems indicated that his perception was not normal. When he was first introduced to a dog, he had to do a lot of touching and feeling to determine that the collar and leash were not actually part of the dog.

RESPONSES TO ANIMALS

Individuals with autism can also have highly variable responses to animals. Many parents have reported to me that their child has a magical connection with their dog that he or she does not have with people. They feel that the dog and child completely understand each other and the dog seeks the child's attention. However, there is another group of children and adults on the autism spectrum who are terrified of dogs. One mother wrote to me that her nonverbal son started screaming when he saw a dog. Why is the relationship with animals so variable for individuals with autism? The individuals who avoid animals do so because the sound or smell of the animal causes pain or sensory overload. For them, a dog barking would hurt their ears the same way that the school bell hurt my ears. Dogs and cats can sometimes be unpredictable, and individuals may avoid them because they never know when the animal will make a noise. For a sound-sensitive individual, a silent animal such as a rabbit might be a better choice. Smell is another problem for some individuals. Strong smells make them gag. Some individuals cannot tolerate the smell of the animal. Keeping the animal clean and well groomed will help prevent problems with smells. In fact, I like the smell of cattle and horses and usually have no problem with animal smells. However, when I stayed at a friend's house I could not tolerate the smell of their dog. The dog had rotten teeth and a bad smell that I could not stand. It was one of the very few dogs that I could not tolerate being near. This experience gave me insight into how some individuals with severe smell sensitivity may respond.

Other individuals start screaming when they see rapid motion. Again, the response to rapid motion is very variable. As a child, I loved automatic doors and rapid motion, yet another child may run screaming from them. Mukhopadhyay was attracted to things that moved rapidly, such as trains and fans. An individual who is sensitive to rapid motion may also avoid an animal because its movements are unpredictable. Again, these individual responses should be taken into consideration when deciding whether animal interaction is a good idea, and if it is, with what type of animal a particular autistic child might successfully interact.

The Magical Connection with Animals

For every individual on the autistic spectrum who avoids animals, there is another individual who has a wonderful bond with them. One of the most beautiful descriptions of the connection was written by Dawn Prince-Hughes in her book *Songs of the Gorilla Nation* (2005). Dawn was a homeless woman with autism who got a job working at the zoo where she made friends with the gorillas. She spent hours watching the gorillas to learn their behavior and their emotions. Being with the gorillas was a sanctuary away from the difficult social world in which she lived.

Many parents have told me that their nonverbal child has a wonderful relationship with their dog. The child is able to get the dog to do anything he wants. Often, nonverbal children or adults with autism have deep relationships with animals. In all of these cases, the animal really bonded with the individual and followed the individual everywhere. *A Friend Like Henry* by Nuala Gardner (2008) is another book about an autistic child's fantastic relationship with a dog.

When I was in high school, being teased, horses were my salvation. Riding horses and working in the horse barn was a refuge away from teasing. The kids who did the teasing were not the same kids who were interested in horses and riding. One might ask, why would an individual with autism understand an animal better than a nonautistic person? I think it is due to different ways of thinking. In my many writings, I have described how I think in pictures (Grandin, 2006, 2009). Words narrate the pictures in my imagination. An animal also lives in a sensory world that is not a world of verbal language.

HOW ANIMALS THINK

Both my thinking and an animal's thinking are sensory based instead of being based on verbal language. A dog will store memories in its brain in the form of images, sounds, tastes, touch feelings, or smells of specific things that it has experienced. Imagine the smell world of a dog. When the dog visits the local tree where every dog has left its mark, that tree contains lots of information. The dog will know who was there, when they were there, whether they are friend or foe, and their rank in the social order. This information can all be conveyed without any words. A person who uses sensory perception instead of verbal thoughts to understand the world is more likely to really relate well with an animal that may perceive the world in similar ways.

Some individuals on the autism spectrum think in pictures like me, others think in sounds, and still others may think in touch or smells. Sensory thoughts consist of sorting sensory information into categories. For example, foods that taste good and foods that taste bad are examples of taste categories. As I write this, I am visualizing fun experiences and frightening ones. Pictures of specific fun and frightening experiences are flashing through my mind. I can access either the "fun" or the "scary" file. Pictures flash through my memory like a series of PowerPoint slides of specific fun and scary events. Examples of specific fun experiences are designing a project with a good friend and water skiing. Examples of scary experiences are driving on an icy freeway and driving near a steep cliff. Each picture is a specific experience. My concept of fun or scary is based on a history of specific past experiences.

A dog also categorizes its behavior. When it is wearing a service dog vest, it must engage in work behavior. When the vest is taken off, it can engage in play activities. It is as if there are two big files in the dog's brain: "work" and "play." The dog must be taught specific behaviors for work. For example, when the vest is on, it cannot bark, chase balls, or jump on people. It must also stay close to its master. A dog has no abstract concept of "work." It knows only specific behaviors and each specific behavior must be put in either the "work" or "play" file in its brain. Brain research shows that the brain sets up file folders with distinct boundaries (Freedman, Riesenhuber, Poggio, & Miller, 2001). For a service dog, the two most important files are "work" and "play." To prevent the dog from becoming confused, it is important to not engage it in play behaviors when the vest is on.

Over the years, I have observed that some of the best horse and dog trainers are either dyslexic or have many Asperger/autism traits. Visual thinking is also common in people with dyslexia. They too may have difficulty understanding people but understanding animals comes easily to them (Grandin & Johnson, 2009).

CHOOSING THE RIGHT DOG

Individuals with autism often refuse to or are unable to socially engage with others. Thus, the best dog to use to engage an autistic child is a friendly dog that keeps trying to engage the child, rather than a dog that cowers in a corner. There are always possible exceptions to this recommendation, and it is important to do some preliminary work to be sure that the child is not afraid of dogs, but friendly, calm dogs will probably be the best choices. A common problem among autistic children is that they sometimes do not know how to pet an animal gently. They may grab and pull at the dog. They need to be taught to stroke an animal and not to squeeze it too tightly. Steady, friendly dogs such as Labradors or golden retrievers usually tolerate this behavior better than small, fragile, nervous dogs. In addition, the small, fragile dogs are more likely to be injured when a child with severe autism has a tantrum. Large, calm dogs also provide the advantage of being less likely to bark and scare a child who has sensitive hearing.

Discussions with teachers and dog trainers indicate that sometimes a child and a dog are instant buddies, and other times it takes time for the child to get to know the dog and bond with it. A child may be afraid of the dog at first, but then grow to really love it. New things are often scary for individuals with autism. Sometimes teachers and parents have to be gently insistent to get a child to try new experiences. It is also important to first introduce the dog in a quiet environment that is free of fluorescent lights and other stimuli that may cause sensory overload. If a lot of noise occurs at the moment the child sees the dog, he or she may associate the animal with the painful stimuli.

HOW ANIMALS CAN HELP

Unfortunately, there is a lack of scientific literature on the benefits of therapy animals for children and adults with autism. I have observed that for some people on the spectrum, an animal has greatly improved their lives. One of the difficulties of studying the human–animal bond in autism is the great variability of the spectrum. An animal works wonders with one individual and may have little positive effect on another. For people who are considering animal-assisted therapy for an individual with autism, there are two excellent books. They are *Animal Assisted Therapy* by M. Pavlides (2008) and *The Golden Bridge* by P.D. Gross (2006). From my own observations and from reports from both parents and individuals on the spectrum, it is obvious that animals are a great benefit for certain individuals. Here are some of the main areas where animals can be beneficial.

Companionship

A pet dog provides companionship and serves as a social icebreaker. Pets offer these same beneficial effects for people who do not have autism. Depression is often a problem in higher functioning individuals with autism. If a pet can help a depressed nonautistic person cope, it may also help a depressed person with autism. I know many people on the spectrum who have greatly improved their lives by acquiring pets. One lady loves her cats, and they cheer her up when she is feeling down. An advantage of having a trained service dog is that it can always be with the person, because it is allowed to enter restaurants and shops. This can be really helpful for shy or anxious people.

Adjunct to Therapy

In this situation, a psychologist or other professional owns the dog and it is present during counseling sessions. The dog's presence can be very beneficial and may help a person open up and discuss problems. Again, this type of service animal can help both people on the autism spectrum and nonautistic people. A creative therapist can use the dog in many different ways to relate with an individual with autism. The dog can help initiate contact with the individual or can take part in an interactive game such as playing fetch. Some therapists encourage individuals with poor speech to ask the dog to follow commands such as sit or shake hands. The dog can help the client open up avenues for social interaction with other people.

Therapeutic Riding

Horseback riding was my favorite activity in high school, and many children and adults on the autism spectrum respond very well to therapeutic riding. One research study showed that therapeutic riding improved social functioning (Bass, Duchowny, & Llabre, 2009). Several parents have told me that their child said his or her first words on a horse. Occupational therapists who work with autistic children may be able to provide an explanation for the beneficial effects of riding on speech. In their therapeutic treatments, they often use rhythmic swinging and balancing activities, which stimulate the vestibular system (Ayres, 1979) and have a calming effect on the brain. Riding involves both rhythm and balancing. Ray, King, and Grandin (1988) found that swinging can stimulate speech sounds. Teachers who adopt the Miller method use activities that involve balancing with autistic children (Miller, Chretien, & Twachtman-Cullen, 2007).

In the book *Horse Boy*, Rupert Isaacson (2009) described the great progress that his young son with autism made when he rode horses in Mongolia and at a ranch in Texas. In both of these places, the environment was quiet and the boy was less likely to become overstimulated. I predict that therapeutic riding may be more effective if it is done in a place that is quiet. A large arena that has multiple horse activities going on at the same time may cause sensory overload. An outdoor setting or an indoor arena dedicated solely to therapeutic riding will provide a more sensory-friendly environment.

It is very important to choose appropriate horses for a therapeutic riding program. For severely autistic nonverbal children, quiet placid horses are the best choice. For nonverbal clients or children with severe sensory problems, it is important to have horses that are not going to make sudden frightening moves. However, some individuals with autism will not want to ride placid horses. I showed horses when I was in high school. Our stable had a wide range of horses ranging from a slow, furry old horse named Teddy, to Lady, who was pretty and spirited. I chose Lady, whereas Teddy would have been the perfect mount for many little kids' riding programs.

Interviews with people who run therapeutic riding centers and the scientific literature both indicate that care must be taken to prevent the horses from becoming stressed or lame. Going around and around a ring all day can become stressful for a horse. Problems with lameness have also been reported. Dr. Lana Kaiser and her associates at Michigan State University found that horses in a well-run therapeutic riding program displayed the same number of stress-related behaviors (e.g., pinned ears, head tossing) when they were ridden by special-education students as when they were ridden by recreational riders (Equine Science Update, 2006; Kaiser, Heleski, Siegford, & Smith, 2006). However, when horses were ridden by nonautistic children who had poor grades or disciplinary actions at school, they showed increased stress behaviors. These children did not have a relationship with the animal, and they often treated it like a tool.

Safety Service Dog

A safety service dog is specially trained to prevent a severely autistic child from running away. These dogs can be very beneficial (Burrows, Adams, & Spiers, 2008). The dog has to be highly trained and the parents have to receive training on how to work with the dog. Dr. K.E. Burrows at the Ontario Veterinary College has done extensive studies of these dogs. Parents reported to her that despite the extra work associated with keeping a dog, the benefits of keeping the child safe and providing companionship to him or her made it worthwhile (Burrows, Adams, & Millman, 2008). When a dog is involved in safeguarding a child, both the child and the dog must be well suited for each other. Suzanne Millman, one of the authors of the Burrows at al. (2008) study, told me that most of the dogs bonded with the parents rather than the child. Her descriptions of some of the parents' problems indicated that they lacked an understanding of how to care for a dog (e.g., failing to recognize the dog's need to have regular breaks so that it could urinate). The best providers of service dogs will not provide a dog to a family that is not able to care for it properly. Unfortunately, less responsible providers are less concerned about the animal being stressed. Service dogs that have the demanding role of safeguarding a child with severe autism must be given time off every day for an hour of fun play.

Training a good service dog is expensive. However, there are some charitable groups such as Tender Loving Canines in San Diego, which assigns dogs to families at no cost. The group selects families in which the dog is more likely to bond with the child. The bottom line is that a service dog that provides safety for a child with severe autism is appropriate for some families and not appropriate for others. The welfare of the animals must always be maintained. When the right dog is paired with the right family, a wonderful relationship can take place.

CONCLUSIONS

Individuals with autism disorders represent a variable spectrum, ranging from people who will remain nonverbal to brilliant verbal people such as Einstein. Animals can improve the lives of many of these individuals. People on the spectrum are socially awkward, and animals can help them open up social interactions.

Interactions with animals can bring significant benefits. Service dogs are beneficial in three basic ways: 1) as companions, 2) as adjuncts to therapy, and 3) to protect the safety of children with severe autism. Horseback riding is also very beneficial for some individuals. Others may not respond well to animals because of a variety of characteristics, such as sensory hypersensitivity, so care must be taken to match the specific autistic individual with an animal that has the right characteristics.

REFERENCES

Ayres, J.A. (1979). Sensory integration and the child. Los Angeles, CA: Western Psychological Services.

Bass, M.M., Duchowny, C.A., & Llabre, M.M. (2009). The effect of therapeutic horseback riding on social functioning in children with autism. Journal of Autism and Developmental Disorders, 39, 1261–1267.

Burrows, K.E., Adams, C.L., & Millman, S.T. (2008). Factors affecting behavior and welfare of service dogs for children with autism spectrum disorder. Journal of Applied Animal Welfare Science, 11, 42–62.

Burrows, K.E., Adams, C.L., & Spiers, J. (2008). Sentinels of safety: Service dogs ensure safety and enhance freedom and well being for families of autistic children. Quality Health Research, 18, 1642–1649.

Coleman, R.S., Frankel, F., Ritvoe, E., & Freeman, B.J. (1976). The effects of
fluorescent and incandescent illumination upon repetitive behaviors in
autistic children. *Journal of Autism and Developmental Disorders, 6,* 157–162.
Davis, R.A., Bockbrader, M.A., Murphy, R.R., Hetrick, W.P., & O'Donnell, B.F.
(2006). Subjective perceptions, distortions, and visual dysfunction in children with autism. *Journal of Autism and Developmental Disorders, 36,* 199–210.
Equine Science Update. (2006). *Do horses find therapeutic riding stressful?*
Retrieved August 21, 2009, from http://www.equinescienceupdate.co.uk/
behav3.htm
Freedman, D.J., Riesenhuber, M., Poggio, T., & Miller, E.K. (2001). Categorical
representation of visual stimuli in the primate prefrontal cortex. *Science, 291,*
312–315.
Gaffney, M.S., Kleinharns, N.M., Haist, F., Akshoomoff, N., Campbell, A.,
Courchesne, E., et al. (2007). Atypical participation of the visual cortex dur-
ing word processing in autism: An fMRI study semantic decision.
Neuropsychologia, 45, 1672–1684.
Gardner, N. (2008). *A friend like Henry.* Naperville, IL: Sourcebooks, Inc.
Grandin, T. (1996). *Thinking in pictures: And other reports of my life with autism.*
New York: Bantam.
Grandin, T. (2006). *Thinking in pictures* (expanded edition). New York: Vintage
Press.
Grandin, T. (2009). How does visual thinking work in the mind of a person
with autism? A personal account. *Philosophical Transactions of the Royal
Society, 364,* 1437–1442.
Grandin T., & Johnson, C. (2009). *Animals make us human.* Boston: Houghton
Mifflin, Harcourt.
Gross, P.D. (2006). *The golden bridge: A guide to assistance dogs for children chal-
lenged by autism or other developmental disorders.* West Lafayette, IN: Purdue
University Press.
Isaacson, R. (2009). *Horse boy.* New York: Little Brown.
Kaiser, L., Heleski, C.R., Siegford, J., & Smith, K.A. (2006). Stress-related behav-
iors among horses used in therapeutic riding programs. *Journal of the
American Veterinary Medical Association, 228,* 39–45.
Kana, R.K., Keller, T.A., Cherkassky, V.L., Minshew, N.J., & Just, M.A. (2006).
Sentence comprehensive in autism thinking in pictures with decreased
functional connectivity. *Brain, 129*(9), 2484–2493.
Landry, R., & Bryson, S.E. (2004). Impaired disengagement of attention in young
children with autism. *Journal of Child Psychology and Psychiatry, 45,* 1115–1122.
Ledgin, N. (2002). *Asperger's and self-esteem: Insight and hope through famous role
models.* Arlington, TX: Future Horizons.
Leekam, S.R., Nieto, C., Libby, S.J., Wing, L., & Gould, J. (2007). Describing the
sensory abnormalities of children and adults with autism. *Journal of Autism
and Developmental Disorders, 37,* 894–910.
Miller, A., Chretien, K., & Twachtman-Cullen, D. (2007). *The Miller Method:
Developing the capacities of children on the autism spectrum.* London: Jessica
Kingsley Publishers.
Mukhopadhyay, T.R. (2008). *How can I talk if my lips don't move?* New York:
Arcade Publishing.
Pavlides, M. (2008). *Animal-assisted therapy.* London: Jessica Kingsley Publishing.
Prince-Hughes, D. (2005). *Songs of the gorilla nation.* New York: Three Rivers
Press.
Ray, T.C., King, L.J., & Grandin, T. (1988). The effectiveness of self-initiated
vestibular stimulation in producing speech sounds in an autistic child.
Journal of Occupational Therapy Research, 8, 186–190.
Russo, N., Zecker, S., Trammer, B., Chen, J., & Kraus, N. (2009). Effects of back-
ground noise on cortical processing of speech in autism spectrum disorders.
Journal of Autism and Developmental Disorders, 39, 1185–1196.

Teder-Sälejärvi, W.A., Pierce, K.A., Courchesne, E., & Hillyard, S.A. (2005). Auditory spatial localization and attention deficits in autistic adults. *Cognitive Brain Research, 23,* 221–234.

Volkmar, F., Carter, A., Grossman, J., & Klin, A. (1997). Social development in autism. In D.J. Cohen & F.R. Volkmar (Eds.), *Handbook of autism and pervasive developmental disorders* (2nd ed., pp. 173–194). New York: John Wiley and Sons.

Wiggens, L.D., Rubins, D.L., Bakemann, R., & Adamson, L.B. (2009). Brief report: Sensory abnormalities and distinguishing symptoms in autism spectrum disorders in young children. *Journal of Autism and Developmental Disorders, 39,* 1087–1091.

Williams, D. (1988). *Autism: An inside out approach.* London: Jessica Kingsley Publishers.

Future Research

This final section of the volume discusses why it is important for research on human–animal interaction (HAI) to provide an evidence base that can be used in practice and to advise parents and teachers about promoting healthy interactions between children and pets. The chapters discuss research designs and methods, as well as some of the challenges in the study of HAI, and argue that greater communication and collaboration between researchers and practitioners in the field would have a number of benefits. The chapters that make up this section present approaches, illustrated with data, concerning how to evaluate existing programs, and describe some of the measures that are currently available to accomplish this task. In Chapter 11, Trujillo, Tedeschi, and Williams tackle the issues of training clinicians on how and when to implement HAI in therapeutic sessions, and describe the evidence for the benefits of such practices. They discuss the types of decisions that must be made in various clinical settings in order to decide whether animal involvement might be warranted and beneficial and to protect both the children and the animals in such interactions. The aim is to weigh the potential advantages and disadvantages of involving animals in the treatment of children as well as the kind of care and research evidence that can be used to inform such decisions.

Thorpe, Serpell, and Suomi then review designs and methods that have been used in the study of HAI to date, some of the challenges in the study of HAI, and what is now needed from the in-the-field perspective to move the field toward evidence-based practice. Finally, in Chapter 13, Griffin, McCune, Maholmes, and Hurley discuss the most important research areas, topics, and specific research questions that the field is poised to answer. They indicate methods and measures that exist to answer those questions or that need to be developed, challenges that exist for the field, the importance of including research in the ongoing design and implementation of therapies that focus on HAI, and why the evidence base that will be built in this way is important. The chapter will serve as a call to action for researchers in the field and a call to practitioners to implement evidence-based practices and to participate in evaluations of ongoing therapies and research to design and study the effectiveness of potential new interventions.

Leon's Postdoctorate in Human–Animal Interaction

Leon was finishing his doctorate in developmental psychology at a prestigious university in the northwest. He had always liked kids and been curious about what factors influenced their development, so it was the perfect field for him. As he progressed through his education, he became increasingly focused on how children developed socially and emotionally. Recently, he had heard a paper at a national meeting of researchers on child development. The title captured his interest, as it addressed how the interactions between children and animals might affect children's ability to deal with grief and loss. The presenter was engaging and made a good case, but Leon's research training made him question some of the sweeping claims that the presenter was making. Were there really enough data? The presenter's conclusions were a composite that she had drawn from five clinical case studies, spread out over time, a collection of her clinical experiences all pulled together in what Leon had to admit was a very convincing way.

In the question-and-answer period, a woman stood up and began to talk about the need for stringent research methods. The audience and presenter then engaged in what Leon found to be an enlightening dialogue about this "new field" of study examining how pets and therapy animals might influence the health and well-being of both children and adults. After the session, he approached the researcher who had first opened this dialogue. She invited him to coffee, and they spent an hour and a half talking about the need for more rigorous research in human–animal interaction (HAI).

Over the course of the next few months, Leon not only began to read more about HAI, but he also stayed in touch with the researcher he had met. She invited him to apply for a postdoctoral fellowship through the government, offered to sponsor him at her university for the fellowship, and agreed to help him write the application. Leon was off on an exciting research adventure. He was committed to applying what he had learned about research in child development to the study of how HAI might affect both children's health and well-being, as well as how therapeutic interactions might optimally be studied to determine their efficacy.

CHAPTER 11

Research Meets Practice

Issues for Evidence-Based Training in Human–Animal Interaction

KATE TRUJILLO, PHILIP TEDESCHI, AND JAMES HERBERT WILLIAMS

The field of human–animal interaction (HAI) is emerging as an academic discipline. Nowhere is this more noticeable than among North American universities, where new courses are consistently being added and new programs developed to meet this need. According to the Animals and Society Institute, a not-for-profit, independent research and educational organization that advances the status of animals in public policy and promotes the study of human–animal relationships, courses in human–animal studies are offered in 26 disciplines at colleges and law schools in the United States and Canada. The organization continues to work alongside other institutions to establish both majors and minors in human–animal studies (Animals and Society Institute, 2009).

The most convincing data to support the investment in expanded research are observational and demographic data that demonstrate the importance of animals in our lives, as professionals and as clients. There are approximately 77.5 million pet dogs and 93.6 million pet cats in the United States; 39% of U.S. households own at least one dog, whereas 34% of U.S. households own at least one cat (American Pet Products Association, 2009).

In a recent study of pet owners in the United States, more than 97% of people agreed with the statement, "My pet is a member of my family." Participants who identified themselves as American Indian were most likely to have companion animals (73.5%; $n = 25/34$), followed by white people (65%; $n = 319/491$), people of Hispanic/Spanish heritage

(56.9%; $n = 41/72$), African Americans (40.9%; $n = 9/22$), Pacific Islanders (40%; $n = 2/5$), and Asians (37.5%; $n = 6/16$). Perhaps the most important finding is that for the subset of study participants who had cats, dogs, or both, there were no significant racial or ethnic differences among participants who reported that they receive emotional support, unconditional love, and companionship from their pets (Risley-Curtiss, Holley, & Wolf, 2006). What should be surprising is not that animals are included in therapeutic practice and research, but that it has taken so long for professions to recognize the importance and prevalence of animals in people's lives.

The relationship between people and animals offers a rich context for professional initiatives to improve a number of areas of human health. HAI, the intentional use of the human–animal relationship to achieve therapeutic goals, constitutes a powerful vehicle for change but remains relatively understudied, and many of the studies that have been done lack verifiable outcomes. As in other promising emerging fields of study, the pioneering efforts of practitioners combined with the participation of researchers allows for movement from practical and anecdotal methods to evidence-supported interventions. It is difficult for scholars and practitioners to keep pace with the changing demands of practice skills and settings.

Some research provides insight into how animals can support human health, and clients should be informed about such options for treatment. For example, the presence of a dog during a child's physical examination can decrease the child's stress (Baun, Oetting, & Bergstrom, 1991). Children who have pets and report a close attachment to their pets rate their family climate significantly better than children who do not have pets (Vizek Vidović, Vlahovic Stetic, & Bratko, 1999). Children with autism who have pets show more prosocial behaviors and fewer autism behaviors such as self-absorption (Redefer & Goodman, 1989). Older clients could benefit from relationships with animals as well. One study showed that seniors who own dogs go to the doctor less often than those who do not (Siegel, 1993). Another review of the literature suggests that visits of animals to long-term care facilities can increase patients' social interactions; decrease apathy, agitation, and aggression; and reduce blood pressure (Williams & Jenkins, 2008).

The University of Denver's Graduate School of Social Work has responded to the intuitive impulse of many social workers to include animals in practice by formalizing the importance of animals in the primary models of the school's educational courses. Since the beginning of this century, the school has progressed from offering one course, Integration of Animals into Therapeutic Settings, to offering an entire certificate program for master's students and a distance-learning professional

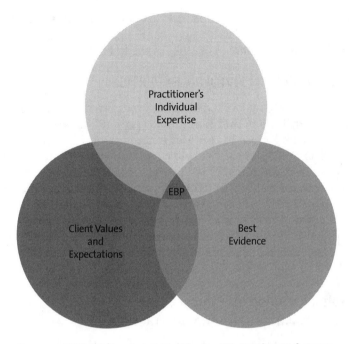

Figure 11.1.   EBP Model. (From Sackett, D.L., Richardson, W.S., Rosenberg, W., & Haynes, R.B. [1997]. *Evidence-based medicine: How to practice and teach EBM*. New York: Churchill Livingstone; reprinted by permission).

development curriculum. As of 2010, three doctoral dissertations on HAI were underway at the Graduate School.

Because social work emphasizes the importance of the person in his or her environment and seeks to recognize the strengths that clients bring to a situation, involving animals in practice is a natural step within the social work field (Gitterman & Germain, 2008; Saleeby, 1992). Because animals are such an integral part of life, it can be easy for well-meaning professionals to try to harness the benefits of the relationships shared with animals without fully considering the difference between having a pet and asking an animal to perform a certain job as part of a structured HAI. Practitioners of this field are striving to develop and implement quality programs and a research agenda that will continue to refine our understanding of how the human–animal bond works in professional capacities. Part of that effort requires us to thoughtfully build programs that are based on a set of principles that will lead us toward best practice.

Evidence-based practice includes three elements (Figure 11.1): 1) the practitioner's individual expertise, 2) best evidence, and 3) client values and expectations (National Institute of Mental Health et al., 2008; Sackett, Richardson, Rosenberg, & Haynes, 1997). This chapter addresses those elements by discussing key principles that have been identified as essential for building ethical HAI programs, the state of the evidence, and client values and expectations as they relate to HAI.

PRACTITIONER'S INDIVIDUAL EXPERTISE

The art and challenge of creating a program that involves living creatures, both human and nonhuman, presents unique ethical concerns that are important to consider in a discussion of evidence-based practice. The principles that we will cover offer a useful framework for developing new programs. They can be applied to existing programs or considered for training practitioners who wish to utilize the context that relationships with animals provide for healing interventions. As the field considers testing models that will lead us toward more evidence-based practice, it is important to select models for rigorous research that professionals agree aspire to the highest standards for human and animal welfare.

Principle 1: Develop an Ethical Compass that Guides Human–Animal Interaction

First and foremost, it is critical that a strong sense of ethics guide any HAI program. Training practitioners who are interested in incorporating animals in their professional work must learn to think critically about what it means to ask another animal to work alongside them. Our culture asks animals to play many roles. They are observed, experimented on, eaten, worn, written about, drawn, played with, and lived with (Bekoff, 2008). It is essential that serious attention be given to the emotional lives of animals (Balcombe, 2006).

The "five freedoms"[1] that follow summarize what most authorities accept as primary considerations for animal welfare that must be accounted for in any HAI (see also Farm Animal Welfare Council, 1993; Serpell, Coppinger, & Fine, 2006, p. 455):

1. Freedom from thirst, hunger, and malnutrition by ready access to fresh water and a diet to maintain full health and vigor.

2. Freedom from discomfort by providing a suitable environment, including shelter and a comfortable resting area.

3. Freedom from pain, injury, and disease by prevention and/or rapid diagnosis and treatment.

---

[1]From the Information and Policy Team Office of Public Sector Information, St. Clements House. (1965). *Report of the Technical Committee to Enquire into the Welfare of Animals Kept Under Intensive Livestock Husbandry Systems, the Brambell Report.* Norwich, United Kingdom: Author; reprinted by permission.

4. Freedom from fear and distress by ensuring conditions that avoid mental suffering.

5. Freedom to express most normal behavior by providing sufficient space, proper facilities, and company of the animal's own kind.

Related to the fifth freedom and perhaps the most difficult to ensure is understanding an animal's social and emotional needs. Marc Beckoff, professor emeritus at the University of Colorado, writes about "anthropomorphic doubletalk," the tendency for people to accept easily that animals feel positive emotions but dismiss occasions when animals have negative emotions as anthropomorphism (Bekoff, 2008). As researchers, we must guard against being self-serving and recognizing animal emotions only when they support our agenda to implement a given HAI. It is unknown what it is like to be another species and how another species may think or feel differently, but there is mounting scientific evidence that helps in understanding that animals do indeed feel and how they feel (Balcombe, 2006; Bekoff, 2008; Rogers, 1998). It is better to use human language to describe animal emotion and take the risk of inaccurately understanding an animal than to disregard the animal's feelings entirely.

Limitations on personal freedom, life determination, training, social disconnection (e.g., separation of an animal from its own kind), and possible injuries as a result of service are all potential consequences for animals that engage in HAI. Practitioners must generate a cost–benefit analysis for the animal as they consider whether to include the animal in the interaction. A strict interpretation of what constitutes exploitation for an animal could lead to the conclusion that only dogs and horses are sufficiently domesticated and gain enough from their interactions that their roles in an HAI would not be exploitative (Zamir, 2006). However, programs already have introduced a variety of species into HAI. For example, Green Chimneys, a residential treatment facility in New York, employs a variety of farm animals, including goats and rabbits, as well as wild animals that have been injured and cannot live in the wild unless they are rehabilitated. Children in this program are assigned animals to care for during their own recovery. When a child is ready to leave Green Chimneys, the residents hold a group ceremony and release an animal that has recuperated as a symbol of the child's own achievement (Haddon, 1994). When this kind of partnership is carefully constructed to benefit both humans and nonhumans, it is an example of an ethical incorporation of an animal into a therapeutic role.

As models for practice the existing arguments for animal welfare must be considered. Human relationships with animals, both as pets and as professional helpers (e.g., Seeing Eye Dogs, police dogs, sheep herders, oxen, horses, therapy animals), are a reflection of human relationships with other humans. Without an ethical, caring, and sensitive approach to the partners in this work, human credibility as helpers is lost. Caring and empathetic relationships and techniques for inclusion of animals and training of animals that preserve people's integrity as caring and empathetic helpers must be modeled. Treating animal partners in any other way undermines the therapeutic process.

Principle 2: Know the Population of People Involved in the Human–Animal Interaction

Often, target populations for HAI are people who have been marginalized due to physical or mental illness, poverty, racial or ethnic discrimination, or other socially isolating factors. These factors, as well as the power disparity that is often experienced in the helper–helped relationship, create a situation in which clients may feel uncomfortable sharing their fears or discomfort with therapists. The introduction of animals to a therapeutic setting can sometimes make the situation less threatening and assist in healing (Tedeschi, Fitchett, & Molidor, 2006). Animals can also act as a "social lubricant," facilitating the relationship-building process between client and professional (Fine, 2006).

However, the impulse to include animals often has more to do with the preference of the practitioner than the desire of the client. Therefore, the practitioner needs to be sensitive to the client's wishes in order to maintain the integrity of the professional environment and healing nature of the intervention. The following questions are helpful in evaluating the situation: Does the client like animals? Does the client have a history of animal cruelty? Has the client been hurt by an animal? Does the client have pets? What has the client's experience with nature been? Is the client afraid of animals? Is the client allergic to any animals? Does the client have religious beliefs that affect his or her views of how animals should interact with people? Does the client's culture teach views of specific animals or species that would affect his or her view of including a particular type of animal in the intervention? Asking these kinds of questions can facilitate the building of a trusting relationship and can open the door to include an animal in the interaction in a way that is beneficial, enjoyable, and healing.

Professionals in a relationship-building, rapport-building stage of working with clients are likely to find some common ground around interest in animals. If there are reasons that an animal should not be included (e.g., allergy, phobia) or should be included with caution (e.g., client physical limitations, history of negative experience), then that knowledge will inform the professional and help the client to feel honored and safe as he or she enters into the professional intervention with the practitioner and animal partner. Certainly, no person should ever be forced to have contact with an animal (Gammonley et al., 1997). This tenet of successful HAI practice is a commonsense one that has been recognized by the Delta Society, but it continues to be a challenge for practitioners, particularly when their enthusiasm prevents them from assessing when and whether it is appropriate for an animal to participate.

Many of the considerations about whether to include an animal in practice should have to do with knowing the client as a person, not his or her diagnosis alone (Saleeby, 1992). It is still important, however, to use diagnosis to help describe and classify behavior for the sake of ongoing evaluation and understanding of how specific kinds of HAI may target specific behaviors. For example, the *DSM-IV-TR* is a useful tool in the discussion of psychological disorders (American Psychiatric Association, 2000). According to the *DSM-IV-TR*, a prominent feature in the diagnosis of a major depressive episode is experiencing depressed mood or no longer finding interest or pleasure in most activities for at least 2 weeks. If the target of an HAI is to help a person with depression learn to experience laughter through the unpredictable play of a friendly dog, then this specific diagnosis and the effects of the intervention can be tracked over time. As more is learned about when and under what conditions HAI is effective, specific language is needed to articulate how these interventions work. Existing criteria must be used to describe human behavior in order to move the field toward a specific understanding of the mechanisms of change that are related to a particular HAI (Melson, 2003).

Principle 3: Know the Species and the Specific Animal

Professionals must know exactly how a therapy animal supports and augments the clinician's ability to work within his or her theoretical orientation (Fine, 2006). The inclusion of an animal to a professional intervention should be purposeful and goal-directed. Animals are not extensions of the practitioner, but bring their own selves to the intervention. Selecting an animal for an intervention may be one of the most important decisions a practitioner makes. For example, a mental health therapist who is working with peer-oriented adolescents and horses, which are herd animals, might purposely pair an oppositional defiant client with a horse that is also oppositional. The goal of the HAI might be for the teen to learn to recognize his own behavior. But if, instead, the goal is for the teen to feel empowered with the experience of successfully completing a task, the same clinician may put the teen with a horse that is docile and easily bridled. It is essential for the handler to know the species and how that species communicates, what situations might be uncomfortable or unsafe for the animal or the client, and finally, what qualities specific animals bring to the intervention. For example, a domesticated therapy dog will provide different approaches from those provided by a horse, which reacts to stimuli as a prey animal.

Dogs demonstrate sensitivity to human gestures that even other nonhuman primates lack (Brauer, Kaminski, Riedel, Call, & Tomasello, 2006; Udell & Wynne, 2008). Their responsiveness and adaptability to human settings has made them "man's best friend" and the number one choice of animal both for HAI programs and as pets in our homes. However, owning a dog does not qualify a person to be a handler for an HAI. Many models of HAI suggest having a handler for the animal who is not the practitioner and who can be completely devoted to the welfare and needs of the animal (Gammonley et al., 1997; Howie, 2008). Often, handlers for these kinds of programs are volunteers. For example, Children's Hospital Boston has a successful visitation program called Pawprints that relies exclusively on volunteers who bring their pets, which have been certified as therapy dogs, to visit children who are in treatment (Children's Hospital Boston, 2009). However, such handlers do require training, and strict guidelines are key to ensuring a positive program. The guidelines should cover the application process, the training of the volunteers, the training of the dogs, and the establishment of policy that ensures safety for all—patients, staff, volunteers, and dogs alike.

Skill testing for dogs who participate in structured HAI is well established. One commonly used test is the American Kennel Club's canine good citizen test (American Kennel Club, 2008). There are 10 components of the test: accepting the approach of a friendly stranger, allowing a stranger to pet them, allowing a stranger to groom and examine them, walking on a loose leash, walking through a crowd of people, sitting on command and staying, coming when called, behaving well with other dogs, not being stressed by distractions, and maintaining all those skills when handled by a different handler. Understanding the value of each of these components of dog obedience is an example of the kind of competence that practitioners should have with the species of their choice for a HAI. Particularly when an animal is asked to work in an environment that it may find unfamiliar or unnatural, there needs to be a high level of understanding of the specific animal and that animal's natural behavior.

One innovative example of a creative HAI and one that illustrates the importance of knowing a particular species comes from the Ohio Reformatory for Women, which is partnering with Magical Farms alpaca farm. Staff are starting a program in which alpacas will live on campus with prison inmates. The inmates will be responsible for the care of the animals, from feeding, cleaning, and grooming them to shearing them and learning about the fiber arts of felting and spinning (Pekarek, 2008; D. Pekarek, personal communication, January 10, 2009). Alpacas are an interesting choice of species for an HAI with inmates because of their sensitive nature as prey and herd animals and because of the highly social nature of the herd. Part of the program includes women spending a significant amount of time in class, learning about the social cues of alpacas and their herd behavior, before interacting with live animals in the program. Understanding alpaca social behavior should provide inmates with insights into their own patterns of social interaction (Pekarek, 2008). In order for an HAI program to be successful, it is critical to ensure that handlers, professionals, and clients are continuously learning about the species involved. Knowing the specific personalities of the animals that will be participating, as well as respecting and responding to their communication about the intervention itself, is also critical.

Principle 4: Know the Environment
Where the Intervention Will Occur

At the University of Denver, considerable time is spent teaching students to assess the environments where an HAI may occur. This knowledge is critical, because without knowing the physical environment where an HAI is to take place, it is impossible to make informed decisions about the risks and benefits that are associated with the HAI for the client, animal, handler, or practitioner. Knowing an environment is not identical to controlling the environment, but certain controls can enhance the safety of participants. Coupled with an understanding of the behavior of a specific species, an environmental assessment can help practitioners create the most healing situation possible that is appropriate for both the animal and the client. Many treatment environments are artificial for animals. Shiny floors, high ceilings, and medical equipment are examples of environmental features that could be distracting or stressful for certain animals (Gammonley et al., 1997; Howie, 2008). Teri Pichot, a mental-health clinician, offers a strong model for how HAI in structured settings can take certain precautions to ensure that the animals and clients are protected. As one enters the Health Department, one sees signs advertising that therapy dogs work there. There are pictures of the therapy dogs, along with brief biographical information about them and an explanation of why they are helpful to the counseling practice. There is a safe place for the dogs to rest and retreat from working, if necessary, and fresh water is available for them (Pichot & Coulter, 2007). All of these features contribute to the animals being valued as partners in the HAI and demonstrate a consciousness about how sensitive living things are to our environments.

Principle 5: Design Programs with Ongoing Evaluation Components

In any field, ongoing evaluation is critical to the successful incorporation of new ideas. Successful HAI programs are characterized by consistently being open to feedback in the form of client satisfaction surveys, standardized tests that relate to the client's therapeutic goals, and internal and external reviews. One example of a program that has a strong evaluation component is Our Farm, which has studied the effectiveness of including animals in a special-education environment. The evaluation has both quantitative and qualitative components and utilizes a standard instrument, the Behavior Assessment System for Children teacher rating scale (Katcher & Teumer, 2006). Also, the evaluation has tracked students according to their *DSM-IV-TR* diagnoses, most commonly autism, attention-deficit/hyperactivity disorder, and other emotional or behavioral disturbances that interfere with students' ability to learn. Tracking the diagnoses was an important step in establishing some credibility for the program. Although program evaluation is important and useful, an even higher level of credibility can be gained from rigorously designed research studies that can test the effectiveness of a therapeutic model and compare it with other models.

BEST EVIDENCE: THE STATE OF THE RESEARCH

Unfortunately, the state of the evidence in the field of HAI is largely anecdotal, and empirical investigations are often characterized by poor research designs and/or small sample sizes (Fawcett & Gullone, 2001). The discipline of HAI has not yet fostered evidence-based practice (Wilson & Barker, 2003). It is understandable that funders, practitioners, and programs trying to demonstrate the efficacy of these models want to be able to provide or indicate with certainty that interventions are achieving verifiable therapeutic goals. In reality, there are many challenges to meeting this level of scientific certainty.

One of the most frustrating features of HAI and one that makes the subject difficult to research is the lack of clear definitions and categorization. For example, HAI has also been termed *pet-assisted therapy, pet therapy, animal-assisted therapy, human–animal bond, human–animal interaction, animal-assisted activities, animal-assisted learning,* and *animal-assisted psychotherapy;* the concept itself is poorly defined (Brodie & Biley, 1999; Butler, 2004; Fine, 2006; Gammonley et al., 1997; Katcher & Beck, 1983).

Depending on the wide range of individual client needs and therapeutic settings, the type of animals and applications vary significantly, making it difficult to compare programs. This variation in programs often develops as a result of the programs being built on the enthusiasm of a program director or volunteers. Such individuals may vary significantly in their theoretical orientation, purpose for becoming involved in the intervention, professional training, and life experience. All of these factors make HAI difficult to standardize and study in a way that leads toward a body of evidence-based knowledge.

The first step in the evaluation of evidence-based interventions is to develop practice manuals that objectively describe intervention methods, allowing other programs to replicate them (Wilson & Barker, 2003). In the arena of evidence-based human intervention practices, researchers struggle with the practical challenge of fidelity of implementation. Replications that stray from the original model eventually lose fidelity to the original model; such variations make them difficult to evaluate on a large scale. Replication is difficult to achieve, especially in HAI, where many programs rely on volunteers to provide the resources for a given intervention. Equine-assisted psychotherapy is a possible exception to this general trend in HAI programming and research. Both the Equine Facilitated Mental Health Association, founded in 1996, and the Equine Assisted Growth and Learning Association, founded in 1999, offer specific techniques and models for working with specific populations and offer training courses in their models (Fawcett & Gullone, 2001). Because both organizations teach similar models and are training practitioners and volunteers on a large scale, the opportunity for developing a multisite evaluation of equine-assisted psychotherapy exists, although it is not yet possible in many other areas of HAI.

HAI has lacked sufficient resources to bring together the skill and talent long enough and in large enough studies to support strong outcome research. Admittedly, outcome research has not been an area of competence or a priority for the professionals who have been doing the work. Practitioners and volunteers in the field often are motivated by the individual results that they see with their clients and are dedicated to the work because of their personal experience. However, now agencies with the capacity to fund the proper type of research are developing a scientific curiosity about the effectiveness of HAI.

HAI research has lacked institutional sponsorship and an accepted place in academia, with the possible exception of several pioneering university veterinary centers. As mentioned earlier, this appears to be changing. In addition, it is important to recognize that many other fields that parallel HAI contribute to studying the usefulness and effectiveness of the human–animal bond. Table 11.1 uses a population-based approach to portray the salient characteristics that researchers

Table 11.1. Characteristics of studies according to level that human–animal interaction (HAI) researchers confront

	Population	Goal Definition	Location/ Environment	Techniques for Animal Inclusion	Provider Expertise	Client Inclusion
Level 1	Well defined (i.e., children ages 10–12 with attention-deficit/ hyperactivity disorder)	Clearly identified (e.g., a 20% increase in attention span as measured by standard tests)	HAI will occur at a predesignated facility dedicated to the intervention (e.g., therapeutic barn)	Clearly defined with specific techniques that are documented for practitioners to follow (e.g., NARHA[a] certification for equine interventions)	Providers/handlers are well trained and certified in a specific intervention, with at least 5 years of experience working with the selected animal and client population, and are able to critically assess how the client and the animal are relating	Clients are consulted regarding the inclusion of animals into their therapy and informed about the use of a given HAI versus conventional treatment; they are willing and able to participate in the HAI. Clients are aware that individual experience, gender, and culture may modify HAI outcomes.
Level 2	Defined (e.g., senior citizens with dementia in a residential care facility)	Identified (e.g., a significant increase in social interaction during a given hour as measured by the frequency of contact with other residents that the client initiates)	HAI will occur in a predesignated space that is dedicated to the intervention (e.g., the recreation room at a senior center)	Clearly defined with specific techniques that are documented for practitioners to follow	Providers/handlers have conventional experience with the target population and moderate experience (2–4 years) in handling animals in HAI	Clients are informed about the use of a given HAI versus conventional treatment. Clients are aware that individual experience, gender, and culture may modify HAI outcomes.
Level 3	Loosely defined (e.g., inmates in a prison)	Defined, but not clearly operationalized (e.g., clients will	HAI is not tied to a specific location (e.g., therapy dogs will	Not clearly defined (e.g., therapy dogs will interact with inmates)	Providers/handlers possess little conventional experience with the	Clients receive limited information about the given HAI versus conventional treatment.

		increase their ability to be empathetic)	visit inmates at the prison)		target population and less than 2 years of experience handling the selected animal in a therapy setting	Clients have limited knowledge of how individual experience, gender, and culture may modify HAI outcomes.
Level 4	Loosely defined (e.g., children in a library on any given Saturday)	Defined, but not clearly operationalized such that results might be assessed (risks might outweigh the benefits of animal inclusion due to lack of professional awareness)	Little assessment of the location/ environment has occurred	Techniques have limited correlation to the therapeutic process and goals	Providers/handlers possess little conventional experience with the target population and limited experience handling the selected animal in a therapy setting	Clients receive limited information about the given HAI versus conventional treatment. Experience with HAI may be based on local media or public relations accounts. Clients do not know that individual experience, gender, and culture may modify HAI outcomes.
Level 5	Service population is inappropriately mixed	Poorly defined to the degree that the cost–benefit analysis of including an animal cannot be conducted	No assessment of the location/ environment has occurred; providers are unaware of this factor	Techniques have undefined correlation to the therapeutic process	Providers/handlers possess no conventional experience with the target population and limited experience handling the selected animal in a therapy setting	Clients receive information about the given HAI based on anecdotal accounts or single reactions. Clients do not know that individual experience, gender, and culture may modify HAI outcomes.

aNorth American Riding for The Handicapped Association.

confront when they approach HAI as a field of study. The variability in technique and expertise is characteristic of an emerging discipline. Because HAI often focuses on an unrehearsed interaction among the provider, animal, and client, the disciplined use of mixed-methods research in the development of evidence-based practices is arguably the best approach to build knowledge for this field. Note that developing evidence-based practices at Level 1 requires investment in facilities that parallels those of investments in laboratories in other fields.

Criteria for evidence-based research are needed. Particularly because the field is interdisciplinary and emerging, it would be helpful to have a centralized database that could help practitioners track new evidence-based research that is specifically related to HAI. For example, the Campbell Collaboration is a database that supports following evidence-based research in education, criminal justice, and social welfare (http://www.campbellcollaboration.org), and the Cochrane Collaboration is an international network of researchers focused on the identification and review of evidence in mental health (http://www.cochrane.org) (National Institute of Mental Health et al., 2008). A database specifically focused on HAI that could coordinate the progress of the field is a fundamental need.

In addition to a database, the field needs to develop centers where professionals can learn how to think critically about HAI and enjoy the benefits of community and scholarship. Knowing how to think critically about human and animal behavior, knowing the limits of our designated professional disciplines, and respecting the lives of our animal partners are key to making HAI both professional and successful. Ongoing conferences, increased sharing through professional organizations dedicated to HAI, and online communication will all contribute to the cohesiveness of the community that will drive this agenda forward.

CLIENT VALUES AND EXPECTATIONS

Client values and expectations are just as important as the practitioner's individual expertise and the best evidence (see Figure 11.1). Regardless of the client population and type of HAI that is being considered, clients should be informed about the research that is available and consulted about their preferences for the inclusion of animals. Certain interventions will not be appropriate for some clients. For example, in Kuwait, families were found to have a less positive view of companion animals than do American families, which is not surprising considering that the Islamic faith teaches that dogs are "dirty" (Al-Fayez, Awadalla, Templer, & Arikawa, 2003). Culturally competent providers who are able to explore the benefits of HAI, are knowledgeable about current research, and can have informed conversations with clients are just as important to evidence-based practice as the evidence itself.

CONCLUSION: MAKING THE CASE FOR EVIDENCE-BASED RESEARCH IN HUMAN–ANIMAL INTERACTION

The scientific study of the human–animal bond is still in its infancy. Gibbs (2003)[2] describes seven steps toward evidence-based practice:

1. Become motivated to apply evidence-based practice.

2. Convert needed information into an answerable question.

3. Find the best available evidence to answer the question.

4. Appraise the evidence critically.

5. Integrate evidence with practice.

6. Evaluate effectiveness and efficacy in exercising these steps.

7. Teach others to do the same.

These steps could offer guideposts for the development of evidence-based HAI. The process depends on practice to inform research and research to inform practice and needs to emerge as a partnership between the research and practice communities that will be mutually beneficial and influential. Future research should concentrate on carefully grounding theory, operationalizing particular kinds of HAI, and defining the population and specific approaches to HAI. Significantly larger sample sizes, control conditions and random assignment, replicated results, and improved measures with strong construct validity will improve the science that evaluates HAI. HAI science cannot develop without practitioner-led research initiatives that are able to convert salient aspects of the oral tradition of practitioners into evidence-based narratives.

Beginning to embed research and training programs in practice-focused, multidisciplinary university centers, creating international collaborations, and seeking institutional support and funding will expedite the process. Finally, adhering to principles that will ensure ethical practice for human and animal well-being must be nonnegotiable. Only when HAI supports the highest ethical standards for animal well-being will it reach the highest healing potential for humans as well.

---

[2]From Gibbs. *Evidence-Based Practice for Social Workers, 1E.* © 2003 Wadsworth, a part of Cengage Learning, Inc. Reproduced by permission. www.cengage/com/permissions

REFERENCES

Al-Fayez, G., Awadalla, A., Templer, D.I., & Arikawa, H. (2003). Companion animal attitude and its family pattern in Kuwait. *Society and Animals, 11*(1), 17–28.

American Kennel Club. (2008). *AKC's Canine Good Citizen (CGC) program.* Retrieved January 25, 2009, from http://www.akc.org/events/cgc/program.cfm

American Pet Products Association. (2009). *2009–2010 National Pet Owners Survey.* Washington, D.C.: Author. Retrieved May 10, 2010, from http://www.americanpetproducts.org/pubs_survey.asp

American Psychiatric Association. (2000). *Diagnostic and statistical manual of mental disorders* (4th ed., text rev.). Washington, DC: Author.

Animals and Society Institute. (2009). *Animals and Society Institute.* Retrieved February 12, 2009, from http://www.animalsandsociety.org

Balcombe, J.P. (2006). *Pleasurable kingdom: Animals and the nature of feeling good.* London: Macmillan.

Baun, M.M., Oetting, K., & Bergstrom, N. (1991). Health benefits of companion animals in relation to the physiologic indices of relaxation. *Holistic Nursing Practice, 5*(2), 16.

Bekoff, M. (2008). Thinkpiece: Increasing our compassion footprint: The animals' manifesto. *Zygon, 43*(4), 771–782.

Brauer, J., Kaminski, J., Riedel, J., Call, J., & Tomasello, M. (2006). Making inferences about the location of hidden food: Social dog, causal ape. *Journal of Comparative Psychology, 120,* 38–47.

Brodie, S.J., & Biley, F.C. (1999). An exploration of the potential benefits of pet-facilitated therapy. *Journal of Clinical Nursing, 8*(4), 329–337.

Butler, K. (2004). *Therapy dogs today: Their gifts, our obligation.* Norman, OK: Funpuddle Publishing Associates.

Children's Hospital Boston. (2009). *Pawprints.* Retrieved February 1, 2009, from http://www.childrenshospital.org/patientsfamilies/Site1393/mainpageS1393P4sublevel55.html

Farm Animal Welfare Council. (1993). *Second report on priorities for research and development in farm animal welfare.* Tolworth, United Kingdom: Ministry of Agriculture, Fisheries, and Food.

Fawcett, N., & Gullone, E. (2001). Cute and cuddly and a whole lot more? A call for empirical investigation into the therapeutic benefits of human–animal interaction for children. *Behaviour Change, 18*(2), 124–133.

Fine, A.H. (2006). *Handbook on animal-assisted therapy: Theoretical foundations and guidelines for practice.* Amsterdam & Boston: Elsevier/Academic Press.

Gammonley, J., Howie, A., Kirwin, S., Zapf, S.A., Frye, J., Freeman, G., et al. (1997). *Animal-assisted therapy: Therapeutic interventions.* Renton, WA: Delta Society.

Gibbs, L.E. (2003). *Evidence-based practice for the helping professions: A practical guide with integrated multimedia.* Pacific Grove, CA: Brooks/Cole Thompson Learning.

Gitterman, A., & Germain, C.B. (2008). *The life model of social work practice.* New York: Columbia University Press.

Haddon, D. (1994, February). Welcome to Green Chimneys: A sanctuary where troubled children and harmed animals recover together and blossom. *Arts Publications.*

Howie, A.R. (2008). *The handler factor: Evaluating handlers for animal-assisted interactions programs.* Seattle, WA: Human–Animal Solutions.

Katcher, A.H., & Beck, A.M. (1983). *New perspectives on our lives with companion animals.* Philadelphia: University of Pennsylvania Press.

Katcher, A., & Teumer, S. (2006). A 4-year trial of animal-assisted therapy with public school special education students. In A. Fine (Ed.), *Animal assisted therapy: Theoretical foundations and guidelines for practice* (2nd ed., pp. 227–242). Boston: Elsevier.

Melson, G.F. (2003). Child development and the human–companion animal bond. *American Behavioral Scientist, 47*(1), 31–39.

National Institute of Mental Health (producer), & Baker, C., Owings-Fonner, N., & Ziegert, A. (directors). (2008). *REACH-SW: Research and empirical applications for curriculum enhancement in social work.* [Video/DVD] (Available from Danya International, Inc., 8737 Colesville Road, Suite 1100, Silver Spring, MD 20910.)

Pekarek, D. (2008). *Animals letting people adopt caring attitudes (ALPACA): A unique prison-based animal program.* Unpublished manuscript.

Pichot, T., & Coulter, M. (2007). *Animal-assisted brief therapy: A solution-focused approach.* New York: Routledge.

Redefer, L.A., & Goodman, J.F. (1989). Brief report: Pet-facilitated therapy with autistic children. *Journal of Autism and Developmental Disorders, 19*(3), 461–467.

Risley-Curtiss, C., Holley, L.C., & Wolf, S. (2006). The animal–human bond and ethnic diversity. *Social Work, 51*(3), 257–268.

Rogers, L.J. (1998). *Minds of their own: Thinking and awareness in animals.* Boulder, CO: Westview Press.

Sackett, D.L., Richardson, W.S., Rosenberg, W., & Haynes, R.B. (1997). *Evidence-based medicine: How to practice and teach EBM.* New York: Churchill Livingstone.

Saleeby, D. (1992). *The strengths perspective in social work practice: Power in the people.* New York: Longman.

Serpell, J.A., Coppinger, R., & Fine, A. (2006). Welfare consideration in therapy and assistance animals. In A.H. Fine (Ed.), *Handbook on animal-assisted therapy* (2nd ed., pp. 453–474). San Diego: Elsevier.

Siegel, J.M. (1993). Companion animals: In sickness and in health. *Journal of Social Issues, 49*(1), 157–167.

Tedeschi, P., Fitchett, J., & Molidor, C.E. (2006). The incorporation of animal-assisted interventions in social work education. *Journal of Family Social Work, 9*(4), 59–77.

Udell, M.A., & Wynne, C.D. (2008). A review of domestic dogs' (*Canis familiaris*) human-like behaviors: Or why behavior analysts should stop worrying and love their dogs. *Journal of the Experimental Analysis of Behavior, 89*(2), 247–261.

Vizek Vidović, V., Vlahovic Stetic, V., & Bratko, D. (1999). Pet ownership, type of pet and socio-emotional development of school children. *Anthrozoös, 12*(4), 211–217.

Williams, E., & Jenkins, R. (2008, October). Dog visitation therapy in dementia care: A literature review. *Nursing Older People, 20,* 31–35.

Wilson, C.C., & Barker, S.B. (2003). Challenges in designing human–animal interaction research. *American Behavioral Scientist, 47*(1), 16–28.

Zamir, T. (2006). The moral basis of animal-assisted therapy. *Society and Animals, 14*(2), 179–200.

CHAPTER 12

Challenges to Human–Animal Interaction Research

Methodological Issues and Barriers to Sustainability

ROLAND J. THORPE, JR., JAMES A. SERPELL, AND STEPHEN J. SUOMI

The relationship between humans and their companion animals dates back to prehistoric times (Rowan, 1991; Serpell, 1989, 2006). Since the 1980s, however, there has been an abundance of interest in the burgeoning research area of human–animal interaction (HAI). Scientific research on the potential health benefits of companion animals has addressed several health-related phenomena, including survival of people following a myocardial infarction (Friedmann, Katcher, Lynch, & Thomas, 1980; Friedmann & Thomas, 1995), contributions of pet attachment to social support (Garrity, Stallones, Marx, & Johnson, 1989; Lago, Delaney, Miller, & Grill, 1989; Robb & Stegman, 1983; Stallones, Marx, Garrity, & Johnson, 1990), levels of happiness (Ory & Goldberg, 1983), measurement of risk factors for cardiovascular disease (Anderson, Reid, & Jennings, 1992; Dembicki & Anderson, 1996), frequency of physician visits (Headey, 1999; Jorm, Jacomb, Christensen, Henderson, Korten, & Rodgers, 1997; Siegel, 1990), amount of physical activity (Bauman, Russell, Furber, & Dobson, 2001; Serpell, 1991; Thorpe, Kreisle, et al., 2006; Cutt, Giles-Corti, Knuiman, & Burke, 2007), and physical function (Raina, Waltner-Toews, Bonnett, Woodward, & Abernathy, 1999; Thorpe, Simonsick, et al., 2006). Although findings from these studies are promising, advances in HAI research continue to be hindered by two vexing problems: research design and sustainability.

RESEARCH DESIGN

Although there is a growing body of research that demonstrates the health benefits of pet ownership, research into this topic has been limited and inconsistent. The inconsistencies are due largely to a number of design issues (Barba, 1995; Beck & Katcher, 2003; Garrity & Stallones, 1998; Melson, 1998; Wilson & Barker, 2003; Zasloff, 1996). First, the cross-sectional design of most of these studies does not permit researchers to assess temporal or causal relationships. The fact that data are collected at one point in time means that it is not known which factors are antecedents (e.g., pet ownership versus good health). Even if pet owner-ship is associated with better health in people, it is not clear whether this relationship is causal or whether it merely reflects a selection bias (i.e., a person's health status may influence his or her pet ownership choices, and/or both health and pet ownership may be related independently to some other variable, such as socioeconomic status).

Second, the studies often lack detailed data. Relevant questions to ask include how attached the individual is to the pet, who the primary caregiver of the pet is, how long the individual has owned the pet, how much time he or she spends with the pet, what the individual's atti-tudes are about companion animals, and what his or her pet ownership history is. The same questions should be repeated each year of a longi-tudinal study. Such information would allow us to examine changes in pet ownership and human health over time and would give us the ability to distinguish between causal and noncausal relationships by using longitudinal study designs. Although there are inherent limitations regarding the use of secondary data, these measures would enhance our knowledge base of pet ownership and human health.

Third, it is very important to ensure that there is an adequate sam-ple size in each pet ownership category to detect significant differences in the outcome variable(s). Some studies have produced inconclusive results with regard to the relationship between pet ownership and health benefits due to the small numbers of pet owners they used. Studies should ensure a sufficiently large sample size within each pet category to eliminate inadequate statistical power as a reason for the unobserved association between pet ownership and human health status. In addition to larger sample sizes, studies should use random sampling techniques when possible to enhance the external validity of the findings.

A fourth shortcoming in work to this point has been the failure to specify a theoretical framework underlying the research hypotheses (Garrity et al., 1989). One suggested theory is that pet ownership sub-stitutes for human social support and buffers stress, which in turn pro-duces health benefits (Dembicki, 1995; Garrity et al., 1989; Siegel, 1990;

Stallones et al., 1990). An alternative hypothesis is that pets encourage behaviors such as increased physical activity that modify the development of age-related diseases and decreases in physical function (Anderson et al., 1992; Dembicki & Anderson, 1996; Headey, 1999; Raina et al., 1999; Thorpe, Kreisle, et al., 2006). However, few studies have been able to demonstrate specific mechanisms that explain the association between pet ownership and health benefits (Dembicki, 1995; Siegel, 1990; Thorpe, Kreisle, et al., 2006).

Confounding variables such as age, gender, race, socioeconomic status, degree of attachment to the pet, number of children, and type and temperament of the animal should be accounted for in all future analyses of pet ownership and human health (Brown & Katcher, 2001; Budge, Spicer, Jones, & St. George, 1998; Friedmann & Thomas, 1985, 1998; Serpell, 2003; Staats & Horner, 1999; Wilson, 1994). Failing to account for those variables in analyses may lead to erroneous conclusions.

Furthermore, it is important for investigators to consider moving beyond simply controlling for those confounders and consider the extent to which these variables potentially moderate or mediate the association between pet ownership and human health. For instance, racial disparities exist among chronic diseases such as hypertension and diabetes that may be influenced by pet ownership; it is plausible to assess whether pets contribute to health benefits by race. Pet ownership may be associated with health only when it is stratified according to specific health or demographic characteristics, such as race or socioeconomic status. It is possible that pets are truly more beneficial among certain populations, such as people with little or no social support, older adults who live in institutional settings, or people who are widowed. Thus, it is important to determine whether the same relationships between pet ownership and health exist across the life course.

SUSTAINABILITY

Research in the area of HAI confronts a number of obstacles that tend to undermine the sustainability of this nascent discipline. Prominent among these is the highly interdisciplinary nature of the field itself. Whereas the majority of established disciplines are represented by relatively coherent bodies of knowledge and theory and by well-defined methods of investigation, the field of HAI is characterized by an eclectic mix of concepts, theories, and methodologies derived from an exceptionally wide variety of different disciplinary origins. This characteristic of the field makes it both fascinating and challenging for those involved, but it can at times appear unfocused and unprofessional when it is viewed from the perspective of more mature and established disciplines. It has also made it difficult for the HAI field to find an appropriate academic home for itself. In the interests of sustainability, the field—or at least the parts of it that address the impact of HAI on human health—should probably be based primarily within institutions that specialize in behavioral medicine, social epidemiology, and/or health psychology. Instead, for largely historical reasons, most of the existing centers and groups that focus on HAI are based either in veterinary colleges, where human health is not an obvious priority, or in schools of social work, where the main focus has been on the putative links between animal abuse and family violence.

A further obstacle to sustainability is the ongoing scarcity of funding for research on HAI. Success in biomedical research is typically measured in terms of peer-reviewed publications in high-quality journals and by the ability to secure long-term research funding from federally supported granting agencies (e.g., National Institutes of Health, National Science Foundation, U.S. Department of Agriculture). Since the 1980s, the field of HAI has been sustained almost entirely by generous but sporadic funding from the pet food industry. It is likely that it could not have developed at all without this support, but the field's dependence on a limited amount of short-term corporate funding has restricted the type and scope of research conducted, raised doubts about the credibility of existing findings, and discouraged young researchers from pursuing careers in this area. More recently, a small number of private foundations have supported short-term HAI studies, but none has shown the kind of sustained interest that might enable the field to become more financially independent, secure, and sustainable. Clearly, in order for the field of HAI to continue to grow and develop in the future, it needs to gain access to more reliable and credible sources of research funding.

Finally, the future of research on HAI is seriously threatened by the lack of appropriate graduate training opportunities for students and young researchers who are seeking entry to the field. Although a number of introductory undergraduate- and certificate-level courses are now available on topics such as animal studies, animals and society, the human–animal bond, and animal-assisted therapy (http://www.animalsandsociety.org/courses), only one established master's degree program currently exists in the United States, at Tufts University School of Veterinary Medicine (http://www.tufts.edu/vet/cfa/mapp_overview.html). The program tends to focus on the philosophical and public policy dimensions of human–animal relations, but it does at least offer courses in both qualitative and quantitative research methods. An informal search of *Dissertation Abstracts* for

2007–2008 using the search terms "pet OR pets OR 'companion animal'" yielded only 22 relevant dissertations completed in North America within that 2-year period, of which only 7 focused on animals and human health. Of those, 4 were classified under the subject heading "psychotherapy" and the remaining 3 belonged to "social psychology," "nursing," and "public health." More ominously, all 7 dissertations were completed in 2007 and none were completed in 2008. Those findings suggest that opportunities for taking advanced degrees in the field of HAI are extremely limited and may be declining. Such evidence does not bode well for the future of HAI research and speaks to the urgent need for new and well-funded graduate training programs in the field.

RECOMMENDATIONS FOR ENHANCING FUTURE RESEARCH

In 1987, the Working Group Summary from the National Institutes of Health Technology Assessment Conference on the Health Benefits of Pets stated that pet exposure should be considered a possible protective factor in scientific studies of human health (National Institutes of Health, 1988). This report also encouraged more research to test explanatory models for health benefits of HAI and stated that the research must evolve from descriptive studies based on random samples to longitudinal studies. Since the publication of this report, the growing body of HAI research supports the notion that companion animals affect human health at different stages of life and in a variety of situations (Boldt & Dellmann-Jenkins, 1992; Stallones et al., 1990; Wilson & Netting, 1987). Here we provide some recommendations for investigators to consider that we believe would enhance the next generation of HAI research.

Future research on pet ownership and human health should include an evaluation of different explanatory mechanisms for the relationship between pet ownership and human health across the life course.

Pet ownership questions should be added to all human health studies, particularly longitudinal studies (National Institutes of Health, 1988). This addition would afford the opportunity to examine the relationship between pet ownership and a variety of health outcomes. A greater understanding of the health benefits of companion animals could be gained if questions regarding pets were added to certain publications (e.g., the *National Health Examination and Nutrition and Health Survey: Epidemiologic Follow-up Study*, the *Cardiovascular Health Study*, the *Atherosclerosis Risk in Communities Study*, the *National Longitudinal Study of Youth, Coronary Artery Risk Development in Young Adults*). Not only is it important to add pet questions, but it is equally important to ensure that sample sizes are large enough to detect statistical differences among the pet ownership categories. Without sufficient statistical power, it becomes difficult to determine whether there is a real effect of pet ownership on human health.

Most of the previous research examining pet ownership has been conducted using a cross-sectional research design. A longitudinal research design examining several aspects of pet ownership at each wave of data collection will provide an opportunity to understand pet ownership from a life course perspective. However, to the authors' knowledge, there are no data available that examine pet ownership histories, or life course events associated with pet ownership. Pet ownership should be investigated from the early stages of life to late life because pets may not play the same role in individuals' lives over time (Boldt & Dellmann-Jenkins, 1992; Stallones et al., 1990; Wilson & Netting, 1987). Most chronic health conditions, such as cardiovascular disease and atherosclerosis, develop over time. Thus, studying the relationship between pets and owners throughout human life spans would provide a better understanding of how pets contribute to the modification of these chronic conditions. Questions about pet ownership, histories of pet ownership (longitudinally or retrospectively), and life course events associated with pet ownership (e.g., housing status, institutionalization) should be included.

A possible reason for inconsistent results in the HAI literature could be that different methodologies are used to measure the exposure variable. Two approaches—functional and structural—have been used to measure pet ownership. The functional approach involves the attachment to the pet, whereas the structural approach merely involves the presence or absence of the pet. The mere fact that a person owns a pet does not ensure that the pet will directly affect the owner's health. Rather, the level of the owner's attachment to the pet may be more important in determining health benefits (Boldt & Dellmann-Jenkins, 1992; Garrity et al., 1989; Ory & Goldberg, 1983; Siegel, 1993). Attachment to a pet could be responsible for differences in cardiovascular benefits to pet owners (Friedmann & Thomas, 1995). Future studies should consider attachment to the pet in the definition of pet ownership, especially among older adults. In addition, pet attachment is known to be affected by the behavior and temperament of the individual animal (Budge et al., 1998; Serpell, 1996), so that, too, needs to be considered in future work.

In sum, the study of HAI presents many challenges, but the opportunities are plentiful. Investigators should continue to develop better measures, research designs, and programs that will ultimately lead to a body of evidence that affects policy. Additional funding needs to be allocated from several sources to train the next cadre of scientists to further enhance our understanding of HAI. As was stated years ago, all future research on human studies should include pet questions and test explanatory models (National Institutes of Health, 1988).

Perhaps two adages that appear in the popular literature—"pets are good for your heath" (American Association of Retired Persons, 1987) and "pets are good for people" (Stauffer, 1982)—will one day be supported by undisputable scientific evidence.

REFERENCES

American Association of Retired Persons. (1987). Matching people with pets. *Highlights, 5,* 16.

Anderson, W.P., Reid, C.M., & Jennings, G.L. (1992). Pet ownership and risk factors for cardiovascular disease. *Medical Journal of Australia, 157,* 298–301.

Barba, B. (1995). A critical review of research on the human/companion animal relationship: 1988–1993. *Anthrozöos, 8,* 9–15.

Bauman, A.E., Russell, S.J., Furber, S.E., & Dobson, A.J. (2001). The epidemiology of dog walking: An unmet need for human and canine health. *Medical Journal of Australia, 175,* 632–634.

Beck, A.M., & Katcher, A.H. (2003). Future directions in human–animal bond research. *The Animal Behavioral Scientist, 47*(1), 79–93.

Boldt, M., & Dellmann-Jenkins, M. (1992). The impact of companion animals in later life and considerations for practice. *Journal of Applied Gerontology, 11*(2), 228–239.

Brown, S., & Katcher, A. (2001). Pet attachment and dissociation. *Society and Animals, 9,* 25–25–41.

Budge, R.C., Spicer, J., Jones, B., & St. George, R. (1998). Health correlates of compatibility and attachment in human–companion animal relationships. *Society & Animals, 6,* 219–234.

Cutt, H., Giles-Corti, B., Knuiman, M., & Burke, V. (2007). Dog ownership, health and physical activity: A critical review of the literature. *Health & Place, 13*(1), 261–272.

Dembicki, D. (1995). *Association of pet ownership with eating, exercise, nutritional status, and heart health of seniors.* Unpublished manuscript, Colorado State University, Department of Food Science and Human Nutrition, Fort Collins.

Dembicki, D., & Anderson, J. (1996). Pet ownership may be a factor in improved health of the elderly. *Journal of Nutrition for the Elderly, 15,* 15–31.

Friedmann, E., Katcher, A.H., Lynch, J.J., & Thomas, S.A. (1980). Animal companions and one-year survival of patients after discharge from a coronary care unit. *Public Health Reports, 95*(4), 307–312.

Friedmann, E., & Thomas, S.A. (1985). Health benefits of pets for families. *Marriage and Family Review, 8,* 191–203.

Friedmann, E., & Thomas, S.A. (1995). Pet ownership, social support, and one-year survival after acute myocardial infarction in the cardiac arrhythmia suppression trial (CAST). *American Journal of Cardiology, 76,* 1213–1217.

Friedmann, E., & Thomas, S.A. (1998). Pet ownership, social support, and one-year survival after acute myocardial infarction int he cardiac arrhythmia suppression trial (CAST). In C.C. Wilson & D.C. Turner (Eds.), *Companion animals in human health* (pp. 187–201). Thousand Oaks: Sage Publications.

Garrity, T.F., & Stallones, L. (1998). Effects of pet contact on human well-being. In C. Wilson & D. Turner (Eds.), *Companion animals in human health* (pp. 3–22). Thousand Oaks, CA: Sage Publications.

Garrity, T.F., Stallones, L., Marx, M., & Johnson, T. (1989). Pet ownership and attachment as supportive factors in the health of the elderly. *Anthrozöos, 3,* 35–44.

Headey, B. (1999). Health benefits and health cost savings due to pets: Preliminary estimates from an Australian national survey. *Social Indicators Research, 47,* 233–243.

Jorm, A., Jacomb, P., Christensen, H., Henderson, S., Korten, A., & Rodgers, B. (1997). Impact of pet ownership on elderly Australians' use of medical services: An analysis using Medicare data. *Medical Journal of Australia, 166,* 376–377.

Lago, D., Delaney, M., Miller, M., & Grill, C. (1989). Companion animals, attitudes toward pets, and health outcome among the elderly: A long term follow-up. *Anthrozöos, 331–332*(1), 25–34.

Melson, G.F. (1998). The role of companion animals in human development. In C. Wilson & D. Turner (Eds.), *Companion animals in human health* (pp. 219–236). Thousand Oaks, CA: Sage Publications.

National Institutes of Health. (1988). *Summary of working group: Health benefits of pets* (DHHS Publication No. 1988-216-107). Washington, DC: U.S. Government Printing Office.

Ory, M., & Goldberg, E. (1983). Pet possession and life satisfaction in elderly women. In A. Katcher & A. Beck (Eds.), *New perspectives on our lives with companion animals* (pp. 803–817). Philadelphia: University of Pennsylvania Press.

Raina, P., Waltner-Toews, D., Bonnett, B., Woodward, C., & Abernathy, T. (1999). Influence of companion animals on the physical and psychological health of older people: An analysis of a one-year longitudinal study. *Journal of the American Geriatrics Society, 47,* 323–329.

Robb, S.S., & Stegman, C.E. (1983). Companion animals and elderly people: A challenge for evaluators of social support. *Gerontologist, 23*(3), 277–282.

Rowan, A.N. (1991). Editorial: Do companion animals provide a health benefit? *Anthrozoos, 4,* 212–213.

Serpell, J.A. (1989). Pet keeping and animal domestication: A reappraisal. In J. Clutton-Brock (Ed.), *The walking larder: Patterns of animal domestication, pastoralism & predation* (pp. 10–21). London: Unwin Hyman.

Serpell, J. (1991). Beneficial effects of pet ownership on some aspects of human health and behaviour. *Journal of the Royal Society of Medicine, 84,* 717–720.

Serpell, J.A. (1996). Evidence for an association between pet behavior and owner attachment levels. *Applied Animal Behavior Science, 47,* 49–60.

Serpell, J.A. (2003). Anthropomorphism and anthropomorphic selection: Beyond the "cute response." *Society & Animals, 11,* 83–100.

Serpell, J.A. (2006). Animal-assisted interventions in historical perspective. In A.H. Fine (Ed.), *Handbook on Animal-Assisted Therapy* (2nd ed., pp. 3–20). New York: Academic Press.

Siegel, J. (1990). Stressful life events and use of physician services among the elderly: The moderating role of pet ownership. *Journal of Personality and Social Psychology, 58*(6), 1081–1086.

Siegel, J. (1993). Companion animals: In sickness and in health. *Journal of Social Issues, 49*(1), 157–167.

Staats, S., & Horner, K. (1999). Allocating time to people and pets: Correlates with income and well-being in a mid-west community sample. *The Journal of Psychology, 133*(5), 541–541–552.

Stallones, L., Marx, M., Garrity, T., & Johnson, T. (1990). Pet ownership and attachment in relation to the health of U.S. adults 21 to 64 years of age. *Anthrozöos, 4*(2), 100–112.

Stauffer, S.B. (1982). Pet programs for the elderly. *Aging, 331–332,* 9.

Thorpe, R.J., Jr., Kreisle, R.A., Glickman, L.T., Simonsick, E.M., Newman, A.B., & Kritchevsky, S. (2006). Relationship between physical activity and pet ownership in Year 3 of the Health ABC Study. *Journal of Aging and Physical Activity, 14*(2), 154–169.

Thorpe, R.J., Jr., Simonsick, E.M., Branch, J.S., Ayonayon, H., Satterfield, S., Harris, T.B., et al. (2006). Dog ownership, walking behavior, and maintained mobility in late life. *Journal of the American Geriatrics Society, 54*(9), 1419–1424.

Wilson, C.C. (1994). A conceptual framework for human–animal interaction research: The challenge revisited. *Anthrozöos, 7*, 4–24.

Wilson, C.C., & Barker, S.B. (2003). Challenges in designing human–animal interaction research. *American Behavioral Scientist, 47*(1), 16–28.

Wilson, C.C., & Netting, F.E. (1987). New directions: Challenges for human–animal bond research and the elderly. *Journal of Applied Gerontology, 6*, 189–200.

Zasloff, R.L. (1996). Measuring attachment to companion animals: A dog is not a cat is not a bird. *Applied Animal Behavior Science, 47*, 43–48.

CHAPTER 13

Scientific Research on Human–Animal Interaction

A Framework for Future Studies

JAMES A. GRIFFIN, SANDRA McCUNE,
VALERIE MAHOLMES, AND KARYL J. HURLEY

A central question addressed by this volume is how well suited to scientific scrutiny are different areas within the field of human–animal interaction (HAI). On one hand, a body of research findings documents the effects of HAI on human health and well-being (see Chapter 3; Friedmann, Barker, & Allen, 2010; Wells, 2009), although many of these studies are characterized by methodological and conceptual weaknesses that limit the interpretation of their findings (Johnson, 2010). However, there is a paucity of research on the role of HAI in typical and atypical child development (Melson, 2003, in press; National Institutes of Health, 1987) and on the efficacy of the use of companion animals in therapeutic settings (see Chapter 6).

A great deal has been written recently about why more research has not been conducted in the HAI field (Griffin, McCune, Maholmes, & Hurley, 2010), the need to study these interactions by using increased methodological rigor and sophisticated research designs (Kazdin, 2010; see also Chapter 12), the need for evidence-based practice in therapeutic applications (see Chapter 11), and directions for future HAI research

(McCardle, McCune, Esposito, Maholmes & Freud, 2010). However, one question that remains unexplored is how the basic and translational research that has been conducted to date has influenced the HAI field, especially therapeutic applications. This chapter will explore this question and provide a broad framework within which progress in research related to HAI may be judged.

> Thought would destroy their paradise. No more;
> where ignorance is bliss, 'Tis folly to be wise.
>
> Thomas Gray, "Ode on a Distant Prospect
> of Eton College" (1747)

Questions about the need to systematically study HAI and the field's ability to employ rigorous methodologies to examine such interactions are not academic questions. More than two thirds of U.S. homes with a child over age 6 include a pet (American Veterinary Medical Association, 2007), and an increasing number of therapeutic interventions involve HAI (Nimer & Lundahl, 2007).

It is tempting to focus on only the positive aspects of HAI (see Chapter 5), but there are risks as well (see Chapter 4). The Centers for Disease Control and Prevention (CDC) reports that 4.5 million Americans are bitten by dogs each year, and one in five of those dog bites results in injuries that require medical attention. Among children, the rate of dog-bite–related injuries has decreased in recent years (Gilchrist, Sacks, White, & Kresnow, 2008), but such injuries remain a serious public health issue.

Although injury statistics are available for the general population, there is no such database available for animal-assisted therapy (AAT) and animal-assisted activities (AAA). We are unaware of any systematic effort to track injuries that are related to the therapeutic use of companion animals in school, hospital, correctional, outpatient, and community settings. There are published guidelines for minimizing the risks associated with disease transmission in health care settings (DiSalvo et al., 2006; Khan & Farrag, 2000; Lefebvre et al., 2008), but there are insufficient data to assess the risks associated with the use of therapy animals in such settings. Given that the various forms of AAT and AAA have flourished without subsequent clinical or news reports of injury or the spread of disease, it is tempting to conclude that the benefits of these activities outweigh the risks. However, it will not be possible to draw any empirical conclusions until both the benefits and risks are quantified in a reliable and valid manner. Ignorance may (or may not) be bliss.

It is often assumed that additional scientific research on HAI will result in a cumulative knowledge base, which in turn will lead to greater conceptual clarity and pragmatic feedback on how to improve AAI. However, this is not necessarily the case. Two meta-analyses of AAA and AAT research studies (Nimer & Lundahl, 2007; Souter & Miller, 2007) revealed moderate effect sizes for the interventions that met their inclusion criteria, but they excluded far more studies from the meta-analyses than they included. Nimer and Lundahl reviewed 250 studies but were able to use only 49 in their meta-analysis, whereas Souter and Miller reviewed 165 studies, of which only 5 met their inclusion criteria. In addition, both meta-analytic studies noted the scattershot nature of the interventions and populations that were under investigation, and the lack of use of common standardized measures across the studies that did meet their criteria. Such difficulties are not limited to studies of AAA and AAT. A recent Cochrane Collaboration meta-analysis of programs that teach children about preventing dog bites (Duperrex, Blackhall, Burri, & Jeannot, 2009) reviewed information on 1,598 such programs. They found only 20 studies on such programs, of which only 2 met their inclusion criterion. Of those 2, neither used a measure of subsequent rate of dog bites as an outcome measure, making it impossible to say much about the efficacy of these interventions. Finally, a meta-analysis examining the relationship between exposure to furry pets and the risk of asthma and allergic rhinitis (Takkouche, Gonzalez-Barcala, Etminan, & Fitzgerald, 2008) reviewed 3,311 studies on this topic, but only 32 met their inclusion criteria. When it comes to HAI research, more is not always better.

Within the HAI field, there is one rare exception to the lack of systematic research on a specific therapeutic intervention: dolphin-assisted therapy (DAT). Beginning with Marino and Lilienfeld (1998) and Humphries (2003), there has been an attempt to systematically review and evaluate the empirical evidence regarding the use of DAT to treat various illnesses and developmental disabilities. Both of these reviews concluded that there was no credible scientific evidence for the effectiveness of DAT. Marino and Lilienfeld later revisited this topic and reviewed five DAT studies that were published subsequent to their original review. Although one of the five studies demonstrated a higher degree of methodological rigor (Antonioli & Reveley, 2005), all were judged to have significant methodological flaws that limited their value in demonstrating the efficacy of DAT (Marino & Lilienfeld, 2007). The later review is instructive to the field, as it systematically reviews the threats to construct and internal validity as they apply to each study and explains why these flaws limit the conclusions that can be drawn from the study. In effect, Marino and Lilienfeld have created a de facto checklist that can (and should) be used by all HAI studies that intend to test the efficacy of a given intervention.

You see, wire telegraph is a kind of a very, very long cat. You pull his tail in New York and his head is meowing in Los Angeles. Do you understand this? And radio operates exactly the same way: you send signals here, they receive them there. The only difference is that there is no cat.

Description of radio widely attributed to Albert Einstein

Ask any dog owner about unconditional love, and he or she will regale the listener with tales of unswerving canine loyalty. Ask any AAA volunteer to describe the effect that his or her visiting animal has on a group of schoolchildren, a resident of a nursing home, or a patient in a hospital, and stories of how such visits have brightened moods, changed behaviors, and altered lives will be presented. Why, then, does scientific research have such a hard time documenting these phenomena? As with Einstein in the quote about radio, a person can "know" that something works, but may have a hard time capturing the essence of the interaction in a way that is faithful to the phenomena being described and that at the same time makes sense to the audience being addressed.

There are several reasons why the HAI field has not generated a more systematic accumulation of scientifically rigorous basic and applied research findings. Perhaps the primary reason is that the field is fragmented and composed of researchers from multiple scientific disciplines who are conducting research isolated from one another. For example, within a single large university researchers might conduct HAI research in the schools of Nursing, Medicine, Social Work, Public Health, Education, and Veterinary Medicine without any awareness of the relevance of the others' work. It is equally plausible that within a single College of Arts and Sciences, HAI research could be conducted within the departments of Psychology, Sociology, Anthropology, Human Development, and Economics to a similar degree of isolation. Finally, outside of academia, professionals and volunteers who are involved with AAI may be interested in participating in and conducting scientific research on their programs, but they may not know how to access the research knowledge and skills that are possessed by the faculty at their local colleges and universities. Isolation is anathema to science. In a field as broad as HAI, ways must be found to connect researchers from various disciplines and research topics and maintain open lines of communication with practitioners and laypeople who are involved with AAT and AAA programs.

Another reason that empirical knowledge in the HAI field has not accumulated more quickly even as more studies have been conducted is the inherent difficulties associated with studying the phenomena in question. For example, the most straightforward way to study the effects of pet ownership on child development would be to randomly assign children at birth to grow up with a dog, cat, fish, horse, snake, and so forth, or no pet at all. Researchers could then monitor both the children's interactions with the pet in question and their overall development, relative to children in the "no pet" control group. Of course, one could never ethically conduct such a study, so researchers are limited to studying children who do or do not have pets for a variety of reasons, knowing that such children and their families may systematically differ on a number of important variables that affect a child's development but have nothing to do with pet ownership per se (e.g., income level, parent's health).

Similarly, a mental health practitioner who uses AAT in his or her practice might want to randomly assign depressed adolescent patients to receive AAT or standard therapy, but could only do so if both the adolescent and his or her parents consent to participate in such a study. Clearly, adolescents with animal phobias or allergies would be less likely to agree to participate, and those who desire AAT might be unwilling to risk being randomly assigned to the control group. After a volunteer subject pool is established, there are design and measurement issues that further complicate how to conduct the study. The most obvious issue is that the adolescent patients will know whether a therapy animal is part of their session. This makes it impossible to tell whether the presence of the therapy animal is affecting the therapy outcome or whether it is just the novelty of having an animal in the room or the desire to produce a positive research outcome that produces results that differ from those of the control group. The inability to conduct "blind" research, in which the subjects and sometimes even the researcher does not know whether the subject is receiving the treatment or a placebo (e.g., a sugar pill) is an inherent limitation of HAI efficacy research. It is possible to create alternative treatment conditions (e.g., presence of a robotic or stuffed animal), but such designs require a larger subject pool and still do not completely rule out the possibility of spurious results.

After a study design has been established, the AAT practitioner also must decide which measures will be used to capture both what takes place in the therapy itself, and whether the hoped-for outcomes are achieved for the patient. Unfortunately, at this stage of the study many HAI researchers decide to create their own measures, either because they have not reviewed the literature on similar studies and the measures that such studies used or because their search of the literature did not reveal any measures that they felt captured what they wanted to measure in their study (the therapeutic process or the patient outcomes). As evidenced by the meta-analyses cited earlier, it is difficult to compare results across studies if they do not use the same or comparable measures. Most homemade measures lack information on their psychometric properties (i.e, their reliability and validity), making it difficult to know whether two different measures of an outcome (e.g., level of depression) are measuring the same thing and would produce the same results if used simultaneously with the same patient. Of course, there are times when researchers have no option other than creating their own measures, but as Marino and Lilienfeld (2007) point out, it should be possible for the HAI field to move toward a limited set of standardized measures that can be used for treatment efficacy studies. A few AAT or AAA studies with a limited set of common outcome measures will advance the field far more than a large number of studies that create their own or use idiosyncratic outcome measures.

As evidenced by this volume, HAI researchers have persisted despite the difficulties that are inherent in conducting research in this field, and they have made significant progress in advancing understanding of the nature of the relationship between children and companion animals, the ways in which such animal companions may influence development, and how the healing power of this relationship may be used within the context of AAI (Wilson, 2006). The research examples listed here only touch on the design, methodology, and data analytic issues that must be addressed in order to increase the rigor and utility of HAI research. Other resources are available that address these issues in more depth (Kazdin, 2010; see also Chapter 12). We now turn our attention to devising a framework within which the broad array of HAI research can be understood and future progress may be judged.

> In proportion as he simplifies his life, the laws of the universe will appear less complex, and solitude will not be solitude, nor poverty poverty, nor weakness weakness. If you have built castles in the air, your work need not be lost; that is where they should be. Now put the foundations under them.
>
> Henry David Thoreau, *Walden* (1854)

As Thoreau advises, the field of HAI need not discard the wide variety of descriptive and empirical research studies that have been conducted up to this point, but rather should build a foundation on which they and future efforts may be understood. In order to make sense of the disparate range of topics encompassed by HAI research, it is necessary to use a multilevel framework to examine how different levels of study relate to one another and how they interact over time with development (e.g., Glass & McAtee, 2006). For the purposes of an HAI research framework, those levels could include genetic, brain, behavioral, family/social, institutional, and cultural levels.

GENETIC STUDIES

The dog genome has been sequenced (Sutter et al., 2007), meaning that it is possible to examine the relationship between the genetic code and behavioral characteristics of different breeds of dogs. Perhaps of greater interest to the HAI field, scientists are now using dogs to study complex behaviors such as social cognition (Morell, 2009), making it possible to examine how such behaviors evolved over time with domestication and providing greater insight into both canine and human behavior (Hare & Tomasello, 2005).

BRAIN STUDIES

HAI research at the neurotransmitter and hormone level is providing exciting advances in understanding how the interactions between humans and animals can alter both of their brain chemistries (Uvnäs-Moberg, Handlin, & Petersson, 2010). Recent research suggests that a dog merely gazing at its owner's eyes increases the level of oxytocin in the owner, suggesting a biochemical basis for the attachment that humans feel toward their pets (Nagasawa, Kikusui, Onaka, & Ohta, 2009). This line of research opens up a new window into understanding the biological basis for complex behaviors such as attachment.

BEHAVIORAL STUDIES

To date, much of the HAI research has been conducted at the behavioral level of the individual, some of it in the context of child development (Chapter 3; DeLoache & Bloom Pickard, 2010; Melson, 2010) and some focusing on children with specific types of disorders or disabilities (see Chapters 8, 9, and 10). As research knowledge evolves, it is likely that studies incorporating genetic, brain, and behavioral levels of analysis will become more common and will validate and enrich findings that currently are limited to observable behaviors.

FAMILY AND SOCIAL STUDIES

All HAIs occur in a social context, whether it is a family home, a neighborhood, or a public park. Therefore, these interactions influence not only the human and animal directly, but also the larger social network. As described in Chapter 2, the presence of companion animals can increase the social capital of a given neighborhood. However, companion animals also bring with them a range of public health issues (see Chapters 3 and 4) that must be addressed in order to protect the safety and welfare of both humans and animals.

INSTITUTIONAL STUDIES

As noted earlier, AAI is becoming more commonplace in a wide range of institutions. In Chapter 7, Nancy Gee provides a comprehensive review of AAA activities in one such institution (schools), but such activities can be found in both inpatient and outpatient mental health settings (see Chapter 8), as well as in hospitals, nursing homes, correctional facilities, and other settings. As such activities become more widespread, researchers must capture the way that the inclusion of AAT and AAA change the social climate of the institutions (see Chapter 2).

CULTURAL STUDIES

In this volume, James Serpell (Chapter 1) provides a fascinating account of the historical and cross-cultural aspects of HAI. As research advances at the other levels, it will be interesting to see what additional cross-cultural similarities and differences emerge as studies are replicated in different cultures and countries. It is hoped that such studies will go beyond cultural differences in attitudes toward different companion animals and explore how different cultural beliefs and practices affect HAI as it relates to child development and therapeutic interventions.

Although this multilevel framework is broad and somewhat arbitrary, it nevertheless provides a starting point to synthesize HAI research results that are conducted at different levels of study. It also serves as a reminder that HAI researchers and AAI practitioners must at least be aware of the advances that are being made at these different levels and the possibility that research conducted at one level has important implications for research or interventions at another level. Overall, it is hoped that this framework has a heuristic value and encourages pet lovers, AAI practitioners, and researchers to pursue a deeper level of understanding of the role that pets play in the lives of humans of all ages.

REFERENCES

American Veterinary Medical Association. (2007). *U.S. pet ownership and demographics sourcebook.* Schaumburg, IL: Author.
Antonioli, C., & Reveley, M.A. (2005). Randomized controlled trial of animal facilitated therapy with dolphins in the treatment of depression. *British Medical Journal, 331,* 1231–1234.

DeLoache, J., & Bloom Pickard, M. (2010). How very young children think about animals. In P. McCardle, M. McCune, J.A. Griffin, & V. Maholmes (Eds.), *How animals affect us: Examining the influence of human–animal interaction on child development and human health.* (pp. 85–99) Washington, DC: American Psychological Association Press.

DiSalvo, H., Haiduven, D., Johnson, N., Reyes, V.V., Hench, C.P., Shaw, R., et al. (2006). Who let the dogs out? Infection Control did: Utility of dogs in health care settings and infection control aspects. *American Journal of Infection Control, 34,* 301–307.

Duperrex, O., Blackhall, K., Burri, M., & Jeannot, E. (2009). Education of children and adolescents for the prevention of dog bite injuries. *Cochrane Database of Systematic Reviews* (Art No: CD004726. DOI: 10.1002/ 14651858.CD004726.pub2), 2.

Friedmann, E., Barker, S., & Allen, K. (2010). Physiological correlates of health benefits from pets. In P. McCardle, S. McCune, J.A. Griffin, & V. Maholmes (Eds.), *How animals affect us: Examining the influence of human–animal interaction on child development and human health.* (pp. 163–182) Washington, DC: American Psychological Association Press.

Gilchrist, J., Sacks, J.J., White, D., & Kresnow, M.J. (2008). Dog bites: Still a problem? *Injury Prevention, 14,* 296–301.

Glass, T., & McAtee, M.J. (2006). Behavioral science at the crossroads in public health: Extending horizons, envisioning the future. *Social Science & Medicine, 62,* 1650–1671.

Griffin, J.A., McCune, S., Maholmes, V., & Hurley, K. (2010). Human-animal interaction research: An introduction to issues and topics. In P. McCardle, M. McCune, J.A. Griffin, & V. Maholmes (Eds.), *How animals affect us: Examining the influence of human–animal interaction on child development and human health.* (pp. 3–9) Washington, DC: American Psychological Association Press.

Hare, B., & Tomasello, M. (2005). Human-like social skills in dogs? *TRENDS in Cognitive Sciences, 9*(9), 439–444.

Humphries, T.L. (2003). Effectiveness of dolphin-assisted therapy as a behavioral intervention for young children with disabilities. *Bridges: Practice-based research synthesis, 1,* 1–9.

Johnson, R. (2010). Health benefits of animal-assisted intervention. In P. McCardle, S. McCune, J.A. Griffin, & V. Maholmes (Eds.), *How animals affect us: Examining the influence of human–animal interaction on child development and human health.* (pp. 183–192) Washington, DC: American Psychological Association Press.

Khan, M.A., & Farrag, N. (2000). Animal-assisted activity and infection control implications in a health care setting. *Journal of Hospital Infection, 46,* 4–11.

Kazdin, A. (2010). Establishing the effectiveness of animal-assisted therapies: What types of research designs and findings would build the field? In P. McCardle, S. McCune, J.A. Griffin, & V. Maholmes (Eds.), *How animals affect us: Examining the influence of human–animal interaction on child development and human health.* (pp. 35–52) Washington, DC: American Psychological Association Press.

Lefebvre, S.L., Golab, G.C., Christensen, E., Castrodale, L., Aureden, K., Bialachowski, A., et al. (2008). Guidelines for animal-assisted interventions in health care facilities. *American Journal of Infection Control, 36,* 78–85.

Marino, L., & Lilienfeld, S.O. (1998). Dolphin-assisted therapy: Flawed data, flawed conclusions. *Anthrozöos, 11,* 194–200.

Marino, L., & Lilienfeld, S.O. (2007). Dolphin-assisted therapy: More flawed data and more flawed conclusions. *Anthrozöos, 20*(3), 239–249.

McCardle, P., McCune, S., Esposito, L., Maholmes, V., & Freund, L. (2010). An agenda for future human–animal interaction research. In P. McCardle, S. McCune, J.A. Griffin, & V. Maholmes (Eds.), *How animals affect us:*

Examining the influence of human–animal interaction on child development and human health. (pp. 193–202) Washington, DC: American Psychological Association Press.

Melson, G.F. (2003). Child development and the human–companion animal bond. *American Behavioral Scientist, 47*(1), 31–39.

Melson, G.F. (2010). Principles for human–animal interaction research. In P. McCardle, S. McCune, J.A. Griffin, & V. Maholmes (Eds.), *How animals affect us: Examining the influence of human–animal interaction on child development and human health.* (pp. 13–34) Washington, DC: American Psychological Association Press.

Morell, V. (2009). Going to the dogs. *Science, 325*(5944), 1062–1065.

Nagasawa, M., Kikusui, T., Onaka, T., & Ohta, M. (2009). Dog's gaze at its owner increases urinary oxytocin during social interaction. *Hormones and Behavior, 55*, 434–441.

National Institutes of Health. (1987). *The health benefits of pets. NIH Technology Assess Statement Online 1987 Sep 10–11.* Retrieved on August 4, 2009, from http://consensus.nih.gov/1987/1987HealthBenefitsPetsta003html.htm

Nimer, J., & Lundahl, B. (2007). Animal-assisted therapy: A meta-analysis. *Anthrozöos, 20*(3), 225–238.

Souter, M.A., & Miller, M.D. (2007). Do animal-assisted activities effectively treat depression? A meta-analysis. *Anthrozöos, 20*(2), 167–180.

Sutter, N.B., Bustamante, C.D., Chase, K., Gray, M.M., Zhao, K., Zhu, L., et al. (2007). A single IGF1 allele is a major determinant of small size in dogs. *Science, 316*, 112–115.

Takkouche, B., Gonzalez-Barcala, F.J., Etminan, M., & Fitzgerald, M. (2008). Exposure to furry pets and the risk of asthma and allergic rhinitis: A meta-analysis. *Allergy, 63*, 857–864.

Wells, D.L. (2009). The effects of animals on human health and well-being. *Journal of Social Issues, 65*(3), 523–543.

Uvnäs-Moberg, K., Handlin, L., & Petersson, M. (2010). Physiological correlates of health benefits from pets. In P. McCardle, S. McCune, J.A. Griffin, & V. Maholmes (Eds.), *How animals affect us: Examining the influence of human–animal interaction on child development and human health.* (pp. 53–82) Washington, DC: American Psychological Association.

Wilson, C.C. (2006). The future of research, education, and clinical practice in the animal–human bond and animal-assisted therapy. In A. Fine (Ed.), *Handbook of animal-assisted therapy* (2nd ed., pp. 499–512). New York: Academic Press.

Index

Page references followed by *f* and *t* denote figures and tables, respectively.